Kids How to Cook Everything

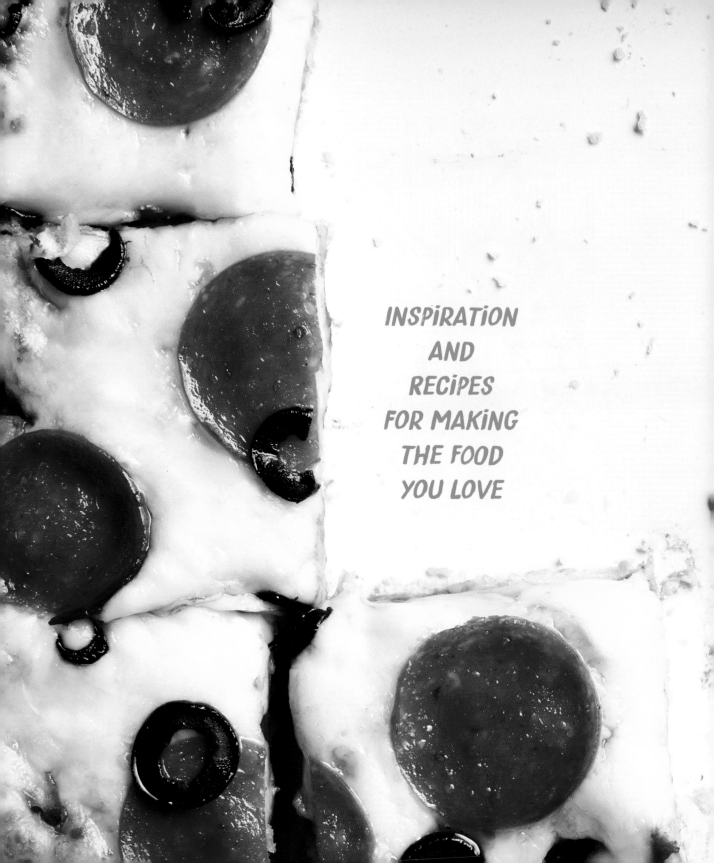

INSPIRATION
AND
RECIPES
FOR MAKING
THE FOOD
YOU LOVE

Kids
~~How to~~ Cook
Everything

Mark Bittman

PHOTOGRAPHY BY GHAZALLE BADIOZAMANI
ILLUSTRATIONS BY APRIL KIM TONIN

HARVEST
An Imprint of WILLIAM MORROW

OTHER BOOKS BY MARK BITTMAN

How to Cook Everything

How to Cook Everything Fast

How to Cook Everything Vegetarian

How to Cook Everything The Basics

How to Grill Everything

How to Bake Everything

How to Cook Everything:
Bittman Takes On America's Chefs

Bittman Bread

Animal, Vegetable, Junk

How to Eat

Dinner for Everyone

A Bone to Pick

Mark Bittman's Kitchen Matrix

VB6: Eat Vegan Before 6:00

The VB6 Cookbook

Food Matters

The Food Matters Cookbook

The Best Recipes in the World

Fish: The Complete Guide to
Buying and Cooking

Leafy Greens

Mark Bittman's Kitchen Express

Mark Bittman's Quick and Easy
Recipes from the *New York Times*

The Mini Minimalist

Jean-Georges: Cooking at Home
with a Four-Star Chef

Simple to Spectacular

HarperCollins books may be purchased for educational, business, or sales promotional use. For information, please email the Special Markets Department at SPsales@harpercollins.com.

FIRST EDITION

Design by MELISSA LOTFY

Photography © GHAZALLE BADIOZAMANI PHOTOGRAPHY

Illustrations © 2023 APRIL KIM TONIN

Food styling by BARRETT WASHBURNE

Prop styling by VANESSA VAZQUEZ

Prep illustrations by OLIVIA DE SALVE VILLEDIEU

Additional photography credits on page 303 (About the Kids)

Library of Congress Cataloging-in-Publication Data
Names: Bittman, Mark, author.
Title: How to cook everything kids / Mark Bittman.
Description: First edition. | New York : Harvest, an imprint of William Morrow, 2024. | Includes index. | Identifiers: LCCN 2024011111 (print) | LCCN 2024011112 (ebook) | ISBN 9780544790322 (hardcover) | ISBN 9780544790810 (ebook)
Subjects: LCSH: Cooking—Juvenile literature. | Cooking for children—Juvenile literature. | LCGFT: Cookbooks.
Classification: LCC TX652.5 .B527 2024 (print) | LCC TX652.5 (ebook) | DDC 641.5/123—dc23/eng/20240327
LC record available at https://lccn.loc.gov/2024011111
LC ebook record available at https://lccn.loc.gov/2024011112

ISBN 978-0-544-79032-2

24 25 26 27 28 IMG 10 9 8 7 6 5 4 3 2 1

FOR HOLDEN

AND MAX

CONTENTS

ACKNOWLEDGMENTS

All of us who worked on this project agreed: It made us feel like kids again. Over the last couple years, my team and I have been fortunate to collaborate with a powerhouse of creatives—and this is the time and place to officially say "thank you" one and all.

First things first: Kerri Conan, as usual, drove this train and pulled it into the station. She's the most valuable cookbook partner I could ever imagine. On this project, we were especially aided by Kate Bittman (my daughter, yes), who's catching up to us in skills even more quickly than we might have hoped.

Together with our excellent editors and designers at Harvest Books and HarperCollins—Stephanie Fletcher, Jacqueline Quirk, Melissa Lotfy, Mumtaz Mustafa, and Yeon Kim—we invited photographer Ghazalle Badiozamani, illustrator April Tonin, food stylist Barrett Washburne, and prop stylist Vanessa Vazquez to help us turn *How to Cook Everything Kids* from an everyday cookbook to a kitchen wonderland that will inspire children to explore new foods with the people who love them most.

And what about these fabulous kids? Thank you—and your parents and guardians—for enthusiastically sharing your experiences cooking some of the recipes in this book. We are so grateful you answered the call for "Kids Candids" when Kate, Kerri, and Ghazalle and her sister Ghazal Badiozamani ("Little G" and "Big G") reached out looking for volunteers. (For more about the young cooks in the book and their photographing family members, see page 303.)

Providing invaluable support to this endeavor were the assistants for the photo shoot: Grace Puffer, Chris Smith, and Joanie Danahy. More thank-yous for our copyeditor and production editor—Leda Scheintaub and Amanda Hong, respectively.

I'd also like to thank my agent, Danielle Svetcov, for landing this beauty. And the readers and supporters of our website, The Bittman Project, and the team behind that endeavor: Kate, Mike Diago, Holly Haines, Samir Rao, and Doc Willoughby. Special thanks to Julianne Kiider and all the folks at Made In Cookware for contributing some of their splendid skillets, pots, and knives for the photo shoot.

Many thanks also to the publishing and sales team at Harvest Books and HarperCollins—publisher Deb Brody, marketer Katie Tull, publicist Tess Day, and the HarperCollins sales team.

As for me, I could not do any of this without the support of my team (largely thanked above, but worth repeating); my beautiful daughters, Emma and Kate; their wonderful partners, Jeff and Nick; my unbelievable grandsons, Max and Holden; and my beloved partner, Kathleen.

INTRODUCTION → YOU DO YOU

This "Introduction" is a chance for us to chat a little about how **cooking is going to change the way you think about food.** But before we dive into the book together, let's say "Hi!" I'm Mark, the guy who is going to help you learn to cook. You'll usually have an adult in the kitchen with you, and not to worry—they'll like these recipes too!

You know what you like to eat. It's probably different from how you ate when you were little, and your choices now are going to be different from when you get older. I'll let the grown-ups in your life talk with you about all that stuff. My job is to share what I know about all kinds of foods and show you lots of delicious and fun ways to prepare them. **I want cooking to be an activity that you love, one that lets your creativity shine.**

I also want to give you the tools you need to discover even more foods to try, choose how you want to cook them, and add seasonings and sauces to them to make them taste the way *you* like best.

But the most important tool for tasting and eating will always be . . . your mouth! Your mouth will tell you if something is crunchy or creamy, soggy in a good way or soggy in a bad way, or too salty or not salty enough. But it's not just your mouth: You'll use your ears to hear food sizzling and bubbling, your nose to sound the alarm when something is burning, and your eyes to decide when something is cooked exactly the way you like it. Don't worry if you don't know how to do this yet—**the more you cook, the better you'll be at using your senses to know when the food is right for you.** So, when

IT LOOKS LIKE MODERN ART!

someone says to you, "Eat your vegetables," you'll able to eat *your* vegetables, **the way** *you* **like them.** Imagine that!

Learning to cook also solves many great mysteries. Why do you like some vegetables cooked and others raw? What are your favorite pasta shapes? How do you like your eggs—scrambled or hard-boiled or both? Have you ever tried fish? Beans? Brown rice? There are *so* many foods out there! What are some of the ones you might explore cooking first? What are you looking forward to trying?

There are always new foods, new seasonings, new combinations, and new skills to learn about and discover. **Every time you try something new, the better you'll get** at shopping, cooking, and eating, the more fun you'll have, and the more you'll learn about yourself as well!

Want to tell me about what you're cooking? Send me a note, anytime: bittman@markbittman.com.

MARK BiTTMAN
SPRiNG 2024

MAKE FRIENDS WITH YOUR KITCHEN

PEEK BEHIND THE DOORS, OPEN SOME DRAWERS, AND EXPLORE

IT'S ALWAYS EXCITING TO MAKE A NEW FRIEND. You know how your time together goes: loud playing and giggling, secrets to share, things to do, lots to talk about, places to explore.

Getting to know your kitchen is sort of the same. And it's a fun way to learn how to cook. So, grab the nearest adult and get ready to prowl around in the fridge. We're going to start by talking about ingredients—all the different foods and seasonings that you want to cook—and how they're used.

Next, we'll look around to see what tools you have and what you might need. That will roll into a bunch of special action words cooks use to describe "techniques" or "skills." These actions are repeated in recipes so you safely use tools, ingredients, and heat to turn food into something delicious to eat.

Then, just before digging into the recipe chapters, we'll go over some tips for setting the table, garnishing dishes, taking photos of what you've cooked, and packing it to go. Ready? Let's meet at the refrigerator.

My favorite kitchen tool is the electric mixer.

I wish someone would teach me how to cook doughnuts.

Holden

FOOD → INGREDIENTS

Ingredients are found in different places in different kitchens. The refrigerator and the freezer. The cupboards or the pantry (or in some kitchens these foods are piled into baskets or bins). And all the different seasonings your family uses, which are usually in one place like a spice cabinet, rack, or spinning shelf that works like a merry-go-round.

In this section, you're going to make friends with the ingredients in your kitchen. Look around, touch, smell, and taste. Ask questions. The idea is to discover what you already know and like, what you want to try next, and what you're not sure you're ready to eat yet.

You can write in the book or make a list on paper if that helps—or take photos. What you're doing now is getting comfortable with the food in your kitchen. And if you already know your way around, here's a chance to see things in a new light and start thinking like a real cook. Seeing what's handy will also help you decide what recipes you can make right away and what ingredients you need to add to your family's shopping list.

TALKING ABOUT WHERE FOOD COMES FROM

You probably know that food is grown on farms (or in gardens) and comes from land or ocean animals. What happens before it gets to your plate is very important to our health, and to our planet Earth. Eating good food—what I like to call "real" food—means that you have to learn more about the in-between parts. Like how far it traveled to get to you and what extra words are on the boxes or cans.

One way to try to eat food that's more real is to cook it yourself. No matter what age you are, it's a good time to start learning. And the best way to learn is to ask questions. You can start by finding out more about where your family shops and looking at what's in your kitchen. Does your food come from the supermarket? Farms and farmers' markets? Special grocery stores or online? Which foods do you eat that come from factories? What does "processed food" mean? Do you know all the tiny words on package labels? Cooking and enjoying meals with the people you love is an excellent time to explore these questions—and other things you're curious about. The answers will be complicated but interesting and lead you on a path toward thinking about how important food is to everyone.

WHAT'S IN THE FRIDGE?

- [ ] Fresh fruits and vegetables—explore the drawers and shelves to see them all!
- [ ] Lettuces—are they in a salad spinner or bag?
- [ ] Milk—dairy and/or nondairy
- [ ] Yogurt
- [ ] Sour cream
- [ ] Cheeses—whole pieces and/or grated
- [ ] Eggs
- [ ] Butter
- [ ] Oils
- [ ] Beef, pork, bacon, sausage, turkey, chicken, fish—either ready for cooking or thawing out
- [ ] Cooked or smoked meats like cold cuts, salami, or ham
- [ ] Tofu
- [ ] Bread, rolls, or buns
- [ ] Peanut butter
- [ ] Jelly, jam, or preserves
- [ ] Pickles
- [ ] Homemade sauces
- [ ] Miso
- [ ] Fresh herbs
- [ ] Bottled sauces and salsas
- [ ] Condiments—mayonnaise, mustard, things like that
- [ ] Cold water
- [ ] Fruit juices
- [ ] Sparkling water
- [ ] Sodas
- [ ] Leftovers!
- [ ] Other foods:
- [ ]

WHAT'S IN THE FREEZER?

- [ ] Frozen fruits and vegetables
- [ ] Frozen beef, pork, bacon, sausage, turkey, chicken, fish
- [ ] Homemade leftovers
- [ ] Cooked beans and grains
- [ ] Packaged snacks and meals
- [ ] Ice cream, sherbet, or sorbet
- [ ] Frozen juices
- [ ] Ice
- [ ] Other foods:
- [ ]

WHAT SEASONINGS DO I HAVE?

- [ ] Salt—more than one kind?
- [ ] Pepper—already ground or in a grinder?
- [ ] Cinnamon
- [ ] Curry powder
- [ ] Chili powder
- [ ] Dried chiles—whole or ground?
- [ ] Cumin
- [ ] Italian seasoning blend
- [ ] Oregano
- [ ] Thyme
- [ ] Rosemary
- [ ] Ginger
- [ ] Nutmeg
- [ ] Bay leaves
- [ ] Allspice
- [ ] Cardamom
- [ ] Cloves
- [ ] Other seasonings:
- [ ]

WHAT'S IN THE CUPBOARDS AND/OR PANTRY?

- [ ] Pasta and noodles
- [ ] Rice and other grains
- [ ] Dried beans
- [ ] Canned beans
- [ ] Canned tomatoes
- [ ] Tomato paste
- [ ] Soups
- [ ] Extra salsas
- [ ] Extra pickles, sauces, and condiments
- [ ] Nuts and seeds
- [ ] Oils
- [ ] Vinegars
- [ ] Peanut butter
- [ ] Soy sauce
- [ ] Jelly, preserves, or jam
- [ ] Sugars, honey, and syrups
- [ ] Flour
- [ ] Cornmeal
- [ ] Cocoa
- [ ] Baking powder
- [ ] Baking soda
- [ ] Bread, rolls, or buns
- [ ] Bread crumbs
- [ ] Crackers
- [ ] Chocolate
- [ ] Candy
- [ ] Packaged snacks
- [ ] Packaged meals
- [ ] Other foods:
- [ ]

WHEN I SAY THIS → I MEAN THIS

These ingredients appear in lots of recipes. This table helps you choose what to use and how to substitute.

SALT
Usually I let you decide how much salt to use. The idea is to start with a little and taste to see if you want more. Kosher salt is salty without any extra flavors, so that's what I like. If you have iodized or sea salt in your house, go ahead and substitute them in recipes, but use a little less when a specific measurement is listed.

PEPPER
Always means black pepper *except* when the recipe includes red chile flakes, which are sometimes called red pepper flakes. For the strongest flavor, grind whole peppercorns in a "mill." Preground pepper is milder.

VEGETABLE OIL
A mild-tasting (or "neutral") oil that works with high heat. Not to confuse you, but my first choices for a neutral oil aren't actually "vegetable oil." I prefer oil made from grapeseed, sunflower, safflower, or peanuts; vegetable oil is made from soybeans. You'll notice a little difference when you taste them, but any are fine. Get a grown-up to show you all the different kinds the next time you're in the store.

OLIVE OIL
For cooking, salads, and drizzling, use an extra virgin olive oil that isn't too expensive and is good for medium-high heat. If you're really into the taste of olive oil and love drizzling it on things, you can try a more expensive bottle—it will be darker in color with big flavor. Just don't use it for cooking.

BUTTER
Unsalted—sometimes called "sweet"—butter is my first choice. If you use salted butter, you will need a little less salt in the recipe.

EGGS
Use large eggs whenever possible. It really only matters when you make batters like for pancakes, cookies, or cakes. With extra-large or medium your batter will end up either a little wet or a little dry, and it's hard to make adjustments.

FLOUR
This almost always means all-purpose flour. Sometimes there will be whole wheat flour too. For gluten-free baking, try substituting one of the blends that measure the same way as all-purpose wheat flour.

SUGAR
Granulated white sugar is listed in recipes as "sugar." When you need something else—like brown sugar—they will both be spelled out in the recipe ingredient list.

TOOLS → EQUIPMENT

These are the nonfood things that appear in the recipes or that you'll need to prepare, serve, or put away the food you cook. You know, stuff like pots, pans, spoons, whisks, and small machines. Many you probably already have. My goal is to keep the size of equipment manageable for smaller hands and bodies, so you might find a mix of adult- and special kid-sized tools works best for you.

Get ready to explore the rest of your kitchen and learn some new words. Whenever you forget the name, it's okay to just say, "You know. That *thingie!*"

POTS AND PANS

SKILLETS. Most recipes call for 8- or 10-inch skillets. When you're cooking more food, or want to double the number of servings, you'll need a 12-inch skillet. It's best if they have metal lids, handles, and knobs (no plastic, wood, or rubber parts) so you can move them from the stove to the oven. (No worries if not! You can just move the food into an ovenproof baking dish or pan to finish it.) Nonstick surfaces are also easier to work with when you're learning. There are many safe, nontoxic choices available now.

POTS. Sometimes these are called "saucepans." The most useful sizes for this book are 1-, 3- and 5-quart. All should have tight-fitting lids for sure, and if they have metal handles and lid knobs, they can go in the oven. Nonstick isn't important for pots. The best are made of stainless steel or cast iron coated with enamel; thick and heavy bottoms will help the pans heat evenly all over. Glass and ceramic don't heat well and are fragile and aluminum or tin inside will make some foods taste and look strange.

BAKING SHEETS. You can use them for roasting too. The best baking sheets for this book have a short rim around the sides to keep liquids from dripping everywhere. A small one, also called a "quarter sheet pan," measures 9 x 13 inches, and a large "half sheet pan" is 13 x 18 inches. There's an in-between size too. If you have that, then you'll need two for the recipes that use what I call in recipes a "large baking pan." Nonstick baking sheets aren't necessary, but if that's what you have, use them.

ROASTING AND BAKING PANS AND DISHES. When you roast foods that have a lot of fat or juices—like meats or chicken—or bake cake batters or bread doughs, the sides of the pan need to be taller than those found on rimmed baking sheets. The recipes in this book use the sizes 9 x 13-inch, 8-inch square, and a standard loaf pan (about 9 x 4 x 3 inches). To make a layer cake or muffins, you'll need two 8-inch cake pans or an 8- or 12-cup standard-sized muffin tin. Metal roasting and baking pans are best if you're only going to have one kind, because they work better in hot ovens or broilers. But for cakes, crisps, or pastas that bake at temperatures below 400°F, glass or ceramic baking dishes are fine and look prettier on the table.

ELECTRIC GRIDDLES, WAFFLE IRONS, AND SKILLETS

Though pancakes are easy to do in a skillet or stovetop griddle, if you're really into them, then you might want to get an electric griddle—also handy for sandwiches—or for waffles a plug-in waffle iron. Electric skillets can be helpful for young cooks or kids not quite comfortable at the stove. They're good for stir-fries, pasta sauces, and even pancakes.

KNIVES AND SCISSORS

Before working with knives, talk things through with the adult you'll be cooking with most. It's important that your cutting tools are comfortable in your hands. The size or shape of the blade doesn't matter much. Some knives specially made for children have extra grips and knobs on them, or smaller handles. To get a good fit, grab the handle like you're shaking hands with someone and make sure your fingers can wrap most of the way around to the other side and it doesn't slide around in your hands.

Older kids will need both small and mid-sized knives (for example 4 and 6 inches) and a long thin knife with a jagged edge—called a "serrated knife"— used to saw back and forth on breads. And here's a surprise—sharp knives grab and cut food better than dull ones so they're safer.

Scissors are great too. You can work downward on a cutting board or in a bowl to chop soft or cooked vegetables, fruit, or salad greens. And they're good for trimming fat from meat and chicken.

No matter what you use, be sure an adult is nearby. They can also help hold food and guide your hand until you get the hang of it. Work slowly and carefully and cut downward onto a solid, nonslip surface. And always know exactly where all your fingers and your other hand are!

SPIRAL SLICERS

A lot of kids—and adults—like to turn vegetables into noodles and ribbons with a special cutting tool. They usually attach to the counter for stability, you lock in the food and blade, and crank away. There's also a hand-held model that works like a grater you twist, but your hands need to be sort of big for it to work. Though I didn't give any special recipes for things like zucchini noodles, you can try spiral-cut vegetables with the different basic cooking recipes in the "Edible Colors" chapter. Noodles and ribbons will cook faster, so you'll need to check sooner than the steps tell you and stir more frequently to prevent the vegetables from getting too brown.

BIG TOOLS

These are the things you don't think about until you need them. And you will need them!

BOWLS. Mixing bowls for mixing and serving bowls for serving. Metal, ceramic (glazed clay), and heavy glass bowls are best for mixing, but of course glass and ceramic can break. All work as serving bowls too, though usually people like something sort of fancy on the table. (I consider a skillet of colorful vegetables or a roasting pan of chicken "fancy," but maybe that's just me!) You'll need different sizes.

PLATTERS. These are big oval or round dishes for serving food family-style. The kind with some kind of raised edge to hold juices and sauces is always a good idea. You don't need platters, but they're a good way to show off and share what you cook.

CUTTING BOARDS. Wooden or heavy plastic doesn't matter, as long as they don't slip around on the counter and you can clean them well with soapy water after every use. Putting a damp towel between the board and the counter also helps keep them still as you work.

MEASURING CUPS AND SPOONS. You will need both liquid and dry ingredient measuring cups. The first has a pour spout and is marked with all the portions of a cup you need. The second has a flat top and comes in 1 cup, ½ cup, ⅓ cup, and ¼ cup sizes. Measuring spoons are different from what you use for cooking and eating. They usually come in a set with a tablespoon, teaspoon, ½ teaspoon, and ¼ teaspoon. (For how to use all these, see "Measure" in the action words on page 13.)

COLANDERS AND STRAINERS. The first have holes to let liquid pass through. The second are made of metal screens or "mesh" that also lets liquid pass through but catches teeny-tiny pieces of food. (Sometimes they're called "sieves.") You'll need a pretty big colander and a smaller strainer. Having a couple different sizes of each is helpful but not necessary.

SALAD SPINNER. Perfect for quickly rinsing lettuces and also all sorts of greens and other vegetables. After spinning, you can pour off the water and use the spinner for refrigerating the clean vegetables. If you don't have a spinner, use a big bowl for rinsing the greens and a colander to drain and shake them. Then wrap them loosely in a clean towel and keep them in a covered container.

fitting lids are best, but bowls covered with a plate or a wrap (see below) can also work.

FOIL AND PLASTIC WRAP. I'm trying to use less plastic and foil, but sometimes you need these wraps for covering containers of leftovers, sealing raw food for the fridge, or fitting into the bottom of pans before cooking. Ask the adults you cook with to help you decide when and where to use both.

PARCHMENT PAPER AND BAKING MATS. "Parchment" is a special paper for cooking that doesn't catch on fire when baking. It helps keep cookies and cakes from sticking to the pans. Some people like to use washable mats made of silicone to do the same thing. A few recipes ask you to use parchment paper; you can find it in any supermarket in the baking section.

SPONGES AND SCRUBBIES. No one wants to talk about cleaning up, but it's a part of cooking. Your choice whether you clean as you go or all at once when you're done. Now let's not say anything else on the topic.

TOWELS. I use cloth towels in the kitchen for everything from cleaning up to draining food and patting it dry. Cotton towels absorb the best. Wash them frequently, use clean towels for draining food, and never try to grab a hot pot or pan with a wet towel or you'll get burned.

MITTS AND HOT PADS. These are a better choice than towels for handling hot pots and pans. Always pay close attention moving these things from one place to another and keep whatever you use away from hot burners and flames.

STORAGE CONTAINERS. The great thing about cooking is that you'll have leftovers. Once they cool off a bit you can put them in glass, stainless steel, silicone, or plastic containers. The kinds with tight-

HAND TOOLS

There's not much on this list, but you probably have more than one of most of them.

SPOONS. I'm talking about the big spoons used for stirring and serving. They can be metal, wooden, silicone, or plastic. And I like the first three best. Using metal on nonstick pans will scratch them, so make sure you have either a wooden or silicone spoon for that.

SPATULAS. The recipes say when to use stiff or soft spatulas. "Stiff" means that you can't bend it easily, so it works for stirring, scraping, flipping, or lifting something in or out of a pan. For nonstick pans the stiff spatula will need to be made of wood, silicone, or plastic. You can use metal spatulas on other pans and baking sheets. "Soft" spatulas are flexible for scraping something soft from the sides of a bowl or sometimes a pot. They're usually not quite straight

at the top and instead form a tip. I like silicone soft spatulas best, but you can use the plastic kind too.

TONGS. When you need to grab something for turning or scooching or moving it from one place to another, you'll need tongs. I like the springy kind that you can snap open and closed, but some people like the kind that have handles like scissors.

WHISKS. These wiry tools for beating liquids and soft foods come in all sorts of sizes and shapes. You want a whisk that's comfortable to hold and fits in your mixing bowls and pots. Long forks can also be used for whisking.

VEGETABLE PEELER. Use this to remove potato or beet skins or the outside of carrots. You can also use a peeler to make ribbons. (See the recipe for making carrot ribbons on page 179.)

POTATO MASHER. The best kind have a disk poked with holes and you smush it down straight into the food you want to make smooth. The squiggly kind will never get food quite as smooth. You can also mash with a fork. It will just take more work.

GRATERS. Most families have a "box grater" with sharp holes on all sides for different kinds of grating. A "Microplane" is a name for an extra sharp grater that makes super-small bits. I say a box grater is great for kids.

CAN OPENER. You're going to need to get into cans once in a while. Electric or hand-crank. Your choice.

GARLIC PRESS. Many home cooks like garlic presses. You put in a peeled clove, squeeze, and out comes smushed garlic and some juice. It's easier than chopping garlic, so go ahead and use one if you like, but the garlic and juice will be stronger tasting than if you use chopped—or even "minced"—garlic.

MACHINES

There are only a few recipes in this book where you must use a food processor (like for the bonbons on page 300) or blender (the smoothies on page 29 is one). An electric mixer—either one you hold in your hand or the kind that sits on a stand—makes cookies, cakes, whipped cream, and frosting a breeze, but you can use other nonelectric tools like whisks. You'll just have to work a little harder and take a few more minutes.

Microwave ovens are perfect for reheating food, warming liquids, and melting butter and chocolate. I also like to use them for steaming vegetables. See page 139 for more on how to do this.

ACTION → TECHNIQUES

Cooking is an activity based on specific ways to change ingredients into something good to eat. In recipes these actions are called "techniques" (or sometimes "methods"). Are you ready to learn a lot of new words? Whenever you need a reminder when you're cooking, you can come back to this section.

PREP

Prep is short for "preparation." This is the work you do before you actually start cooking.

RINSE. It's a good idea to rub fruit and vegetables under cold tap water to rinse away dirt or germs or other things you don't want to eat. A colander set in the clean sink is a good tool to use because you can shake it a little and drain everything afterward.

DRY. Remove the last bit of water by patting the food dry with a clean towel. (Or use a salad spinner. See page 8.)

TRIM. This is how you remove any parts of a food you don't want to eat. For fruits and vegetables, work downward with a knife on a cutting board to trim away the hard parts like stems, cores, ends, and also parts that are bruised or rotten. Tear off the outer leaves on greens and cabbage. For meats and poultry, you want to cut away any extra fat.

PEEL. Use either a vegetable peeler or a small sharp knife to get rid of tough skin you can't—or don't want to—eat. Work with the blade moving away from you to keep from cutting your fingers. You'll probably need help with big thick-skinned foods like pineapple or winter squash.

SLICE. Think of what sliced sandwich bread or cake looks like—you get thick or thin solid pieces by slicing. You can cut food into slices either before or after cooking it. You also need to cut slices as the first step in chopping. Hold the food in a way so that your fingers are far away from the knife blade, make sure the knife and the board aren't wobbling, and cut downward. Slicing evenly takes the most practice. Luckily, you will usually be slicing to chop in this book, so you don't have to do it perfectly.

CHOP. This is the general word for cutting slices into smaller pieces. The recipes in this book will tell you whether to make chunks (big pieces) or to chop into smaller pieces. There will be a description of the way to chop when it's important to do something special. Otherwise the idea is to cut downward into bite-sized pieces or smaller. As always when using a knife, make sure everything is stable and keep your fingers out of the way of the blade. This is especially important with small things like nuts and garlic cloves. And remember, you can use scissors for a lot of foods too. (See page 7.)

MINCE AND DICE. We don't do much "mincing" or "dicing" in this book, but you might in other books or you might want to try when you get more practice. Mincing is when you chop and chop, holding the top of your knife with one hand and rocking the handle until the food is in teeny-tiny bits. Dicing is cutting the food into almost perfect cubes.

TEAR. Same action with your hands as ripping paper; you might tear lettuce or herb leaves or other greens. The pieces will look more jagged than when you cut and it's also easier and more fun.

CRUMBLE. You know when you rub things between your fingers to bust them into chunks? That's exactly how you crumble food. Soft cheeses like feta and blue cheese are usually better to crumble than chop. And dry ingredients—bread, cookies, cakes, and crackers—are easy to crumble.

MEASURE

To measure liquids, fill the cup—the kind with a pour spout that you can see through—to the line you need for the recipe. Put the cup on a counter or table so that your eyes are looking straight at the measuring line. There may be a little dip that looks like a bubble. Add or pour off liquid until the bottom of that bubble is right where the measuring line is.

For measuring dry foods like flour, sugar, grains, and cut vegetables or fruit, use the flat-topped cups. For fine ingredients such as flour or sugar, scoop up the ingredient into the measuring cup, letting it pile up a little bit above the edge. Then use the flat side of a butter knife to swoosh the excess ingredient back into its container. For looser, bigger foods—like chopped vegetables—just pack them in as best you can without too much peeking over the top.

You use the same measuring spoons for both liquid and dry ingredients. Fill the spoons with liquid all the way to the very top. For dry ingredients, dip the spoon in so the food is heaped over the top, then swoosh the extra away with the flat side of a butter knife, just as you do when measuring dry ingredients in a cup.

MOVE

These are the words for using a tool, appliance, or hands to make foods do something they can't do by themselves. After these movements, ingredients will look totally different from before you moved them.

STIR. Usually you stir with a spoon, swirling food around in a pot, pan, or bowl. You can also stir with a stiff or soft spatula, fork, tongs, chopsticks, or your hands. "Mix" and "combine" are other recipe words to describe stirring to bring different foods together. Sometimes—as with salads or stir-fries—you'll still be able to see the separate ingredients after stirring. Other times—as with pancake batter or sauces—the ingredients come together into one thing after stirring so you no longer see each food by itself.

BEAT. Fast stirring basically. The idea with beating is to combine two or more things into one thing. Like when you beat an egg yolk with the white for scrambled eggs. Forks and whisks are usually the best tools to beat with.

TOSS. Gently lifting something—like salad or noodles—from the bottom and sides up into the air and letting it tumble back down. That's tossing. The best tools for tossing are tongs, a big fork and spoon, or your hands.

WHISK. When you beat with a whisk or a fork until something becomes creamy, foamy, frothy, or fluffy. An electric mixer fitted with either two beaters or a whisk attachment makes this work much faster.

MASH. Pulverizing a soft food by smushing or smashing. Potatoes are the most popular thing to mash. Some other mashable foods are bananas and other soft fruit, or cooked vegetables like sweet potatoes, carrots, eggplant, or tomatoes. You can use a fork or a potato masher for mashing.

PURÉE. Making food totally smooth is called puréeing. It's like super-mashing. You'll need a food processor or blender. And sometimes the recipe will say to add some liquid.

SPREAD. Another word for smear. It's what you do when you put butter on bread, cream cheese on a bagel, or frosting on cake. A dull knife or a small stiff or soft spatula are the best tools for spreading.

SPRINKLE. Just like rain or snow, sprinkling is putting a thin layer of a wet or dry ingredient on top of another food. You can use your fingers or a spoon. Salt, pepper, spices, herbs, and sugar are the usual things you'll sprinkle during cooking. Other words for sprinkle are scatter, dust, and shake.

DRIZZLE. One of my favorite things to do is to add a few drops of a liquid (like olive oil or a sauce) over food before eating.

RUB. You've got to use your hands to rub. It's the best way to move seasonings or oil all over meat or vegetables before cooking so that you can get into the cracks and crevices.

COOK

The words on this list describe the techniques all cooks use to heat food. So, you're joining a very special club! In the recipes in this book, I also use even more detailed words to describe how something looks, smells, tastes, or feels when you touch it with your hands or press it with a tool. Those words will be more familiar to you since they relate directly to your senses.

BOIL. Water and other liquids boil when they're hot enough to start bubbling. Just seeing little bubbles forming at the bottom of the pan doesn't count. The water has to be going crazy and throwing off steam to be boiling.

SIMMER. In cooking, gently bubbling liquid is called simmering. I usually like to say "gently bubbling" whether the recipes are for kids or adults. But this is a cookbook, so everyone should learn the word most people use.

SOME FACTS ABOUT HEAT

* Cooking is what happens when we raise the inside and outside temperature of ingredients.
* Heat turns raw food into cooked food.
* Some cooking actions like boiling or steaming change food with hot liquids.
* Pan-cooking, baking, and roasting are examples of dry heat cooking methods.
* You can see steam, sizzling oil, boiling water, and smoke.
* You can see flames, red cooking surfaces, and other sources of heat.
* But you can only feel heat.

STEAM. Yes, you can cook with steam, which is actually hotter than boiling water. Be extra careful to take lids off pots or work near a boiling kettle so the steam blasts away from you! Instead of covering the food in water as you do with boiling, you put the food above the boiling water. (The recipe on page 139 explains how.) You can also steam food in the microwave with little or no added liquid.

PAN-COOK. When you cook ingredients in a pan—or pot—with a thin layer of oil or butter, I call that pan-cooking. Or just plain cooking in the recipes here. The official word for this technique is "sautéing." That just makes it seem more complicated than it is. You might also see the words "sear" or "brown" in the steps during pan-cooking. Those are used to alert you that the food is going to be cooked until it darkens without burning.

STIR-FRY. Like pan-cooking, only hotter and faster with more stirring.

STEW. Also called "braising." Both words describe cooking slowly with liquid, usually in a big covered pot, on the stove or in the oven. The recipe may say to precook some or all of the ingredients first. I love stewed and braised dishes, and you probably have had them without knowing what they were called. But since they take a while to cook and usually have a lot of steps, I've only included some soups and chili in this book.

BAKE. Cooking in the oven with low to medium heat. Baking is used for cookies, cakes, breads, and other treats. But it also appears in recipes for not-sweet, "savory" dishes like pizza, pot pies, and casseroles.

ROAST. Raise the heat in the oven so that food browns and maybe even gets crunchy, and that's roasting. There's almost always a little oil or butter involved in roasting, but there are exceptions. (That's the thing I love about cooking—there's always a lot of rule-breaking going on, and you never stop learning.)

BROIL AND GRILL. This is when you cook directly over or under a flame or electric heating element. There is a little broiling in this book, where the heat comes from the top and the pan is super-close to it.

FRY. With both "deep" and "shallow" frying, you use more oil than with pan-cooking (see "Pan-Cook" on this page). If you make your own crisp taco shells (page 105), you'll be shallow frying. Recipes where you cook food in a few inches of hot oil are for more advanced cooks, but you'll get there someday soon if you practice the easier techniques first.

HOW TO PREP MANY FOODS FOR COOKING

The prep steps in the recipes tell when—and, in most cases, how—to get food ready for cooking. This visual guide demonstrates the most efficient ways to slice, chop, snip, and grate.

APPLES AND PEARS

1. Peeling is optional. Slice downward around the core, removing flesh in pieces.

2. Cut the pieces into slices or wedges.

3. Or cut the pieces in a crosshatch pattern to chop.

AVOCADOS

1. Make sure the avocado isn't wobbling. Cut downward from top to bottom until you hit the big seed in the center.

2. Turn the avocado and cut the same way in another place, close enough so you can wiggle the knife to loosen a wedge away from the seed.

3. Use your fingers to pull the wedge away. Then scoop the flesh away from the skin with a spoon. Repeat until you get as much avocado as you need.

BELL PEPPERS

1. Cut downward around the core; turn and repeat all around.

2. Remove any remaining white pith with a paring knife (or not).

3. Cut the pepper into strips.

4. Gather the strips and cut them crosswise to chop.

BROCCOLI

1. Trim away the tough end, then cut off and save the stalk.

2. Cut downwards to remove the florets (or break them off), rotating the head as you go.

3. Chop the florets into smaller pieces if you like.

4. Peel the stalk and slice into coins or chop in bits.

BUTTERNUT (OR WINTER) SQUASH

1. Cut crosswise into two halves and put flat-side down.

2. Cut downward to remove the skin; trim off the ends.

3. Halve again to access the seeds and remove them.

4. Slice into manageable pieces of relatively equal thickness.

5. Following the contours of the squash, cut into cubes.

CABBAGE

1. If the core isn't flat, trim some off so it is.

2. Slice downward at a slight angle around the core to remove the leaves.

3. Slice into thin shreds (or cut in a crosshatch pattern to chop).

CARROTS

1. Peeling is optional, depending on how they look and will be used.

2. Slice carrots crosswise into manageable chunks; halve thick pieces lengthwise.

3. Slice the carrots lengthwise into sticks.

4. Gather the carrot sticks together, and slice across to chop.

CAULIFLOWER

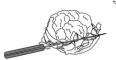   

1. If the core isn't flat trim some off so it is.

2. Slice downward to cut the head in half; remove any leaves.

3. Cut around the core to make florets (or break them off).

4. It's even faster to cut florets from an upside-down cauliflower.

5. For chopped cauliflower, rock the knife over the florets.

CHILES

   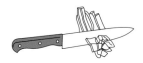

1. To quickly mince, remove the stem and rock a knife over the whole chile.

2. For less heat, hold the stem and cut off a piece of flesh.

3. Roll the chile over and repeat until cored.

4. Then rock a knife over the slices until minced.

CITRUS

1. For zest, run the fruit back and forth along a fine grater.

2. For juice, squeeze a half over a strainer (or your loosely cupped hand).

3. For segments, peel; then break the fruit apart and remove the seeds.

4. Or cut peeled fruit crosswise into attractive wheels.

CORN

  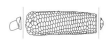

1. Grab the husk and pull down; repeat to reveal as much of the cob as you can.

2. Run the ear under water and pull off the remaining threads of silk.

3. Trim off any rough-looking tops or bottoms if necessary.

4. To remove the kernels, stand up the ear, cut downward, turn, and repeat.

CUCUMBER

   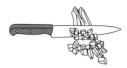

1. Trim the ends. Then peel only if the skin is thick or waxy.

2. Cut lengthwise, then spoon out the seeds if you'd like.

3. Or cut around the seeds to remove the flesh in pieces.

4. Cut lengthwise into spears.

5. To chop, cut the spears crosswise.

GARLIC

1. Lightly crush with the flat side of a knife, pressing it down with your hand.

2. Peel and trim or pinch off the stem end. (Or not.)

3. Rock the knife over the cloves until minced.

GINGER

1. Scrape off most of the skin with a spoon or remove it all with a paring knife.

2. Cut lengthwise into thin slices.

3. Rock the knife over the slices until minced.

HERBS

1. Most of the cilantro sprig is edible; for other herbs discard any tough stems.

2. Cut to remove the leaves and most tender stems.

3. Rock the knife over a pile of leaves and tender stems to chop.

4. Or hold a sturdy herb sprig and pull down to strip it.

5. Then rock the knife over the leaves to chop.

ONIONS

   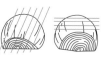 

1. Cut off both ends.

2. Slit through the skin and first layer, then remove them.

3. Cut the onion in half from top to bottom.

4. For slices, cut from top to bottom or crosswise in any thickness.

5. To chop, bundle slices and cut across them.

SCALLIONS

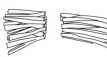 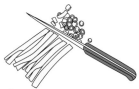 

1. Trim off the darkest part of the tops and the root ends.

2. Cut at an angle (or straight) across all the scallions at once for slices.

3. For chopped scallions, rock the knife over them.

STONE FRUIT

1. Slice downward around the pit, removing flesh in 3 or 4 pieces.

2. Cut the pieces into slices.

3. Or cut the pieces in a crosshatch pattern to chop.

STURDY GREENS

1. Trim the ends. Separate the leaves from the stems (if you like).

2. Gather the leaves into a bunch, and cut crosswise into "ribbons."

3. For smaller pieces, rock your knife over the slices a few times to chop.

4. For fast stems and leaves together: cut crosswise from the top.

TOMATOES

1. Put the fruit upside down and slice downward at an angle to remove the core.

2. Slice each piece lengthwise into wedges.

3. Slice the wedges crosswise into chunks if you'd like.

4. Make sure to capture the juice.

CHOPPING WITH SCISSORS

1. It's super-fast to chop cooked or tender raw vegetables with scissors.

2. Keep working the scissors through the vegetables as you turn the bowl.

MAKING THIN RIBBONS

1. Work in either direction to make ribbons of vegetables or cheese with a vegetable peeler.

GRATING BY HAND

1. For faster chopping and cooking: Stand the box grater up on a cutting board.

2. Push the vegetable up and down over the largest holes on the grater; be assertive.

3. As they accumulate inside the grater, empty the pieces onto the board.

4. To grate hard cheese by hand, run it back and forth along a fine grater.

PREPARING MEAT

1. Trimming fat from meat takes time; I don't usually bother.

2. Slice thinly against the grain; it's easier if you freeze the meat for a few minutes.

3. Or cut into chunks. The smaller the piece, the faster it cooks.

STAY SAFE!

The recipes are intended for you to cook with an adult, especially when you're beginning. You obviously need to be careful working with knives, stoves, ovens, and reaching into high places. But it doesn't have to be a big deal. Just pay attention to what you're doing. You'll enjoy cooking much more if you take your time to set up everything that you need to be comfortable. Taste and ask questions as you go. Have a drink and a snack handy if you like. And if you need to take a break, that's okay too.

HAVE FUN!

Sure, the cooking is fun, but so is the garnishing, serving, and eating. A lot of cooks like to set the table first or at least get out whatever plates, silverware, glasses, and napkins you need. Think about what sauces and extra seasonings you might like to add to the dish before eating. And if you have extra time between steps, cleaning up some of the mess always makes things taste better. I don't know why, but it does!

Some ideas for drinks are milk—from a cow or goat or a plant like oats or nuts—or water or sparkling water. Both milk and juices can be pretty filling and distract you from the taste of the food, so if water is too boring for you, think about trying a splash of juice in your water or sparkling water, with or without ice. And I don't know what the rule about sugary or even diet soda is at your house, but I do know that food tastes best when there's not a lot of competing flavors in your mouth.

Taking photos of what you cook is a great way to show off what you're learning and share recipes and garnishing and serving ideas. Natural lighting from windows in daylight is always the best for shooting food. But of course it's often dark at dinnertime. Setting up a little desk lamp to shine on the plates or using the light above your stove usually gives better results than the flash in your camera.

Have you ever heard or read the advice, "Don't let perfection be the enemy of good"? It means that the important thing is doing something at all, not being perfect at it. I believe in that advice for sure. Sometimes I take great photos and sometimes not. Who cares? The important thing is that I created something good to eat. Sharing your food photos is fun if you can have a laugh at the ones you call "ugly delicious." Or just keep them for yourself so you can track your progress. You'll see. What's most important is enjoying and sharing what you made. Cooking with and for the people you love makes every day a whole lot better.

PACKING FOOD TO GO

Taking what you made to school or a friend's house, or on a road trip or picnic, is always a great idea. And now there are so many reusable containers that are easy to pack into a cooler. Some even come with their own cooler. There are lunchboxes with separate compartments—that look like toolboxes—and squishy sealed bags and pouches made from washable silicone. Sandwiches usually only need wrapping in parchment paper or cloth, and metal thermoses keep soups hot and cold drinks cold. There are even some cool travel utensils out there now. Don't forget the napkins!

HOW THESE RECIPES WORK

The recipes in this book are written just like most other cookbooks so that you will be able to learn skills you can use your whole life. I added extra details to help you know what exactly to look for at every step. Here are more extras in these recipes:

1

OPENING NOTES. These describe the recipe and the finished dish to help you decide if you want to try it.

2

SERVING SIZES. When you're learning to cook, handling less food gives you more chances for success. You'll need to prep fewer ingredients, the pan and pot sizes can be smaller, and the cooking time is usually faster. So, most of the recipes in this book are written using small quantities for fewer servings. Because little kids eat less than big kids or adults, the portions appear in a range that covers all appetites. It's easy to feed more people by doubling the ingredients. If you do this, you'll also need to use bigger pots and pans. An adult can help you decide if you need to do that.

3

TIME. The estimated time it will take to cook a recipe includes both prep and cook activities. Let's call it an average time for you and an adult to work together. But it's not a race—take your time and try not to feel rushed or stressed, especially when you're just starting out. It's supposed to be fun, right? The more you cook, the faster you'll be able to pull a recipe together.

4

SYMBOLS. These flag recipes that are best for Beginner (★), Intermediate (★ ★), or Advanced (★ ★ ★) cooks; recipes that freeze well (❄); and recipes that are vegetarian or can easily be adjusted for vegetarians (🍃).

5

INGREDIENTS AND STEPS. These are the main parts of recipes. The ingredients tell you what foods you need and maybe some advance prep to do. I suggest you read the recipe through all the way and get everything on that list chopped, measured, and ready to go. You can separate things in little bowls, on parchment paper, or on cutting boards. After that, you only have to focus on the steps themselves. Sometimes some of the prep is explained in the steps so that I can add details about how to do the action. Follow the directions in order to mix, cook, and bake your way to delicious food.

6

OTHER NOTES. Each recipe includes ideas for other dishes to eat along with whatever you've chosen to make. There are also variations and lists after some recipes so you can change or substitute ingredients and seasonings or add your own touches to create something totally "you."

7

"DID YOU KNOW" SECTIONS. Little boxes tell you more about an ingredient or cooking action.

1 What isn't a good time for buttery egg noodles? They're like silky birthday-present ribbons you can eat. Since they go with everything, the recipe here gives you enough to refrigerate for reheating later—or to share now!

BUTTERY EGG NOODLES

2 MAKES: 2 TO 4 SERVINGS ⟩→ **3** TIME: 20 MINUTES ❄️🖐️ **4**

INGREDIENTS

5

Salt

8 ounces egg noodles (about half a 1-pound package, long or short strands)

1 to 2 tablespoons butter

Pepper (if you like)

EAT WITH: any meat-and-vegetable stir-fry (page 229), Chicken with Orange Sauce (page 219), or Scrambled or Fried Eggs (pages 39 and 43).

6
VARIATION

BUTTERY WHOLE GRAIN NOODLES. You might not be able to find whole wheat egg noodles, so look for whole wheat fettuccine if you want strands or whole wheat fusilli (corkscrews) or farfalle (butterflies) for cut pastas that are sort of thick and chewy. Cook these the same way as regular egg noodles, checking early and often because they go from firm to mushy pretty fast.

STEPS

1 Fill a 5-quart pot halfway with water and bring it to a boil over high heat. Add 2 big pinches salt.

2 When the water boils, add the noodles. If you have long strands, gently swirl them with tongs until they soften and sink all the way in the water. Adjust the heat so the water boils without bubbling over and cook, stirring every 2 or 3 minutes with the tongs, until the noodles are as tender or mushy as you want. Start checking after 5 minutes. They're going to keep cooking a little after draining.

3 When the noodles are ready, dip a ladle into the pot and save 1 cup of the cooking water near the stove. Drain the noodles into a colander in the sink and return the noodles to the pot with the butter. If you're adding more stuff from the list below, put that in the pot now too.

4 Set the pot over medium-low heat and stir with the tongs until the butter melts. Add a small splash of the cooking water to keep the noodles from sticking and make a little sauce. Eat hot, with a sprinkle of pepper—or not.

7

DID YOU KNOW

You can substitute any kind of oil—like olive or other vegetable or nut oils—for the butter here. Pick one that tastes good to you and stick with it or try a different kind every time you make a pot of noodles.

PASTA AND NOODLES 165

⭐ Some mornings you've just got to have a milkshake. Choose from the main recipe, which tastes like a Creamsicle, or from a rainbow of colors that magically includes chocolate.

ORANGE SMOOTHIE

MAKES: 1 TO 2 SERVINGS (ABOUT 1½ CUPS) ⟩⟩ *TIME: 10 MINUTES* 🍃

INGREDIENTS

1 large orange

½ large banana

½ cup yogurt

¼ teaspoon vanilla extract (if you like)

1 cup ice cubes, plus more as needed

EAT WITH: Crunchy Bread (page 242).

STEPS

1 Peel the orange and separate the fruit into sections. Pinch out any seeds and put the sections in the blender. In this order, add the banana, yogurt, vanilla, if you're using it, and ice.

2 Put the lid on the blender and turn the machine on at the lowest speed. As the ingredients begin to purée, increase the speed slowly until the smoothie is the texture you want. To make it slushier, add another ice cube or two. Or to make it thinner (or help the machine grind better), add water, 1 tablespoon at a time. Drink the smoothie as soon as possible so it stays icy. (Or put it in a stay-cold cup so you can sip it slowly.)

RECIPE CONTINUES ➡

Mark and Holden make a Blue Smoothie.

BLUE SMOOTHIE. Instead of the orange, use 1 cup fresh or frozen blueberries. If you use frozen fruit, you might not need any ice, so add it, if you like, after the rest of the ingredients are blended.

RED SMOOTHIE. Instead of the orange, use 1 cup fresh or frozen strawberries or raspberries. If you use frozen fruit, you might not need any ice, so add it, if you like, after the rest of the ingredients are blended.

GREEN SMOOTHIE. You won't taste any vegetables in here. Instead of the orange, use 1 cup packed baby spinach leaves and the juice of ½ lemon.

CHOCOLATE CHIP SMOOTHIE. Use a whole banana for this and skip the orange. Add 1 ounce dark chocolate—2 tablespoons of chocolate chips or about ⅓ of a 3-ounce chocolate bar (broken into big pieces).

DID YOU KNOW

You can make smoothies with any kind of plain yogurt. That includes nonfat, 1%, 2%, or whole yogurt made with cow or goat milk, or nondairy yogurt made from oat, soy, almond, cashew, rice, or coconut milk. Or use soft silken tofu. They will all taste different, and some will be creamier than others, so try the yogurt by itself before adding it to the blender. When I say "yogurt" in the ingredient list, you can use any of these. What's most important is that it's plain and not sweetened.

The same is true for whenever you see milk in recipes. Even though cow's milk is the usual first choice, go ahead and use whatever you drink at home. There will be differences in how some things turn out, but no big deal.

⭐ At last, a breakfast cereal that's all you: You decide how crunchy and sweet to make the oats, whether you want cinnamon, and what to stir in for extras. For a mellower, oatier flavor and softer texture, see what you think of the variation for muesli.

GRANOLA,
JUST THE WAY YOU LIKE IT

MAKES: 6 TO 12 SERVINGS (ABOUT 4 CUPS) ⇒ TiME: 30 TO 50 MiNUTES ❄️ 🍃

INGREDiENTS

3 cups rolled oats (not instant)

¼ cup packed brown sugar, honey, maple syrup, or other syrup, plus more to taste

1 teaspoon cinnamon, plus more to taste (if you like)

¼ teaspoon salt

EAT WiTH: milk, fresh fruit, yogurt, or Applesauce (page 261).

VARiATiON

MUESLI. No need to bake this cereal. Combine all the ingredients in a big bowl and stir to combine. Store in the refrigerator for up to a couple weeks and eat just like you would granola.

STEPS

1 Heat the oven to 350°F. Line a large rimmed baking sheet with a sheet of parchment paper and spread the oats into the pan. Sprinkle with the sugar (or drizzle with the honey or syrup). Sprinkle the cinnamon, if you're using it, and salt on top of that. Use a stiff spatula to toss and stir the oats until they're coated.

2 Put the pan in the oven and bake for 10 minutes, then stir with the spatula. Take a taste and add 1 or 2 tablespoons more sweetener and a pinch of cinnamon, if you like, and stir again.

3 Return the pan to the oven and repeat Step 2 every 10 minutes until the oats are as dark as you'd like them. (You won't need to add sweetener every time, though!) Choose your stir-ins from the list that follows and measure them out so they're ready.

4 When the granola is ready, scatter your choice of stir-ins over the top of the mixture and toss with the spatula to combine. Let cool and then transfer to an airtight container. The granola will keep in the refrigerator for up to a couple months. *RECiPE CONTiNUES ➡*

GRANOLA STIR-INS

- 1 cup chopped nuts (any kind you like)
- 1 cup whole seeds (like sunflower, sesame, or pumpkin)
- ½ cup unsweetened shredded coconut
- ½ cup raisins
- ½ cup dried berries or chopped dried fruit
- ½ cup candied ginger (sweet and spicy!)
- ½ cup chocolate chips or chopped chocolate

DESSERT FOR BREAKFAST

In a glass, spoon alternating layers of granola with yogurt and fresh fruit or Applesauce (or another fruit sauce) (page 261) and suddenly you're eating a parfait. Or for a breakfast sundae, warm some frozen berries in the microwave, spoon them on top of a bowl of yogurt, and top with a sprinkle of granola.

★ ★   Start with your own granola (see the recipe on page 31) or one you like to buy and end up with a satisfying breakfast that's as fun to make as it is to eat. If you choose store-bought granola—you can even use other whole grain cereals—break up any clumps by crumbling the cereal with your hands in the bowl in Step 3. These are sweetened with your favorite dried fruit—you'll need a food processor for that part—so they're just the right kind of sweet for a strong start to the day, especially if you start with a good-for-you cereal. And any extras are perfect for saving in the fridge or freezer for snacking emergencies. Just wrap each in a small piece of parchment and stick them in an airtight container.

NO-BAKE BREAKFAST BARS

MAKES: 12 TO 16 BARS ⟫ TIME: 20 MINUTES PLUS TIME FOR CHILLING ❄ 🗨

INGREDIENTS

Vegetable oil for greasing the pan

1½ cups dried fruit (like apricots, plums, raisins, or cherries)

2 tablespoons honey or maple syrup

3 cups Granola, Just the Way You Like It (page 31) or other granola or whole grain cereal

EAT WITH: fresh fruit or berries, or peanut or another nut butter; or dip in yogurt.

STEPS

1 Use your fingers or a clean towel to grease an 8- or 9-inch square baking pan by smearing a thin layer of vegetable oil all over the bottom and sides. (The bars will be thicker when made in an 8-inch pan, a little thinner in a 9-inch one.)

2 Put the dried fruit in a food processor with the honey or syrup. Push and let go of the start button quickly to pulse the blade until the mixture is thick and sticky. Add water 1 tablespoon at a time to chop up the fruit and help get things moving. It's okay if you can still see bits of fruit. The idea is to end up with fruit "glue," so you don't want it to be at all soupy.

3 Put the cereal in a big bowl. Lift the blade out of the food processor by its plastic knob and use a soft spatula to carefully scrape the fruit glue into the bowl with the cereal. Then scrape the rest of the fruit mixture into the bowl too. Keep using the spatula to lift the cereal from the bottom, folding and stirring to mix it evenly with the fruit.

4 Scrape the mixture out of the bowl with a soft spatula and use a fork to press it evenly into the prepared pan. Chill in the fridge until firm, about 2 hours. Cut into squares or rectangles. Store in an airtight container for up to 4 days (see the recipe note).

★ One recipe fits all: oatmeal (of course), cornmeal and grits (also known as mush or polenta), cream of wheat (the real kind), and rice (white or brown). These are the common grains eaten hot for breakfast around the world, and chances are you'll like at least one of them. Once you decide, it's easy to adjust the recipe during cooking. Do you want the spoonfuls to be soupy like porridge? Or thicker, on the clumpy side?

HOT CEREAL, STARTING WITH OATMEAL

MAKES: 2 TO 4 SERVINGS ⇛ TIME: 15 MINUTES

INGREDIENTS

1 cup rolled oats (not instant)

Small pinch salt

1 tablespoon butter (if you like)

1/2 teaspoon cinnamon (if you like)

EAT WITH: See the list that follows for both sweet and savory flavoring and topping ideas.

STEPS

1 For soupy oatmeal, put 2 1/4 cups water in a medium saucepan. (For hot cereal on the dry side, start with 1 3/4 cups water.) Add the oats and salt and turn the heat to high. When the water boils, turn the heat down to low and cook, stirring a lot, until the water soaks into the oats and there are big bubbles popping on top. This takes about 5 minutes.

2 Stir in the butter and cinnamon if you're using them. If the cereal looks thicker than you like it, stir in more water, 1 tablespoon at a time. Cover the pan and remove it from the heat. Get your flavorings and toppings ready.

3 After 5 minutes off heat, either stir your flavoring or topping into the pot or serve the oatmeal and then add what you like to your bowl.

RECIPE CONTINUES ➡

REAL CREAM OF WHEAT. A little creamy, a little chewy. Use bulgur instead of the oats. Everything else stays the same.

RICE FOR BREAKFAST. Grab your favorite spoon! Put 1 cup cooked rice (white or brown) in the pot with 1 cup milk or water. Follow the directions for oatmeal in the main recipe.

MUSH. More stirring means no lumps, so be prepared to work a little. You can make this with finely ground cornmeal (the kind used for baking), medium-grind cornmeal (for what's also called "polenta"), or white or yellow grits (for a different, popcorny flavor). Whatever you choose, extra butter is a good idea. Instead of the oatmeal in Step 1, start with ½ cup cornmeal and ¾ cup water and add the pinch of salt. Put 2 cups water in a pitcher or measuring cup near the stove. Use a whisk to stir the mixture constantly while it comes to a boil. Turn the heat down so the bubbles plop on top of the mush sometimes and change to a big spoon. Add small splashes of water from the pitcher and stir around the inside of the pot so the cornmeal or grits don't stick. (You probably won't use all the water in the pitcher.) They're ready when they're creamy and soft and pull away from the sides of the pot as you stir (you'll have to taste). It will take 20 to 30 minutes.

DID YOU KNOW

If you make extra and refrigerate leftover hot cereal, you can heat a bowlful in the microwave and top it the same as usual—or totally differently—for fast hot breakfasts for up to 1 week.

11 FLAVORINGS AND TOPPINGS FOR HOT CEREAL

Go sweet or savory. To flavor the whole batch, stir 2 tablespoons of any of these into the pot. Or add 1 or 2 teaspoons to each bowl. Taste, then decide if you need a little more.

1. Milk (for richer hot cereal, you can replace some or all of the water with milk in the main recipe or the variations)
2. Yogurt
3. Berries or chopped fresh fruit (you'll probably want extra!)
4. Jam, preserves, or jelly
5. Brown sugar, honey, or maple or other syrup
6. Raisins or chopped dried fruit
7. Peanut or other nut butter
8. Unsweetened shredded coconut
9. Salsa
10. Soy sauce
11. Grated cheese

⭐ There's no reason to rush scrambled eggs. With my favorite low-and-slow way, it still only takes a few minutes, and they turn out exactly the way you like them. If you're cooking a big breakfast—or even if you're just having toast on the side—get everything else ready before you start the eggs. They're best right out of the skillet.

SCRAMBLED EGGS

MAKES: 1 OR 2 SERVINGS »» *TIME: 20 MINUTES* 🌿

INGREDIENTS

2 eggs

Salt

Pepper (if you like)

1 tablespoon butter or olive oil

EAT WITH: Crunchy Bread (page 242), warm corn or flour tortillas (page 107), bacon or any breakfast meat (page 58), and/or Big French Fries (page 155).

STEPS

1 Put a small bowl on the counter, with a small plate right next to it. Smack the side of an egg on the plate hard enough to hear it crack but gently enough that the shell doesn't break into pieces. Use both hands to carefully hold the egg over the bowl and open it so the insides slide out.

2 Repeat with the other egg. Add a small pinch of salt and pepper to the bowl if you like. Use a fork or a whisk to beat the eggs, making circles with your hand or moving back and forth. Keep beating until the eggs are golden yellow and no longer have any streaks.

3 Put the butter or oil in an 8-inch skillet over medium-high heat. (This is a good time to use a nonstick pan.) When the butter melts or the oil shimmers, pour in the eggs, count to five, then turn the heat down to medium-low. Begin slowly stirring with a large spoon or soft spatula, scraping the sides of the pan where the eggs are firmer toward the center to help the eggs cook evenly.

4 Keep stirring until the eggs are as soft and jiggly or dry and firm as you want them. The longer eggs cook, the more tough and rubbery they get (you might also start to see some golden brown spots), so as soon as they look the way you like, move the skillet off the heat and immediately spoon the eggs onto a plate so they don't keep cooking. After tasting, you can sprinkle with more salt and pepper.

RECIPE CONTINUES ➡

SCRAMBLED TOFU. In Step 1, instead of the eggs, divide a block of firm tofu into 3 or 4 even pieces, depending on how big it is and how much you want to eat. Put one piece in the bowl and refrigerate the rest in an airtight container (use it within a few days). Use your hands or a fork to crumble and mash the tofu into small bits. Follow the recipe from Step 2, cooking and stirring until the tofu is hot and maybe a little crisp in places.

MORE SCRAMBLED EGGS OR TOFU. You can make more breakfast for more people simply by increasing everything—the size of the bowl, the number of eggs (or pieces of tofu block), the butter or oil, and the size of the pan (a 12-inch skillet will hold up to 8 eggs).

SCRAMBLED EGG NOODLES. Turn scrambled eggs into strands you can eat like pasta. All you need is a 12-inch nonstick skillet and a gentle touch. Follow the recipe through Step 2, then beat either 1½ teaspoons soy sauce or water into the eggs. In Step 3, put the skillet over medium-low heat and add 1 tablespoon vegetable oil. Use a brush or towel to spread the oil evenly over the pan. When the oil is hot, pour in the egg mixture, tilting the pan so the bottom of the pan is covered in a thin layer. Cook, undisturbed, until the top is dry, about 1 minute. The easiest way to remove the eggs is to use a soft spatula and a big spoon to roll the eggs up like a piece of paper. Carefully transfer to a cutting board and let cool for a minute or 2. Then cut across the roll to form strips. Gently toss the eggs with your fingers on the cutting board to unravel the strips. You can use these to garnish stir-fries, noodles, or rice, or sauce them as if they're noodles themselves.

9 WAYS TO FLAVOR SCRAMBLED EGGS

Whisk any of these extras into the eggs in Step 2:

1. 2 tablespoons grated or crumbled cheese (any kind you like)
2. 2 tablespoons chopped cooked vegetables (maybe leftover from dinner)
3. 2 tablespoons crumbled crackers or chips
4. 1 tablespoon chopped herbs (like chives, basil, or mint)
5. 1 tablespoon chopped olives
6. 1 tablespoon chopped green onion
7. 1 tablespoon salsa
8. 1 teaspoon ketchup
9. A dash of hot sauce

DID YOU KNOW You can make scrambled eggs fluffier by adding 1 teaspoon water to the bowl for every 2 eggs before beating. Or to make them creamier, whisk in 1 teaspoon milk.

★ ★ Sure, eggs cooked in buttery toasted bread are fun to eat and super-delicious. Just ask my oldest daughter (and Holden's mom), Kate, who always requested them when she was little. And in a lot of ways, it's also easier to cook both things together in one pan. You can make the eggs as runny or firm as you like—the directions tell you how.

EGGS IN A HOLE
À LA LITTLE KATE

MAKES: 1 OR 2 SERVINGS ⟫ → TIME: 15 MINUTES

INGREDIENTS

2 slices bread

1 tablespoon butter or olive oil

2 eggs

Salt

Pepper (if you like)

EAT WITH: any breakfast meat (page 58).

Cheese is excellent here. After you crack the egg into the bread, sprinkle a thin layer of your favorite grated cheese over the top. When you flip it, the cheese will melt and get crisp in places. If it spreads in the pan past the crust, you'll have made a "cheese skirt"!

STEPS

1 Use a biscuit cutter or a drinking glass to cut a big hole out of both bread slices. Get a small plate on the counter by the burner you'll be using. Put a 10-inch skillet over medium heat for about 1 minute. Add the butter or oil and swirl it around the pan. When the butter stops foaming or the oil is hot, after about 1 minute, add the bread slices and circles to the pan.

2 As soon as you can, smack the side of an egg on the plate hard enough to hear it crack but gently enough that the shell doesn't break into pieces. Use both hands to carefully hold the egg over one of the holes in the bread and open the egg so the insides slide out. Repeat with the other egg and hole.

3 Watch for a couple minutes until the egg whites turn white on the bottom and the bread starts to smell like toast. Slide a stiff spatula under the piece that seems the most ready, lift it above the pan, and gently turn it over. Turn the circles over with the spatula and move them around the pan to soak up any extra butter.

4 Cook the second side until the eggs are as firm as you like them, 1 to 3 minutes. To check, press gently on the yolk with the spatula to see if it's at all jiggly. If it turns totally light yellow and feels solid when you press, there should be no more runniness. Watch the circles because they'll be ready before the eggs in the holes. Sprinkle the eggs with salt and pepper too if you like and eat while they're hot.

VARIATIONS

SUNNY—SIDE UP EGGS. Also known as fried eggs. Toast the bread separately in a toaster. To cook the eggs, follow the recipe, but skip the bread and open the eggs directly into the skillet in Step 2. Cover the pan and cook, checking every minute, until the eggs are as runny or firm as you want them; you don't need to flip them.

SUNNY—SIDE DOWN EGGS. Also known as over-easy, over-medium, or over-hard eggs, depending on how long you cook them. This is the best way to cook fried eggs if you want the whites a little crusty and the yolks only a little or not at all runny. It just takes a little practice to turn the eggs without the bread. Do everything the recipe says only without any bread.

⭐ ⭐ When eggs and toast come together, it's almost like eating pancakes, except French toast is crunchier and faster. All the better for making a big batch and wowing your family or friends with your cooking. As for the choice of bread, use whatever you like for toast or sandwiches and be sure to check out the variations for some new ideas.

FRENCH TOAST

MAKES: 2 SLICES ➢➢ TIME: 20 MINUTES 🍃

INGREDIENTS

1 egg

⅓ cup milk

1 teaspoon sugar or a teeny pinch of salt (if you like)

2 slices white or whole wheat bread, each no more than 1 inch thick

1 tablespoon butter or vegetable oil, plus more as needed

EAT WITH: any of the toppings from the list that follows or bacon or sausage (page 58).

STEPS

1   Crack the egg and open it into a wide, shallow bowl or pie plate as described in Scrambled Eggs on page 39. Add the milk and the sugar if you want the toast to be a little sweet (or the salt if you don't). Whisk with a fork until the mixture—called a custard—is a light yellow color without streaks.

2   Set the bowl of custard near the skillet. Put the butter or oil in a 10-inch skillet over low heat. Add the first piece of bread to the custard and turn it over with a fork a couple times until it gets a little soggy.

3   Turn the heat under the pan to medium. When the butter foams or the oil shimmers, carefully put the soaked bread in the pan and add the other slice to the custard. Let the French toast cook without touching for 3 to 5 minutes while you turn the second bread slice in the bowl and let it sit, just like you did the first one.

4   Look at the bread in the pan. When the edges turn brown and you notice a toasty smell, lift one corner with a stiff spatula and peek to see if it's the golden color you like and either let it cook some more or slip the spatula all the way under, lift it up from the pan, and turn the bread over. Cook the other side the same way, peeking after another 2 minutes or so.

RECIPE CONTINUES ➡

French toast is even good cold. Or try warming leftovers in the microwave on a low setting.

5 The French toast is ready when you press down in the middle with the spatula and it's no longer squishy. If you need to turn it again, go ahead. When that slice is ready, move it to a plate and repeat with the second slice. While the second slice is cooking, you can top the first one as you like and begin eating. (Be sure you come back in a couple minutes or ask someone to watch the pan!) Or wait to eat both at the same time.

VARIATIONS

TORTILLA TOAST. Corn or flour. Instead of bread, soak and cook 3 small or 2 large tortillas in batches as described in the main recipe. You can either stack them on the plate with toppings in between or roll each so the toppings become filling.

ENGLISH MUFFIN TOAST. Instead of sliced bread, soak and cook both halves of an English muffin. (You might be able to fit them both in the bowl and skillet at the same time.) Be sure to give them time to soak up all the custard before cooking.

WAFFLED FRENCH TOAST. For when you really want waffles but there just isn't time to make a batter. Instead of a skillet, prepare a waffle iron. Smear or brush both sides with the butter or oil, then close it and turn the heat to the medium-high setting. Prepare the custard and soak the bread as described in Steps 1 and 2 in the main recipe. When the waffle iron is hot, carefully open and put the bread on the bottom (one or both pieces, depending on if they fit in a single layer). Close and cook until golden and crisp. The time depends on your waffle iron, but you'll be able to tell by watching and smelling.

10 TOPPINGS FOR FRENCH TOAST, PANCAKES, OR WAFFLES

Pick one or two and start with small amounts. You can always add, but you can't take away.

1. Soft or melted butter
2. Maple (or other) syrup
3. Honey
4. Powdered or granulated sugar
5. Yogurt or sour cream
6. Cut fresh or frozen fruit or berries
7. Applesauce or other cooked fruit (page 261)
8. Jam or preserves
9. Grated or sliced cheese
10. Salsa

★ ★ In the Dr. Seuss book *Green Eggs and Ham*, the eggs have green yolks and are fried sunny-side up—a tough trick for us normal humans to do. Instead, let's tint scrambled eggs with a top-secret ingredient. I'll give you a hint: It's creamy, mild, and used for guacamole.

GREEN EGGS AND HAM

MAKES: 1 OR 2 SERVINGS ≫→ TiME: 30 MiNUTES

INGREDiENTS

2 ounces cooked ham

4 teaspoons butter or olive oil

¼ large avocado

1 tablespoon maple syrup

Salt

Pepper (if you like)

2 eggs

EAT WiTH: Fresh Tomato (or Fruit) Salsa (page 80) with tortillas or toast, pages 107 and 242.

STEPS

1   Heat the oven to 200°F and put an ovenproof plate or pan near the stove. Cut the ham into bite-sized pieces; you should have about ½ cup. Put 2 teaspoons of the butter (or oil) in a medium skillet (preferably nonstick) over medium heat.

2   When the butter melts (or the oil is hot and shimmers), add the ham and cook, stirring enough so it cooks without burning, until the chunks brown and get crisp in places, about 5 minutes.

3   While the ham cooks, prepare the avocado as shown on page 16: Cut downward toward the center in 2 places so you can pull about ¼ of the fruit away from the pit; scoop the avocado out of the peel in big chunks, and put them in a medium bowl. (Wrap the rest of the avocado tightly and save for another use.)

4   Remove the skillet from the heat, add the maple syrup, and stir until the ham pieces are shiny. Scrape the ham and glaze from the pan onto the plate and transfer to the oven to keep warm. Rinse out the skillet and wipe it dry.

5   Mash the avocado with a fork or potato masher until most of the lumps are gone. Sprinkle with salt and pepper too if you like. Put a small plate right next to the bowl with the avocado. Smack the side of an egg on the plate hard enough to hear it crack but gently enough that the shell doesn't break into pieces. Use both hands to carefully hold the egg over the bowl and open it so the insides slide

RECiPE CONTiNUES ➡

out. Use a fork or a whisk to beat them with the avocado until the mixture is smooth. (The eggs will turn a little green!) Now's a good time to make any sides you want ready to eat.

6 Put the skillet over medium heat and add the last 2 teaspoons of butter or oil. When it's hot, add the egg mixture. Use a stiff spatula or spoon to cook and stir, scraping the sides and bottom of the pan.

7 As the eggs begin to form clumps, some parts might dry out; whenever you see that, remove the pan from the heat and continue to stir until the cooking slows down a bit. Then return to the heat and continue cooking. The eggs are done when they look good to you (I like them creamy, soft, and still a bit runny, but some people prefer them drier). Serve the eggs right away with the ham and whatever else you like on the side.

⭐ There are many ways to boil eggs in their shell. I like this way the best for kids: the shells are less likely to crack when you put them into the pot and the peel almost always comes off easily. Plus, the timing in this recipe for the levels from runny (soft-boiled) to solid (hard-boiled) is almost always perfect with large-sized eggs.

BOILED EGGS
HARD, SOFT, AND IN-BETWEEN

MAKES: AS MANY EGGS AS YOU WANT ⟫ TIME: ABOUT 15 MINUTES 🌿

INGREDIENTS

2 to 6 eggs
Salt
Pepper (if you like)

EAT WITH: any kind of toast (page 242).

STEPS

1 Find a pot that will hold all the eggs you want to cook with several inches above them and make sure it has a lid that fits tightly. Put the eggs in the pot, then fill the pot with enough water to cover the eggs by about 2 inches.

2 Put the pot over medium-high heat and bring to a gentle boil. Once the water boils, turn off the heat, cover the pot, and set a timer. For soft-boiled eggs, you'll want to cook them for 6 minutes; for medium-boiled, go for 8; and let hard-boiled eggs with firm yolks stay in at least 10 minutes (11 if you like them sort of chalky). The photo on page 51 gives you an idea what each stage looks like. While the eggs sit, fill a bowl big enough to hold the eggs with lots of ice and some water—cooks call that an ice bath.

3 When the eggs are cooked how you want them, use a slotted spoon to move them from the pot to the ice bath. Let the eggs stay in the ice water until they feel cool or warm. Then peel and break or cut them open. Eat them with a sprinkle of salt and pepper too if you like. (You can also refrigerate the eggs in their shells for up to several days and eat them cold.)

You can make egg salad with either hard-boiled or scrambled eggs. (Like you would with the Tuna Sandwich recipe on page 96.) All you do is put a cold cooked egg or 2 (or however many you want) in a shallow bowl and mash them with a fork. Add a sprinkle of salt and pepper and 1 teaspoon mayonnaise for every egg. Stir with the fork, then decide if you want more mayo. You can also add chopped pickles, herbs, or green onions. Or maybe you might stir in mustard, dried chile flakes, or hot sauce to wake up your mouth. Egg salad is good in sandwiches, on crackers, stuffed into celery, or on top of green salad.

★ ★ Stirring stuff into scrambled eggs is sort of like eating an omelet, only with omelets the scrambled eggs wrap around the stir-ins so they're more like a filling. Sure, you get to choose how to fold your omelet—in half or thirds or sort of roll it—and there are directions here for all ways. But if things don't go exactly how you expected the first few times, that's fine. You'll get the hang of it.

OMELET

MAKES: 1 OMELET ⇉ TIME: 15 MINUTES 🌿

INGREDIENTS

Fillings from the list that follows

2 eggs

1 tablespoon milk (if you like)

Salt

Pepper (if you like)

1 tablespoon butter or olive oil, plus more as needed

EAT WITH: any kind of toast (page 242) or Big French Fries (page 155).

STEPS

1 Pick out a filling from the list that follows and get it ready. If you're using vegetables or a sauce, you want to warm them a little in the microwave before starting.

2 Put a small bowl on the counter, with a small plate right next to it. Smack the side of an egg on the plate hard enough to hear it crack but gently enough that the shell doesn't break into pieces. Use both hands to carefully hold the egg over the bowl and open it so the insides slide out. Repeat with the other egg. Pour in the milk if you'd like the eggs a little creamier and easier to fold. Add a small pinch of salt and pepper too if you like.

3 Use a fork or a whisk to beat the eggs, moving the whisk in circles or back and forth. Keep beating until the eggs are yellow colored and no longer have any streaks.

4 Put the butter or oil in an 8-inch skillet over medium heat. (This is a good time to use a nonstick pan.) Once the butter is melted or the oil is hot, swirl the butter or oil around the pan and then pour in the eggs. Cook without doing anything for about 30 seconds. Use a stiff spatula to push one edge toward the center and tip the pan so that uncooked eggs run in to fill the space in the bottom.

RECIPE CONTINUES ➡

5 Scatter the filling across the middle of the eggs and cook until the center is almost as firm as you like your eggs, then turn off the heat. Slip the spatula under one edge of the eggs and, in one motion, lift and push so that the flap of eggs covers the filling. You can push all the way to the other edge to fold the omelet in half. Or you can try using the spatula to roll the center of the omelet over to flip onto the other side. And if neither of those work out, slip the spatula under the other edge and fold the eggs toward the middle of the omelet to cover the filling from that side too. To eat, tip the pan over your plate and scootch the omelet out of the pan with the spatula.

8 YUMMY OMELET FILLINGS

You can mix and match, but don't use more than ¼ cup total or the omelet will be hard to fold.

1. Your favorite grated cheese
2. Chopped cooked vegetables like broccoli, carrots, spinach, or peas
3. Chopped cooked ham, bacon, sausage, turkey, chicken, crab, or shrimp
4. Sliced fresh fruit or berries
5. Applesauce or other cooked fruit (page 261)
6. Chopped fresh tomatoes, tomato sauce, or salsa
7. Chopped fresh herbs
8. Sliced olives

★ ★ The official name for this sort of flat omelet is "frittata," an Italian dish that describes anything from pasta to vegetables to bread crumbs held together with scrambled eggs. I love that my grandson Holden dubbed this "egg pizza," though. Now we can spin the recipe so it's more like a crust—you can eat it plain or add toppings. And just like pizza, the leftovers are good cold, right out of the fridge.

EGG PIZZA

MAKES: 2 TO 4 SERVINGS ⇉ TIME: 30 MINUTES

INGREDIENTS

1 or 2 or 3 handfuls crackers (like saltines or goldfish), chips (tortilla or potato), or dry bread (like croutons or bread crumbs)

4 eggs

2 tablespoons butter or olive oil

EAT WITH: Tomato or Meaty Sauce (page 170), Fresh Tomato (or Fruit) Salsa (page 80), or Cherry Tomato Candy (page 146).

STEPS

1 Put a handful of the crackers, chips, or bread in a sealed bag (unless you've got Goldfish or another small-shaped cracker you want to keep whole). Close the bag, lay it flat it on a cutting board, and bash it until the crumbs are as big or small as you like. Transfer the crumbs to a measuring cup and repeat until you have a packed ½ cup.

2 Put a small bowl on the counter, with a small plate right next to it. Smack the side of an egg on the plate hard enough to hear it crack but gently enough that the shell doesn't break into pieces. Use both hands to carefully hold the egg over the bowl and open it so the insides slide out. Repeat with the other eggs.

3 Use a fork or a whisk to beat the eggs, moving the whisk in circles or back and forth. Keep beating until the eggs no longer have any streaks and are all one color. Add the crumbs to the eggs and stir a few times with the fork or a spoon to coat them evenly.

4 Put the butter or oil in a 10-inch nonstick skillet over medium heat. Make sure the pan has a tight-fitting lid. When the butter melts or the oil shimmers, spoon in the egg mixture and tip the pan slightly or run the spoon over the top so the egg covers the bottom of the pan. Turn the heat down to medium-low and cook without stirring until the eggs look firm around the edges but aren't getting too brown on the bottom, 3 to 5 minutes.

RECIPE CONTINUES ➡

CLASSIC FRITTATA. Instead of stirring in the crumbled chips or crackers, after you beat the eggs in Step 2, heat up to 1 cup chopped cooked vegetables (maybe with some crumbled cooked bacon, ham, or sausage) until warm and stir them into the eggs. Then keep going with the recipe.

5 Put the lid on the pan and keep cooking the pizza until the eggs are no longer jiggly in the center, another 3 to 5 minutes. Use a stiff spatula to slide the pizza out of the pan onto a cutting board. Slice in wedges or squares and eat soon or refrigerate for up to a couple days.

DID YOU KNOW

You can top Egg Pizza like regular pizza. Before you cover the pan, dab on some small spoonfuls of tomato sauce or salsa and sprinkle with grated mozzarella or Parmesan cheese. Bake until the cheese melts and let sit for a couple minutes before slicing.

⭐ Cooking breakfast meats (and hot dogs!) is a great way to learn how to adjust heat and recognize doneness. They're ready in a flash and also make excellent sandwiches or easy dinners with rice, grains, noodles, or salads. Some people even have them for snacks.

CRISP BACON
(AND OTHER STUFF LIKE THAT)

MAKES: 1 TO 4 SERVINGS ≫ **TIME: 10 TO 20 MINUTES DEPENDING ON THE MEAT**

INGREDIENTS

4 slices bacon (thick or thin)

EAT WITH: any of the egg recipes in this chapter, Crunchy Bread (page 242), or all the ways described in the recipe note above.

STEPS

1 Set a dinner plate on the counter and fold a clean towel in the bottom. Put the bacon in a cold, dry 10-inch skillet. It's okay if it doesn't quite fit because the bacon will shrink as it cooks, but if you want smaller pieces, use scissors to cut the strips in the pan. Turn the heat to medium-high and stand by. When the meat starts to sizzle in a couple minutes, turn the heat down to medium, but don't try to move the slices yet.

2 In 2 or 3 minutes some fat will begin shining in the bottom of the pan. Now grab tongs and start turning the pieces, moving them around so they cook evenly. Fuss just enough to keep them from burning while giving them a chance to stay in one place to cook.

3 The meat will get darker and smaller, with more fat in the bottom of the skillet. Chewy, fatty bacon will be ready to eat after 5 to 10 minutes of cooking. Crisper bacon takes 10 to 15 minutes total time. Once the slices are cooked the way you want them, use the tongs to put them on the plate with the towel to drain. What you don't eat right now you can refrigerate in an airtight container for a couple of days and eat cold or heat in the microwave on low for a few seconds.

RECIPE CONTINUES ➡

VARIATIONS

CRISP SAUSAGE LINKS. Cook 4 large or 8 small links, smoked and fully cooked or raw. You can cut them up or leave them whole before putting them in the cold skillet and following the steps in the recipe. The idea is to roll them around, adjusting the heat so the raw kind are brown on the outside and no longer pink inside. These will take 10 to 20 minutes, depending on their thickness. (Fully cooked smoked sausages might still look pink but should be hot all the way through.)

CRISP SAUSAGE PATTIES. For when you have "loose" sausage that's not packed in casing. For this recipe, shape 8 ounces of meat like tiny hamburgers (see page 224) so that they're in patties about ½ inch thick and 3 inches across. Cook them the same way, only wait to turn them for the first time until you can slip a stiff spatula under one and it's brown on the bottom and releases from the pan easily. These will take 10 to 15 minutes to crisp on the outside and no longer be pink in the middle.

CRISP HAM. Prosciutto works this way too—as will any fully cooked ham or even salami. Start with 8 ounces of sliced meat or cut a bigger chunk into cubes. Put 1 tablespoon olive oil in the cold skillet before adding the ham. Cook it the same way as the bacon, only watch it more closely, stirring with a spoon or moving with tongs as it cooks, because it will brown and crisp faster, in 5 to 10 minutes.

CRISP HOT DOGS. Maybe not exactly breakfast meat, but it cooks the same way. Leave 2 or 4 hot dogs whole, slice them across into rounds, or cut them in half lengthwise into 2 strips. (Scissors are the easiest tool here.) Put 1 tablespoon olive oil in the cold skillet before adding the hot dogs. Cook them the same way as bacon, only watch them more closely, rolling them around with tongs as they cook, because they will brown and crisp faster, in 5 to 10 minutes.

DID YOU KNOW

Cooking eggs in the skillet after cooking the meat helps season and flavor the eggs. After taking out the bacon (or other meat), turn off the heat or carefully move the skillet to a cool burner. Tip the pan a little so you can spoon off all but 1 or 2 tablespoons of the fat. Then follow the egg recipe you want, only don't add any butter or oil.

★ ★ The trickiest part of cooking pancakes is the flipping. With a small batch of batter, a big skillet (or griddle), and a little practice, you can make pancakes any day of the week. One fact of life you need to know: The first few pancakes are never as brown as the last. That's a plus. Everyone likes them a little different.

FLIPPY PANCAKES

MAKES: 2 TO 4 SERVINGS ➢➢ **TIME: 30 MINUTES** ❄ 🌱

INGREDIENTS

1 tablespoon butter

1 cup all-purpose flour

1 teaspoon baking powder

¼ teaspoon salt

1 teaspoon sugar

1 egg

¾ to 1 cup milk

Butter or vegetable oil for cooking

EAT WITH: anything you'd put on French toast (that goes for waffles too!). See the list on page 46.

STEPS

1 Put the butter in a very small bowl and warm it in the microwave on low until it melts. This takes just a few seconds, so watch it. When it's ready, let it sit to cool.

2 Measure the flour into a medium bowl. Add the baking powder, salt, and sugar and stir with a big spoon a few times. In a smaller bowl, crack in the egg (see page 39 if you need help) and add ¾ cup milk and the melted butter. Use a whisk or fork to beat everything together until there are no streaks. The butter might turn into specks, but that's okay.

3 Pour the egg mixture into the bowl with the dry ingredients and stir gently, just long enough to make a lumpy batter. You want all the flour wet, but don't overmix. The batter should plop easily from the spoon. If it's too thick, stir in some or all of the last ¼ cup milk.

4 Put a 12-inch skillet over medium-low heat (or heat a griddle to the same temperature). Put 1 tablespoon butter or oil into the skillet. When the butter foams and melts or the oil shimmers, use a measuring cup or ladle to pour a little batter into the pan. Hold the utensil at least an inch above the pan and watch how the batter spreads. You always want it to bubble gently so the pancakes brown without burning. Raise the heat a little to make that happen and be prepared to adjust the heat as the pancakes cook.

RECIPE CONTINUES ➡

5   Don't rush. Wait until bubbles appear in the center of the pancakes, about 3 minutes. Slip a stiff spatula under an edge to peek and check the color. When the bottom is golden brown, lift the pancake with a spatula and turn it, aiming to land it back in the empty spot. Do the same with the other pancakes. Keep cooking and checking the bottom until they feel a little firm when pressed and both sides are golden brown, another minute or 2 on the second side.

6   Move the pancakes to a plate and repeat the steps until all of the batter is gone, starting with adding butter or oil to the pan. You should be able to cook all the batter in 2 or 3 batches. Top with whatever you like best and eat.

DID YOU KNOW

A small ladle or a ¼-cup measuring cup with a long handle are the perfect tools for making pancakes and waffles.

VARIATIONS

FLIPPY BLUEBERRY PANCAKES. Before starting, rinse and drain 1 cup blueberries. After spooning in the batter in Step 4, scatter a few blueberries on top of each pancake. Be a little extra careful when you turn them to cook the other side.

FLIPPY CORNY PANCAKES. These taste like corn bread. Also good with blueberries. Instead of 1 cup flour, use ¾ cup flour and ¼ cup finely ground cornmeal.

FLIPPY WHEATY PANCAKES. Less fluff, more flavor. Instead of 1 cup all-purpose flour, use ¾ cup all-purpose flour and ¼ cup whole wheat flour.

WAFFLES!

You can use pancake batter to make waffles. Heat the waffle iron to medium and make sure the surface is brushed with a little oil or is totally nonstick. Spoon the batter into the center until it spreads to about 1 inch from the edges of the waffle iron, then close and cook until you can open it easily and check on how brown the waffle is.

OTHER THINGS YOU CAN COOK IN A WAFFLE IRON:

* Toast (buttered side down)
* Sandwiches (butter the outsides of both slices of bread)
* English muffins (buttered side down)
* French toast (see the recipe on page 45)
* Rice or noodles (make sure they're not too saucy and that the iron is well oiled)

★ Now is your chance to show off a bit and make breakfast for your friends and family. The only tricky thing about this giant crisp and poofy pancake—also called a "Dutch Baby"—is getting the big skillet in and out of the oven. The batter isn't heavy, though, so you can do it with a little help. If you're comfortable using a blender, then you can use one to make the batter. In Step 1, put all the ingredients in the container and pulse the machine until the mixture is smooth.

PUFFY PANCAKE

MAKES: 4 SERVINGS ⟩⟩ TIME: 30 MINUTES

INGREDIENTS

4 eggs

1 cup milk

¾ cup all-purpose flour

½ teaspoon salt

4 tablespoons (½ stick) butter

½ cup powdered sugar for dusting

EAT WITH: Crisp Bacon (and Other Stuff Like That) (page 58); Applesauce (page 261); any cooked or fresh fruit; maple syrup, honey, or jam.

STEPS

1 Heat the oven to 425°F. Put a large bowl on the counter, with a small plate right next to it. Smack the side of an egg on the plate hard enough to hear it crack but gently enough that the shell doesn't break into pieces. Use both hands to carefully hold the egg over the bowl and open it so the insides slide out. Repeat with the other eggs. Pour in the milk and add the flour and salt.

2 Use a fork or a whisk to beat the mixture, moving it in circles until a pretty smooth batter forms. It's okay to have some small bits of flour showing but no big lumps.

3 Put the butter in a 12-inch skillet over medium heat. It doesn't need to be nonstick, but it must be safe to use in the oven. Heat the butter, stirring once or twice until it melts and stops foaming, a minute or 2. Turn off the heat and pour the batter into the pan. Carefully and quickly put it in the oven.

4 Bake the pancake until it's puffed and browned, 15 to 20 minutes. Get the powdered sugar measured and ready to use. As soon as you take the skillet out of the oven, use a spoon or a mesh strainer to dust the top of the pancake with the powdered sugar. (See Did You Know below.) It will lose its puffiness as it cools, but that's fine. Use tongs or two forks to tear it into pieces and move them to plates.

RECIPE CONTINUES ➡

CHEESY PUFFY PANCAKE.
You won't need powdered sugar. When you make the batter in Step 1, add ½ cup grated cheddar or Jack cheese or ¼ cup grated Parmesan cheese. Beat it in as directed and keep going with the recipe.

PUFFY POPOVERS. Like egg cupcakes. You'll need an 8-cup muffin or popover tin (or use 8 cups of a 12-cup pan). Instead of using a skillet to melt the butter, put it in a glass measuring cup and microwave it on a low setting until it melts and foams. (Or use a small saucepan over medium heat.) Put about 1½ teaspoons butter in each cup and use a ladle or big spoon to divide the batter evenly into the buttered cups. The popovers will take 5 to 10 minutes to bake. You can dust them with powdered sugar, or skip it.

DID YOU KNOW

To dust powdered sugar on top of something so it looks like snow, just put it in a mesh strainer and gently tap it with your hand. Small tea strainers are easiest to control, but any size will work.

FLAVOR BURSTS

ALL THE SAUCES, DIPS, DRIZZLES, AND SPRINKLES THAT MAKE EVERYTHING TASTE EXACTLY HOW YOU LIKE

⭐ I'm guessing you like to eat a lot of things with butter or maybe a few drops of olive oil. Let's say you melt that butter (or warm the olive oil as explained below) and maybe add a little extra flavor with a teeny bit of what's known as "aromatic vegetables" (that's the name for onions, garlic, ginger, and other seasoning vegetables). Or if that's not your thing, try another food from the list that follows. Suddenly you have a homemade drizzling sauce that will make everything it touches even more delicious. And by trying different stir-ins, you'll learn a lot about the taste of different ingredients.

MELTED BUTTER
DRIZZLING AND DIPPING SAUCE

MAKES: ½ CUP ⟩⟩ *TIME: 10 MINUTES* 🌿

INGREDIENTS

4 tablespoons (½ stick) butter

1 tablespoon chopped onion, garlic, or ginger

2 tablespoons water

2 tablespoons fresh lemon juice

Salt

EAT WITH: raw or steamed vegetables (pages 133 and 139); simply cooked meats, chicken, or seafood; on rice, noodles, or grains; bread for dipping.

STEPS

1 Put the butter in a small pot over medium heat. When the butter is melted, add the onion, garlic, or ginger and cook, stirring slowly and stopping once in a while until the pieces puff and soften, 1 to 2 minutes. If they start to get brown, turn the heat down.

2 Stir in the water and lemon juice and sprinkle with a teeny pinch of salt. Adjust the heat so the drizzle sauce bubbles gently and thickens a little, about 2 minutes more. Remove it from the heat and let it cool while you make the rest of your meal. Then drizzle or dip away.

DID YOU KNOW

You can make extra and refrigerate leftover butter or olive oil drizzle in a small jar, where it will become almost solid. Then you can use it as a spread or melt it again in the microwave on low.

WARM OLIVE OIL DRIZZLING AND DIPPING SAUCE. Instead of the butter, use ¼ cup olive oil. Wait for the oil to smell good and start to look a little thinner at the beginning of Step 1, then follow the recipe.

10 THINGS TO STIR INTO MELTED BUTTER OR OLIVE OIL DRIZZLING AND DIPPING SAUCE

Add any of these flavoring ingredients after the butter melts (or the oil is warm) in Step 1. You can even pick a couple different things from the list at the same time. I'm giving you some measurements, but after you taste it, you can add more if you like. Eat these the same way as you would the main recipe, or drizzle on popcorn, nuts, or toast.

1. Chopped fresh herbs like mint, basil, dill, chives, or parsley (1 teaspoon)
2. Dried herbs or spices like oregano, curry or chili powder, or cinnamon (¼ teaspoon)
3. Mustard (½ teaspoon)
4. Balsamic vinegar (1 teaspoon)
5. Black pepper (¼ teaspoon)
6. Red chile flakes (¼ teaspoon)
7. Hot sauce (1 or 2 shakes)
8. Any chopped nuts (2 tablespoons)
9. Poppy seeds (1 tablespoon)
10. Sesame seeds (1 tablespoon)

⭐ Now here's a sweet-and-savory sauce that works for drizzling, dipping, and cooking. It's called a "glaze" because the sugars in the syrup will make the sauce shiny and a little sticky. Making the main recipe and trying the ideas that follow will help you learn to taste the difference between sweet, salty, savory, tangy, and spicy flavors. So be prepared to add a few drops here and there to make it your own.

SOY SAUCE GLAZE

MAKES: ½ CUP ⟫ *TIME: 10 MINUTES* 🌿

INGREDIENTS

½ cup maple syrup, plus more to taste

1 teaspoon soy sauce, plus more to taste

Water if needed

STEPS

Stir the maple syrup and soy sauce together in a small bowl until the glaze is smooth and shiny. It will be on the thin side, but that's okay. Taste and add syrup to make it sweeter, soy sauce to make it more savory and salty, or 1 or 2 teaspoons water to make it milder.

EAT WITH: Once you make this you'll want it on everything. But my favorite foods for this are carrots, cabbage, chicken, tofu, meatballs, and egg noodles.

It's easy to cook with Soy Sauce Glaze. Stir it into the pan with vegetables, fish, or meat when they're ready to eat and toss everything around with tongs or a spatula until it's shiny all over.

VARIATIONS

SWEET-AND-SOUR SOY SAUCE. Perfect on salad or steamed vegetables. Instead of ½ cup maple syrup, use ⅓ cup maple syrup and 1 tablespoon rice vinegar.

PEANUT SAUCE. Thick and nutty. Try this on noodles or rice. Instead of ½ cup maple syrup, use ⅓ cup peanut butter and 2 tablespoons maple syrup. Then decide if you want to thin the mixture by adding 1 or 2 teaspoons water. Stirring with a fork will make the sauce smoother faster.

HOT SOY SAUCE SYRUP. Use the same way but . . . Spicy! Sweet! Salty! Follow the steps in the main recipe, only add a dash or 2 (or 3) of your favorite hot sauce. You can also try this after making either of the ideas above.

SPICES & HERBS

Part of becoming a good cook is learning to season plain foods in ways that help you enjoy what you eat while being a little adventurous and creative—as with painting or drawing. This section explains the basics of salt and pepper for sure, and fresh and dried herbs and ground spices.

Shocking but true: Tasting is not the best way to try seasonings. They will be much stronger tasting on their own than they are when you actually eat them with food. And sticking your nose up close will make the smell more intense than they'll be when you use them.

So, if you don't want to dive into a recipe that uses a seasoning you've never tried (or tried before and didn't like much), start by waving your hand over the sprigs of herbs or the jar of dried herbs or spices and smelling the air. Chop up a few leaves of fresh herbs or take a pinch of dried herbs or spices, put them in some warm olive oil or melted butter, and dip a piece of bread in there to taste. Then see what you think.

The following descriptions will give you some idea of what you're getting into.

FROM THE SPICE CABINET

SALT. Kosher salt has the mildest flavor. Sometimes the recipes give a measurement, but since everyone likes different amounts, start with a small pinch between your thumb and first finger, stir into your dish, taste, and add more if you want.

BLACK PEPPER. Can be mild or sharp tasting, especially if it's freshly ground into coarse bits. Start with a smaller pinch than salt (or one grind with a pepper mill) and test before adding more until you get a feel for what you like.

CINNAMON. You know this flavor. Bold and sort of sweet, even without sugar. Used mostly for baking but not always.

RED CHILE FLAKES. The spicy stuff that comes with pizza. It's ground from dried chiles, not from the same plant as black pepper, so the heat tastes different.

CHILI POWDER. A brick-colored blend of cumin and other spices with mild finely ground chiles (yes, the powder is spelled differently than the pepper by itself). When you eat the dish chili, this is mostly what you're tasting.

CURRY POWDER. A bright yellowish-orange blend that can include as many as ten different spices. In America, we give it one name, but there are many different styles and each tastes a little different.

FIVE-SPICE. A strong and super-interesting blend of spices used in Chinese and other Asian dishes. If you like black licorice, try it.

CUMIN. Sweet and sort of grassy, with a green-brown color. It features in chili powder, a lot of Mexican food, and some Mediterranean and Indian dishes.

GROUND GINGER. The flavor is different from fresh ginger—still sharp and sort of hot but slower to hit your taste buds.

SMOKED PAPRIKA. One of my favorites. Not hot like chiles. It's a little sweet, and the smokiness will remind you of barbecue sauce.

DRIED ITALIAN HERBS. A mix of herbs like oregano, parsley, rosemary, basil, sage, and thyme. Sometimes there's garlic in there. Read the label because brands are different.

DRIED THYME. Whenever you want to add a mild sweetness with a little garden taste, this is the herb.

DRIED OREGANO. A little bolder than thyme with a taste that always makes me think of Italian food.

DRIED SAGE. Thanksgiving. That's the flavor of sage. Great with chicken and pork.

FRESH HERBS (KEEP IN THE REFRIGERATOR)

BASIL. Big and tender green mild leaves. Often eaten with mozzarella cheese in a salad or sandwich but also good on pizza or stirred into pasta sauce.

CILANTRO. Love it or hate it, but you've got to try it. To some people it actually tastes like soap! Used in salsa but also popular in Thai, Indian, and Vietnamese food.

CHIVES. Perfect if raw onions are too strong for you. Chives are like onion grass.

MINT. That candy-cane-and-toothpaste flavor you know, only without the sweets. Great in yogurt or with cucumbers.

PARSLEY. Probably the most popular fresh herb garnish, either chopped or in sprigs. I prefer the texture of the kind with flat leaves. Both that and curly parsley have a grassy flavor.

DILL. Wispy leaves that look more like grass on stems. It might remind you of pickles, but the taste is milder and more interesting than parsley and is perfect with most vegetables.

ROSEMARY. Tastes like mild pine cones, so be sure to ditch the stems and chop the needle-like leaves into teeny bits. Awesome to cook with chicken and in tomato sauce for pasta and pizza.

★ The famous fast-food sauce is easy to make at home, exactly how you like it.

HONEY MUSTARD SAUCE

MAKES: ½ CUP ⟫ *TIME: 10 MINUTES* 🌿

INGREDIENTS

¼ cup mustard (any kind; see page 78), plus more if you like

3 tablespoons water

1 tablespoon honey

EAT WITH: raw or cooked vegetables; chicken, fish, or pork; or spread on bread for sandwiches.

VARIATION

CREAMY HONEY MUSTARD SAUCE. Milder flavor, lighter color, slightly thicker. Instead of water, use mayonnaise or sour cream.

STEPS

1 Put the mustard in a small bowl. Add the water and honey and stir with a spoon or fork until it all comes together into a smooth sauce.

2 Take a taste and see what you think. To make it sharper, add another teaspoon of mustard. To make it sweeter, add a teaspoon of honey.

⭐ You probably didn't think ranch dressing could get any better than what you've eaten in restaurants or out of the bottle. Trust me: It can. You'll need a secret ingredient, though. Fortunately, it's available in the baking section of a regular supermarket.

RANCH FOR REAL

MAKES: ABOUT 1 CUP ➡➡ **TIME: 15 MINUTES** 🌿

INGREDIENTS

½ cup mayonnaise

½ cup buttermilk

2 tablespoons buttermilk powder

Salt

Pepper (if you like)

1 teaspoon dried dill (if you like)

EAT WITH: Hello? How about everything?

VARIATION

PINK AND SWEET RANCH. In Step 1, add 2 tablespoons ketchup before whisking. You can skip the salt, pepper, and dill.

STEPS

1 Put the mayonnaise, buttermilk, and buttermilk powder in a medium bowl. Sprinkle with a little salt, and then a lot of pepper and the dill if you like them.

2 Whisk until the dressing is smooth. Taste and add more salt or pepper if it needs some. Transfer to a small airtight container, refrigerate, and eat within 1 week.

⭐ When you combine oil and vinegar, and maybe some other flavorful ingredients, you get the salad dressing called "vinaigrette." The rice vinegar and olive oil combo in this recipe is mild, with a slightly sweet tang. Changing the kind of vinegar and oil will make your dressing taste different, so salads will never be boring. See the variations below and the descriptions of these two important pantry ingredients on page 5.

SALAD DRESSING

MAKES: ABOUT ¾ CUP ≫→ TIME: 10 MINUTES 🌿

INGREDIENTS

½ cup olive oil

3 tablespoons rice vinegar, plus more to taste

Salt

Pepper (if you like)

EAT WITH: salad (of course); cold or hot chicken and seafood; or as a dip or drizzle for raw or cooked vegetables.

STEPS

1 Put the oil and vinegar in a small jar or airtight container with a tight seal. Add a small pinch of salt and pepper too if you like. (If adding any extras from the list below, now is the time.)

2 Close the container and shake until the dressing thickens. Taste and add more vinegar 1 teaspoon at a time to make the dressing tangier. Or add salt and pepper.

3 Shake the jar again and eat right away or refrigerate for up to 1 week. Shake again every time you use it.

When a fat (like oil) and a watery liquid (like vinegar) are whisked or shaken, they come together in a thick mixture called an "emulsion." Sometimes when you emulsify liquids they stay together and sometimes they separate again with the oil on top. That's why I like to make dressing in a jar. All it takes is a quick shake to bring the dressing back together again.

DIJON DRESSING. In Step 1, add 1 teaspoon Dijon mustard to the jar before shaking.

LEMONY DRESSING. Use lemon juice instead of the vinegar.

BALSAMIC DRESSING. For a sweeter, deeper flavor that works with most of the variations or extras too. Instead of the rice vinegar, use balsamic vinegar.

RASPBERRY DRESSING. Really any fruity jam or preserves are awesome in this. For a sweeter dressing, try raspberry jam instead of the vinegar. After shaking, taste and see if you want to add a teaspoon or 2 of vinegar to add some tang.

3 EXTRAS TO TRY IN SALAD DRESSING

1. 1 teaspoon dried herbs or spices like Italian seasoning blend or chili powder
2. 1 tablespoon chopped fresh herbs like dill, mint, or chives (best to eat this dressing within 3 days)
3. 2 tablespoons chopped nuts like almonds or peanuts

THE CONDIMENT LAB

These are the sauces—called condiments—that you usually get from the store. I like to keep them all in the refrigerator after opening so they'll last longer. Then eat 'em straight from the bottle or jar or mix and match to make your own special sauces.

KETCHUP. Most kids love the sweet, slightly tomatoey, slightly spicy taste. Just remember it's already pretty sugary when you're thinking of what to mix it with.

MUSTARD. Yellow mustard is the neon-colored tangy kind. You might also like the spicier French-style creamy golden mustards usually called Dijon (pronounced dee-jawn) or German-style brown kinds, which are flecked with ground mustard seeds. Coarse mustard is when the seeds are barely ground at all.

MAYONNAISE. True mayonnaise is made by blending eggs with vegetable oil until smooth and creamy. You can substitute eggless mayo—often called after the brand name Vegenaise—or silken tofu or even plain yogurt (see page 30).

SALSA. Made from tomatoes, tomatillos, fruits, even beans or corn—all with different levels of spiciness from chiles. The jarred salsas on store shelves are cooked. Fresh salsas are sold refrigerated. There are recipes for them both on page 80.

MISO. A thick and bold-tasting aged paste made from soy or other beans and sometimes rice or barley. The lighter it is, the milder the flavor. Get the refrigerated kind in tubs.

HOT SAUCE. Made from all different kinds of chiles. There

are hundreds of kinds, from mild to mouth-explodingly hot, from watery thin to ketchupy thick. I count chile crisp—ground dried chiles or pepper flakes soaked in vegetable oil and sometimes spelled "chili crisp"—as a hot sauce too. You can have a lot of fun finding your favorite as long as you taste a drop at a time.

SOY SAUCE. Have you heard of "umami"? It's the flavor described as being savory-salty and sort of meaty or mushroomy without having either of those things in it. And soy sauce—which is made by aging soybeans—is the perfect example of something that has umami. Be sure to get one that only has soybeans (and sometimes wheat) in it with no added sugar or other flavors.

BBQ SAUCE. Like ketchup only smokier and spicier.

PICKLES. You can pickle anything, but what we usually think of when we say pickles are cucumbers soaked in a "brine" of salt, water, and often vinegar. The brine is then flavored with dill, garlic, or sugar. Relishes are just pickles chopped up, so let's count them here too.

READY TO MIX?

Let's get started with a few classic combos for dipping, drizzling, and smearing on bread. One note: "Equal parts" means the same quantity. And 2-to-1 means twice as much of the first ingredient as the second. Start with tablespoons or quarter cups and taste as you go. And remember that you can also add the herbs and spices explained on page 73.

FRENCH DRESSING: Equal parts ketchup and mayonnaise.

THOUSAND ISLAND: Add chopped pickles to French Dressing.

MUSTARD–AISE: Equal parts mustard and mayonnaise.

TARTAR SAUCE: Add chopped pickles to Mustard-aise.

SOY MAYONNAISE: Add a splash of soy sauce to mayo.

HOT MAYO: Add a couple drops of hot sauce to mayo.

ORANGE SAUCE: Equal parts mustard and ketchup. Try it on French fries!

★ ★ A lot of chopping makes this an "intermediate" recipe. Fresh salsa is totally worth the work, though. And best of all, you decide exactly what goes in it and how hot you want it (or not). To make the salsa with fruit, see the list that follows. And to use other chiles or spices to raise the heat level, see the spices on page 73 and "Hot Sauce" starting on page 78.

FRESH TOMATO (OR FRUIT) SALSA

MAKES: 2 CUPS ⟩⟩ *TIME: 30 MINUTES* 🌿

INGREDIENTS

2 large ripe tomatoes (about 12 ounces)

1 or 2 scallions (if you like)

1 or 2 cloves garlic (if you like)

Several sprigs fresh cilantro (if you like)

¼ teaspoon red chile flakes, plus more to taste (if you like)

1 lime

Salt

Pepper (if you like)

EAT WITH: tortilla chips; or spooned on eggs, tacos, shrimp, chicken, or vegetables.

STEPS

1 Put the tomato upside down so it doesn't wobble and cut it downward in half. Cut each half into wedges around the core and chop the wedges into small chunks. (See the illustrations on page 21.) Scrape the pieces and all the juice on the cutting board into a medium bowl.

2 Now for the optional ingredients to add to the bowl: Trim and chop the white and green parts of the scallions. Peel the garlic and chop it into tiny bits. Strip the leaves and tender stems from the cilantro and chop them too. Measure the chile flakes into the bowl.

3 Cut the lime in half and squeeze some juice into the bowl. Sprinkle with a little salt and pepper too if you like. Stir and taste. Adjust the seasoning with more chile flakes, lime juice, salt, and/or pepper. Eat right away or refrigerate for up to a couple days.

VARIATIONS

COOKED SALSA. Take the finished tomato or fruit salsa and put it in a small pot over medium heat. When the juices start to bubble, cover with a tight-fitting lid and turn the heat down to medium-low. Cook, stirring every 2 or 3 minutes, until the salsa is as soft as you like, 10 to 15 minutes.

SMOOTH SALSA. You can transform any fresh or cooked salsa. Just put it in a blender or food processor and pulse the machine until the salsa is as smooth or chunky as you like. (It's safest to let cooked salsa cool to room temperature before blending or processing.)

5 FRESH FRUITS TO TRY IN SALSA

For directions peeling and chopping, see the illustrations beginning on page 16. You'll need to substitute about 2 cups chopped fruit or berries for the tomatoes in this recipe. Everything else stays the same.

1. Oranges or tangerines (perfect in winter)
2. Berries (strawberries, blueberries, and blackberries will be less mushy than raspberries)
3. Melons (like watermelon, cantaloupe, or honeydew)
4. Mango (creamy and sweet)
5. Plums (so colorful—use the skin and all)

DID YOU KNOW

If you use sweet onions like Vidalia or Walla Walla here, they'll cook down a little faster and be even jammier.

A lot of kids—and many adults—find raw and stir-fried onions too sharp tasting. Cooking them slowly, called "caramelizing," turns them brown, sweet, and mellow, almost like fruit jam. They keep in the fridge for a week so you can use them whenever, wherever. This recipe is also a good lesson in watching and tasting how an ingredient can change right before your eyes.

JAMMY ONIONS

MAKES: ABOUT 1 CUP (4 TO 8 SERVINGS) >> TIME: ABOUT 1 HOUR, WITHOUT MUCH WORK

INGREDIENTS

1 pound white or yellow onions

1 tablespoon olive oil

1 teaspoon sugar

EAT WITH: sandwiches or toast; eggs; or tossed with rice, beans, or noodles; or use them instead of raw onions for stir-fries or sauces.

STEPS

1 Trim the onions and peel them. Cut the onions in half from top to bottom, then lay each half flat side down and cut it into thin slices. (Either direction is fine.) For small pieces, slice or chop them in the other direction too.

2 Put the onions in a 10-inch skillet over medium heat. (Don't add the oil yet.) Cover and cook, stirring every 3 minutes, until the onions are dry and beginning to stick to the pan, 10 to 15 minutes.

3 Add the oil and sugar and turn the heat down to medium-low. Cook uncovered, stirring every 5 minutes, until the onions are super-soft and as dark as you want them. That might be as little as 10 or as many as 40 more minutes. (Or somewhere in between.) Eat them right away or let them cool a bit. Put leftovers in a sealed container in the refrigerator.

HOLD ON!

SANDWICHES, TACOS, BURRITOS, AND SNACKY THINGS TO EAT WITH YOUR HANDS

⭐ Popcorn teaches you to cook with your nose and your ears. All the action happens in a covered pot, so you can't even sneak a peek without getting popcorn everywhere.

POPCORN IN A POT

MAKES: 4 SERVINGS (ABOUT 6 CUPS) »» **TIME: 10 MINUTES**

INGREDIENTS

1 tablespoon vegetable oil

¼ cup popping corn

2 tablespoons butter

Salt

EAT WITH: Toss the buttered popcorn with a little grated Parmesan or cheddar cheese if you like. Or add chopped nuts and dried fruit or raisins. And check out all the choices in Melted Butter Drizzling and Dipping Sauce (page 68).

STEPS

1 Put the oil in a 2- or 3-quart pot with a tight-fitting lid over medium heat. Add 3 kernels of the popcorn.

2 While you wait for the oil to heat, melt the butter in the microwave or in a small pot over medium heat. When it's melted, put it near the stove and get a large bowl out.

3 As soon as you smell the oil and hear the 3 kernels pop, take the lid off the pot and add all of the corn. Cover and shake the pot back and forth on the stove once or twice, holding the lid on. Cook, shaking every minute as the corn begins to go crazy popping.

4 Adjust the heat so the oil and popcorn smell toasty, not like they're burning. You can move the pot off the burner to cool it down fast. When you can count to 3 between pops, 3 to 5 minutes after adding the corn, take the pot off the heat.

5 Carefully transfer the popcorn to the bowl with a big spoon, drizzle with the butter, sprinkle with salt, and scoop with the spoon from the bottom of the bowl to toss everything evenly. Eat right away or store in an airtight container for up to a day or 2.

★ Flour tortillas make awesome mini pizzas in a flash, especially if you keep a tube of tomato paste and some cheese in the fridge. The recipe here is for one pizza to bake crisp in the toaster oven. To turn other breads into pizza or to make them with soft crusts, which is even faster, see the ideas that follow. If your tortilla is bigger or smaller than the one in the recipe, you'll want to add a little more or a little less of the toppings; see page 90 for how to measure. You can also make a bunch by increasing the amount of ingredients and baking them in a larger pan in the regular oven. See the list that follows for topping ideas.

PIZZILLA

MAKES: 1 INDIVIDUAL THIN-CRUST PIZZA ⇒⇒ TIME: LESS THAN 15 MINUTES

INGREDIENTS

1 flour tortilla (about 8 inches)

1 teaspoon olive oil

1 teaspoon tomato paste (if you like)

2 tablespoons grated mozzarella cheese

EAT WITH: Raw Snacking Vegetables (page 133) or Leafy Salad (page 137).

STEPS

1 Heat the toaster or regular oven to 400°F.

2 Put the tortilla on the toaster oven tray. Or if you're baking more in the regular oven, spread them out on a big baking sheet without touching. Measure 1 teaspoon olive oil and 1 teaspoon tomato paste (if you like) onto each tortilla. Smear them all over the top with the back of a spoon or your fingers.

3 Scatter the cheese over the tortilla, being careful not to get too much on the pan. If you're using more toppings, add them now too.

4 When the oven is hot, put the pan in. Set the timer for 5 minutes, then start checking. Bake until the top is bubbling and the edges of the tortilla are golden.

5 Remove the pan from the oven and let the pizzilla sit for at least a minute before eating whole or cutting into wedges.

RECIPE CONTINUES ➡

PIZZA TOAST. Instead of the tortilla, use 1 slice any white or whole wheat bread or the bottom half of a sandwich roll or hamburger bun. Everything else stays the same.

PITA PIZZA. Instead of the tortilla, try 1 pita, white or whole wheat. Everything else stays the same.

SOFT AND SUPER-FAST PIZZILLA, PIZZA BREAD, OR PITA PIZZA. Skip Step 1. Follow Steps 2 and 3, only assemble the pizzilla on a microwave-safe plate. For Step 4, cook the pizza in the microwave on high for 30 seconds and check. You might need a few more seconds to get it all bubbly. Pick up the recipe again with Step 5.

10 EXTRA TOPPINGS FOR PIZZILLA

Easy does it. The more you pile on, the soggier the crust will get.

1. A pinch of salt and black pepper or red chile flakes
2. A sprinkle of dried Italian seasoning blend
3. A sprinkle of garlic powder
4. Extra grated cheese like more mozzarella, cheddar, Jack, or Parmesan
5. Sliced button mushrooms
6. Sliced black or green olives
7. Chopped red or green bell pepper
8. Chopped pickles (hey, try it!)
9. Sliced or chopped pepperoni or salami
10. Cooked and crumbled sausage or bacon

HOW TO MEASURE CIRCLES

This recipe calls for an 8-inch tortilla. Sometimes that appears on the package and sometimes it doesn't. So, to find out the size you have, you'll need to measure the diameter. Put a ruler or tape measure across the widest part and see what you've got. This works for pots, pans, baking dishes, pie crusts—anything round. The number doesn't have to be exact, just to the closest inch. That's how to know what you're working with and if you need to make adjustments to a recipe.

★ ★ Smushing a cheese sandwich in the pan leaves you with a crisp outside and a gooey inside. You will need a couple cans from the pantry or a small heavy pot for this one.

GRILLED CHEESE SANDWICH

MAKES: 1 SANDWICH ⟫ *TIME: 5 MINUTES* 🥬

INGREDIENTS

1 tablespoon butter or olive oil

2 slices any bread (about ½ inch thick)

⅓ cup grated (or 1 or 2 slices) melting cheese (like cheddar, Jack, or Swiss; about 1 ounce)

EAT WITH: pickles, raw vegetable sticks, salad, a cup of Creamy Tomato Soup (page 110) or Only-the-Vegetables-You-Like Soup (page 117), or chips.

STEPS

1 Put an 8-inch skillet over medium heat and add the butter or oil. Make a sandwich with the bread and cheese; try to keep the cheese in an even layer not too close to the crusts of the bread.

2 When the butter melts or the oil is hot, put the sandwich in the skillet. Set a small plate on top of the bread and weigh it down with the cans or heavy pot. Adjust the heat so the butter or oil sizzles without burning.

3 Cook until the bottom of the bread smells like toast and is lightly browned and crisp, 2 to 3 minutes. Take all the stuff off the sandwich, slip a spatula underneath, lift it off the pan, and turn it over.

4 Swoosh the sandwich around in the pan to sop up all the butter or oil. If you want the sandwich even flatter, pile the plate and cans back on. The other side will also take 2 to 3 minutes to brown. Use the spatula to transfer the sandwich to a plate. Wait a minute for the cheese to cool and set, then dig in.

RECIPE CONTINUES ➡

NOOTCHY SANDWICH. For times when you or your friends aren't eating any cheese or dairy. Make the Nootchy Butter on page 94 and spread ¼ cup on one slice of the bread before closing the sandwich. Use olive oil, not butter, in the pan and follow the recipe.

GRILLED CHOCOLATE SANDWICH. Like dessert. Instead of the cheese, use 1 small chocolate bar between the bread. Your choice what kind, but I like mine pretty dark.

INSIDE-OUT GRILLED CHEESE SANDWICH. That's right. Crisp cheese on the outside, bread on the inside. You'll need a nonstick skillet for this. Use one piece of bread and twice as much cheese. Don't put butter or oil in the pan or use the plate and weights. Scatter half the cheese in the bottom of the pan, top with the bread slice, and scatter the rest of the cheese on top. Put the pan over medium heat and cook without touching anything until the cheese bubbles and melts and turns brown, 3 to 5 minutes. It should be crisp enough to slip a spatula underneath and turn it over. Cook the second side the same way. When the sandwich is ready, tip the pan so the extra fat pours away from the bread before lifting it out with the spatula.

CHEESE TOAST. This time the sandwich is open. You can use any of the cheeses listed in the recipe or try grated Parmesan. Turn on the broiler to the highest setting (or use a toaster oven) and put the rack about 4 inches from the heat source. Keep the bread dry at first and put both slices on a baking sheet (or the pan for the toaster oven) and move the pan under the heat. Watch it until the top is toasted as dark as you like it. Remove the pan, use tongs to turn the bread, then put a pat of butter on each uncooked side or drizzle with half the oil. Top the slices with the cheese and put the pan back under the heat until the cheese is as melted and bubbly or brown as you want it.

CREATE YOUR OWN

Start

BREAD

SLICED

SPLIT ROLL OR BUN

HAMBURGER OR HOT DOG BUNS

SUB OR HERO ROLL

DINNER ROLLS

ENGLISH MUFFIN

BIG FLOUR TORTILLA

PITA

TOAST? CRISP or SOFT?

SMEAR

Mayo, Mustard, or Mashed Beans

or

PB & J

NOOTCHY BUTTER

For toast, crackers, or sandwiches—a great-tasting spread that contains no nuts or dairy. Here's how: Drain a 15-ounce can of cannellini beans into a colander and rinse under running water. Put them in a shallow bowl or plate with 2 tablespoons each brown sugar, olive oil, and nutritional yeast. (These golden flakes have a slightly nutty-cheesy taste and are usually found in supermarkets near the spices.) Use a fork or potato masher to smush and stir everything into a spread. Add water 1 tablespoon at a time if the nootchy butter is too thick. (A food processor will make the butter even smoother but be careful not to add so much water that it looks soupy.) Taste and add more sugar or yeast if you like and mix it in. Makes about 1 cup and will keep in a sealed container in the fridge for 1 week.

SANDWICH

Layer

Cheese

Meat

Veggies

TOMATO

ONION

PICKLES

LETTUCE

Eggs

Leftovers!

SMUSH

ROLL

CLOSE

BUT I LIKE WHITE BREAD!

You know everyone wants you to eat whole grains, right? They're more nutritious, more filling, and you won't get hungry again as fast. Whole wheat sandwiches are a good place to start. They've already got a lot of other flavors and textures going, so you won't be focused on the bread. How about trying a whole wheat pita or English muffin to start? Or your favorite wrap or Pizzilla (page 88) with a whole wheat tortilla?

⭐ No problem if tuna isn't your thing. Skip to the other ideas that follow the main recipe. Let me just say for tuna eaters and anyone who thinks they're not a fan: The fish in cans and jars has a better texture than what comes in pouches. You can get water-packed, but I think oil-packed tuna tastes better.

TUNA SANDWICH

MAKES: 2 SANDWICHES (ABOUT ¾ CUP FILLING) ⟫→ *TIME: 15 MINUTES*

INGREDIENTS

1 small can tuna (about 5 ounces), water- or oil-packed

¼ cup mayonnaise, plus more as needed

1 teaspoon yellow or Dijon mustard (if you like)

Salt and pepper (if you like)

Bread or rolls for 2 sandwiches

Extras like lettuce, tomato, or sliced pickles for finishing the sandwiches

EAT WITH: Instead of a sandwich, try the tuna on crackers or chips, or wrapping a spoonful in big lettuce leaves.

STEPS

1 After you open the can of tuna, carefully turn it upside down over a bowl (or the sink) to drain off the water or oil. You can press down on the fish with the lid of the can to keep it from tumbling out and make it drier as long as your fingers stay away from the sharp edges. Use a fork to scrape the tuna into a clean bowl and break it up.

2 Add the mayonnaise and the mustard if you're using it. Keep using the fork to mash and stir the tuna until it's evenly coated and there are no more big chunks. Taste and decide if you want to add a sprinkle of salt and pepper. (You can refrigerate the tuna at this point in a sealed container for up to a couple days. If you want to chill it down fast, stick it in the freezer for 10 minutes.)

3 Toast the bread and spread the slices thinly with more mayonnaise if you like. Fill the sandwiches with the tuna and add whatever extras you like. Cut into halves or quarters and eat.

RECIPE CONTINUES ➡

 If you don't like mayonnaise, you can moisten these salads with the same amount of olive oil, plain yogurt, or sour cream.

VARiATiONS

**CHICKEN OR TURKEY
SANDWICH.** Instead of the tuna,
chop or shred ¾ cup cooked
chicken or turkey. Be sure to pack
it in the measuring cup. Then
follow the recipe.

SALMON SANDWICH. Instead
of the tuna, use a small can of
salmon (about 5 ounces). Drain
and follow the recipe.

CHICKPEA SANDWICH. A great
meatless idea. Drain and rinse
one 15-ounce can of chickpeas.
Measure 1 cup into a bowl and
mash with a fork into bits. Follow
the recipe from Step 2.

IDEAS FOR SPIKING TUNA, CHICKEN, TURKEY, SALMON, OR CHICKPEA SANDWICHES

The quantities below are starting
points. Add as much as you
want. But be prepared to add
more mayonnaise to keep the
mixture moist.

- 2 tablespoons chopped sweet
  or dill pickles
- 2 tablespoons chopped celery
- 1 tablespoon chopped scallion
  or red onion
- 1 tablespoon lemon juice (or
  1 teaspoon grated lemon zest)
- 1 or 2 splashes hot sauce
- 1 tablespoon sweet or dill relish
- 1 chopped hard-boiled egg

★ ★   There are two secrets to crisp quesadillas that are easy to flip and cut. The first is to not overload them with too much cheese. Better to make more of them or have something on the side. The second is instead of filling and stacking two tortillas, just cook one at a time and fold it in half.

QUESADILLAS

MAKES: 2 TO 4 SERVINGS ⇢⇢ *TIME: 30 MINUTES*

INGREDIENTS

4 (8-inch) flour tortillas

1 cup grated melting cheese (like cheddar or Jack; about 3 ounces)

4 teaspoons vegetable oil

EAT WITH: Fresh Tomato (or Fruit) Salsa (page 80), Guacamole (page 134), sour cream, hot sauce, and Coleslaw (page 138).

STEPS

1   Spread the tortillas out on a clean, flat work surface and scatter the cheese evenly on top of each. Scootch the cheese away from the edges so it has room to melt and spread.

2   Put 1 teaspoon of the oil in a 10-inch nonstick skillet over medium heat. When it's hot and shimmering, use a spatula to move one of the tortillas to the pan. Cook, watching for the cheese to melt and the tortilla to look golden, 2 to 3 minutes. You can use the spatula to lift a corner and peek. Adjust the heat so it's sizzling without burning.

3   Slip the spatula under one side of the tortilla and fold it in half. Let the quesadilla cook until the bottom half is brown and crisp, about 1 minute. Then use the spatula to turn the tortilla and brown the other side the same way. Move the quesadilla to a cutting board and repeat the recipe from Step 2 until all the oil and tortillas are gone.

4   While the next tortillas are cooking, you can cut the finished quesadilla into wedges and put on plates and get all the sides ready to start eating.

RECIPE CONTINUES ➡

DID YOU KNOW

You can use non-cheese fillings to fill tortillas the same way. Mashed sweet potatoes, potatoes, or beans will act like the "glue" to hold the tortilla together and let it crisp up; just make sure the filling is hot and you only spread it about ¼ inch thick on each tortilla.

CHEESE CRISPS. Perfect for snacking with friends. Heat the oven to 400°F and spread the tortillas into 2 large baking sheets. Scatter the cheese evenly on top of all the tortillas and bake until the cheese is bubbly and the edges of the tortillas brown, 5 to 10 minutes. Cut into wedges or let the crisps cool enough to tear them apart.

BEAN QUESADILLAS. Reduce the cheese to ¾ cup. Heat 1 cup refried beans in the microwave (or mash 1 cup any drained cooked or canned beans with a fork and heat them). Before topping the tortillas with the cheese, spread ¼ of the beans on each tortilla. Then follow the recipe from Step 2.

CHICKEN QUESADILLAS. Or really you could use any leftover cooked beef or pork. Reduce the cheese to ¾ cup. Chop or shred 1 cup cooked chicken and heat it in the microwave on a medium setting for 1 minute. After topping the tortillas with cheese in Step 1, scatter ¼ cup chicken on each. Then follow the recipe from Step 2.

5 THINGS TO ADD TO QUESADILLAS OR CHEESE CRISPS

Remember . . . not too much, just scatter a fistful on top of the cheese.

1. Chopped scallion
2. Chopped black or green olives
3. Sprinkle of red chile flakes or chili powder
4. Chopped dill or sweet pickles (try it!)
5. Jammy Onions (page 83)

⭐ A super-easy recipe with two important lessons: how to roll burritos and wraps, and how to make your own refried beans. I mean, you can buy them already seasoned in a can—or thaw a packaged frozen burrito—but why would you after trying this?

BEAN BURRITOS

MAKES: 1 TO 2 SERVINGS ⟫ *TIME: ABOUT 30 MINUTES* ❄️🍃

INGREDIENTS

1 (15-ounce) can pinto or black beans

1 tablespoon vegetable or olive oil

1 scallion or 1 thick slice of onion, chopped (if you like)

2 teaspoons chili powder

¼ cup water, plus more as needed

Salt

Pepper (if you like)

2 (8-inch) flour tortillas

Extra filling choices: shredded lettuce, chopped tomatoes, sour cream

EAT WITH: Fresh Tomato (or Fruit) Salsa (page 80) and Guacamole (page 134).

STEPS

1 Drain the beans in a colander and rinse. Put them on a dinner plate or in a shallow bowl and use a fork or a potato masher to break them up. Stir as you work to make sure they all get mashed. Keep going until they're as smooth or chunky as you like, then let them sit by the stove ready to go.

2 Put the oil in a 10-inch skillet over medium heat. When it's hot and shimmers, add the scallion or onion if you're using it and stir until it gets soft and starts to turn golden, 2 to 3 minutes. Add the chili powder, stir once or twice, then add the beans and ¼ cup water and stir until everything is combined.

3 Cook the beans, stirring almost always and mashing a little if you want them smoother. Add more water 1 tablespoon at a time until the mixture is as thick or thin as you like and the beans are bubbling. If you add too much water, just keep cooking until it boils away. Turn the heat down to low, taste, and add salt and pepper too if you like.

4 Heat the tortillas one at a time on a plate in the microwave on high until soft and warm, about 30 seconds. Turn the tortilla with a spatula and get ready to fill and roll your burrito. (To heat without a microwave, warm a dry 8- or 10-inch skillet over medium-high heat and soften the tortillas one at a time, about 30 seconds on each side. Transfer to the plate.)

RECIPE CONTINUES ➡

10 MORE FILLINGS FOR BURRITOS AND TACOS

Or maybe we call them wraps, because some of the fillings might not be considered Mexican style.

1. Peanut butter and jelly
2. Sliced ham and cheese
3. Tuna, chicken, turkey, salmon, or chickpea sandwich filling (pages 96 and 98)
4. Scrambled Eggs (page 39)
5. Scrambled Tofu (page 41)
6. Green Eggs and Ham (page 47)
7. Crisp Bacon (page 58) with or without lettuce and tomato
8. The fillings from Crispy and Meaty Tacos (page 105)
9. Any chili (page 127)
10. Chicken, fish, pork, or beef Mark Nuggets (page 217)

BEAN AND CHEESE BURRITOS.
You'll need to skip the extras or there will be too much filling to roll. For melted cheese in the burritos, when you heat the beans in Step 2, stir in ½ cup grated cheddar, mozzarella, or Jack cheese. For raw cheese inside, scatter ¼ cup cheese on top of the beans before rolling in Step 4.

5   Put about ½ to ¾ cup of the beans on one side of the tortilla so that they're in a pile not too close to the edges. If you want any of the optional filling choices, scatter them on top of the beans, but don't go crazy or you won't be able to close the burrito. Grab both sides of the tortilla and fold them partway over the filling. Keep holding while you slip your thumbs under the edge by the beans and start rolling. The idea is to keep the sides wrapped tight while you roll the tortilla over itself to make the burrito rest on the plate with the seam side down. If the ends fly open or any filling escapes, no problem, you'll get the hang of it with practice.

6   Now repeat Steps 4 and 5 with the other tortilla. Cut the burritos in half or leave whole and eat with whatever sides you like. (If you have beans left over, refrigerate them for another burrito or bowl. They'll keep for several days.)

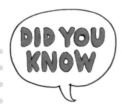

DID YOU KNOW

If you make extra burritos with just the beans inside (or beans and cheese), you can freeze them in an airtight container for up to a few months? To thaw and heat one, put it in the microwave on a medium setting until piping hot inside, 4 to 5 minutes.

★ ★ ★ (if you fry your own shells) ★ ★ (if you make soft tacos or buy crisp shells)   Frying in oil is an important cooking skill, and tortillas are an easy food for practicing. You'll still want an adult working with you. If you don't feel like the extra work, make the Soft Tacos idea that follows or use store-bought crisp shells and skip to Step 3. To host taco night for family or friends with you at the stove, just double or triple the recipe. I bet someone will be happy to come help in the kitchen.

CRISP AND MEATY TACOS
(OR TOSTADAS)

MAKES: 4 TACOS (1 TO 4 SERVINGS) ⟫ **TIME: 45 MINUTES**

INGREDIENTS

¼ cup vegetable oil, plus more as needed

4 (6-inch) corn tortillas

8 ounces ground meat (beef, pork, chicken, or turkey)

Salt and pepper

1 small onion, chopped (if you like)

1 or 2 cloves garlic, chopped

2 teaspoons chili powder

½ teaspoon ground cumin

1 tablespoon tomato paste

2 tablespoons water

1 lime, quartered, for serving

STEPS

1 Put a wire rack on a rimmed baking sheet by the stove. Pour the oil into a 10-inch skillet over medium-high heat. When it's hot and shimmering, use tongs to put a tortilla in the pan and count to 10. It should start blistering and the oil should be bubbling. (If not, count to an additional 5 or 10 until it does.) Carefully grab an edge with the tongs and turn it over. For tacos, keep holding on with the tongs and fold the tortilla in half to form a taco shell. (For tostadas, let go of the tongs and leave the tortilla flat.)

2 Keep cooking, either holding the taco shell with tongs to keep its shape or letting the tortilla lay flat for tostadas. Either way, turn the tortilla over once or twice, until it turns golden. This takes less than 1 minute. Lift it out of the oil and set it on the wire rack. Repeat with the other three tortillas, adjusting the heat so you have sizzling without burning. Add more oil if the pan starts to look dry.

RECIPE CONTINUES ➡

EAT WITH: chopped lettuce or cabbage; chopped tomatoes; Fresh Tomato (or Fruit) Salsa (page 80); grated cheddar, mozzarella, or Jack cheese (or try crumbled queso fresco, a mild Mexican cheese that's perfect for tacos). For other filling ideas, see the list on page 103.

DID YOU KNOW

You can use flour tortillas for tacos too. Fry them as described in the main recipe and use them in the variations that follow or anytime you want crisp-fried flour tortillas. For soft and warm flour tortillas see page 107.

VARIATIONS

CRISP BEANY TACOS (OR TOSTADAS). This vegetarian filling works with kidney, pinto, cannellini, or black beans. Drain a 15-ounce can in a colander and rinse. Mash the beans with a fork on a plate to break them into bits and use them instead of the ground meat in the recipe, only in Step 3, leave 2 tablespoons of oil in the pan after frying the tortillas.

SOFT MEATY OR BEANY TACOS. Works for any of the meat or bean fillings. Skip to Step 3 and add 1 tablespoon oil to the skillet for meat tacos (or 2 tablespoons for bean). Keep the filling on medium-low heat while you warm the tortillas. Warm the tortillas in one of the ways talked about in the box on the right.

3 Remove the pan from the heat and carefully spoon all but 1 tablespoon of the oil into a small heatproof bowl. Keep the reserved oil near the stove. Return the skillet to medium heat and add the meat. Sprinkle with salt and pepper and cook, stirring every couple minutes with a stiff spatula and breaking the chunks up until the meat starts to brown, 5 to 10 minutes.

4 Add the onion and garlic and some or all of the reserved oil if the pan looks dry. Cook, stirring every minute or so, until the vegetables soften and the meat looks pretty brown all over, 1 to 3 minutes. Add the chili powder, cumin, and tomato paste and stir all the time to mix everything into the meat and warm the spices, less than 1 minute. Stir in the water and scrape up any browned bits from the bottom of the pan. When the water bubbles away a few seconds later, remove the skillet from the heat.

5 Use the spatula or a large spoon to slip the taco filling carefully into the shells. Top with whatever you like from the "Eat With" list on page 105 and eat right away.

HOW TO WARM TORTILLAS

When you don't feel like frying taco or tostada shells, here are two easy ways to warm soft flour or corn tortillas:

OVEN. Heat the oven to 375°F. Stack as many tortillas as you want on a piece of foil and fold in the corners so they're covered all over. Put the package in the oven and bake until heated through, 5 to 10 minutes. Keep the tortillas wrapped in the foil (or put them in a pretty cloth napkin) until you're ready to serve.

MICROWAVE. Instead of foil, sprinkle a clean towel with tap water and use that to wrap your stack. You'll need about 15 seconds per tortilla. So 4 tortillas will take about 1 minute.

SIPS AND SPOONFULS

SOUPS YOU CAN
DRINK FROM A MUG
OR EAT FROM A BOWL

★ ★   Let me explain why a soup made from canned tomatoes is better than tomato soup from a can or one of those microwave cups. Not counting salt and pepper, there are only four ingredients in this recipe. And you and I can pronounce all of them.

CREAMY TOMATO SOUP

MAKES: 3 TO 4 SERVINGS ⟩⟩ *TIME: 30 MINUTES* ❄ 🍃

INGREDIENTS

1 (28-ounce) can whole tomatoes

1 cup cream, half-and-half, or milk, plus more as needed

1 tablespoon tomato paste

1 teaspoon sugar

Salt

Pepper (if you like)

Olive oil for drizzling

EAT WITH: bread or crackers; rice or noodles (on the side or stirred in); steamed vegetables; Leafy Salad (page 137); or, of course, a Grilled Cheese Sandwich (page 91).

STEPS

1 After opening the can, put all the tomatoes and their juice in a blender. Pour the 1 cup cream, half-and-half, or milk into the empty tomato can and set it by the stove.

2 Start the blender on low and slowly crank up the speed until the tomatoes are smooth and look like thick juice. You are making a "purée" with an action called "puréeing." This may take a minute or 2.

3 Put the tomato paste in a medium pot over medium heat. When it starts to sizzle, stir in the puréed tomatoes and raise the heat so the liquid bubbles gently. Cook, stirring once every 2 or 3 minutes, until the soup thickens and darkens, about 15 minutes.

4 Stir in the cream, half-and-half, or milk and let the soup just start to bubble again. Then adjust the heat so the soup continues to bubble and cook, stirring once or twice more until you decide if you want the soup thicker or thinner. If thicker, keep cooking and stirring for another few minutes until it looks right. For thinner soup, add more of the cream or whatever liquid you used.

5 Carefully take a taste and add salt and pepper too if you like. Keep the soup covered over low heat until you're ready to eat. After it's in a cup or bowl, drizzle with a little olive oil. Refrigerate any leftovers in an airtight container for up to 1 week. You can reheat in the microwave or eat it cold (really!). Or freeze for a few months.

CURRIED TOMATO SOUP. When you cook the tomato paste in Step 3, add 1 or 2 teaspoons curry powder, depending on how much curry flavor you want for the soup. Use coconut milk instead of the dairy in the main recipe.

FRESH TOMATO SOUP. You've got to make this in the summer when the tomatoes are the juiciest. Instead of canned tomatoes, start with about 2 pounds fresh tomatoes. (Anything but cherry tomatoes because they're so seedy. If you use colors besides red, your soup will be those colors!) Cut around the core of each tomato to remove it, then toss the whole tomatoes in the blender—seeds and skins and all. In Step 3, increase the cooking time by 15 minutes so the tomato purée can thicken. Then keep going with the recipe.

DID YOU KNOW

Your soup will be thickest with cream, second thickest with half-and-half, and thinnest with milk. And for nondairy tomato soup, unsweetened oat or soy milk are your best choices.

DECORATE YOUR SOUP BOWL . . .

. . . WITH SOMETHING DELICIOUS TO TOP AND STIR IN

FOR FRESHNESS
- Chopped fresh herbs
- Chopped raw vegetables
- Steamed or roasted vegetables

FOR CRUNCH
- Croutons (page 243)
- Crumbled crackers or chips
- Chopped nuts

FOR TANG
- Fresh Tomato (or Fruit) Salsa (page 80)
- Chopped pickles
- A squeeze of fresh lemon or lime juice

FOR RICHNESS
- Pat of butter
- Drizzle of olive oil
- Swirl of cream
- Spoonful of yogurt or sour cream

FOR SPICE
- Red chile flakes
- Chopped fresh chiles
- Dash of curry or chili powder

FOR HEARTINESS
- A scoop of rice or grains
- A spoonful of beans
- A fried or scrambled egg
- A blizzard of grated cheese
- Crumbled cooked bacon or sausage
- Leftover seafood or chicken

★★ A super-fast and hearty soup that starts with either canned beans or beans you cook yourself from dried. (The recipe for that, if you'd like to try it, is on page 210.) I'm not joking—you can use any bean here.

ANY-BEAN SOUP
WITH OR WITHOUT HAM

MAKES: 2 TO 3 SERVINGS ⟫ *TIME: 40 MINUTES* ❄ 🗍

INGREDIENTS

1 (15-ounce) can or 1¾ cups cooked beans (like chickpeas, navy or cannellini, pinto, or black)

1 tablespoon olive oil

2 thick slices ham (about 3 ounces), chopped (if you like)

1 celery stalk, chopped

1 carrot, chopped

½ small onion, chopped

1 clove garlic, chopped

1 teaspoon dried Italian seasoning blend

2 cups water or vegetable or chicken stock (or bean cooking liquid if you have it)

Salt

Pepper (if you like)

EAT WITH: see Decorate Your Soup Bowl on page 112. On the side, warm bread or tortillas; Leafy Salad (page 137); or Steamed Vegetables (page 139).

STEPS

1 If you're using canned beans, put them in a colander and rinse under running water. (If you have already cooked beans, measure them and whatever liquid you saved from the pot and keep them separate.)

2 Put the oil in a medium pot over medium heat. Add the ham if you're using it, the celery, carrot, onion, and garlic, and stir once or twice. Adjust the heat so the mixture sizzles without burning and cook, stirring every minute or so, until everything looks a little darker than when you started and the vegetables are soft, 5 to 10 minutes.

3 Add the Italian seasoning and stir a couple times until you smell it, less than a minute. Add the reserved beans. If you used canned, also add the 2 cups water or stock; if using cooked beans, add enough water or stock to the cooking liquid you saved to equal 2 cups and stir that into the pot. Bring the soup to a boil, then turn the heat down so the bubbling slows down a bit and cook, stirring every 3 minutes or so, until the vegetables are totally soft and the liquid thickens, 5 to 10 minutes.

4 Take the pot off the heat and use a slotted spoon to carefully remove about ½ cup of beans and vegetables to a large plate. Break them up with a fork or potato masher and return them to the pot. (This will give the soup a great flavor and texture.) Taste and add salt and pepper too if you like and eat as soon as it's cool enough.

RECIPE CONTINUES ➡

BEANS-N-NOODLE SOUP.
An Italian soup called pasta e fagioli (fa-jol-eh) and one of the best soups ever. Use pinto or cannellini beans. In Step 3, when you add the beans and liquid, stir in ⅓ cup dried cut pasta (like small shells, orzo, or macaroni) and an extra cup of water or stock. Keep checking the noodles for tenderness, but they should be ready when the vegetables are soft. Don't bother to remove and mash any of the soup in Step 4. Just start serving it up. Sprinkling the top of each bowl with Parmesan cheese is an excellent idea.

LENTIL SOUP WITH HAM.
Lentils are available in cans in many supermarkets. But they only take about 30 minutes to cook from dried (see page 210). You can use either canned or homemade in this recipe.

SMOOTH YOU-PICK-THE-BEAN SOUP. A creamy vegetarian soup that you can top with any chopped or crumbled cooked meat (see the recipe on page 58). Or leave it meatless after puréeing. Skip the ham in Step 2 and follow the recipe to Step 4. Carefully use a ladle to spoon the soup into a blender. It's important NOT to fill the container more than halfway and that you get some help to hold down the lid and start the machine on its lowest setting to start breaking everything up. Stop and scrape down the sides with a silicone or rubber spatula. Keep going faster and faster as long as the soup isn't splattering high in the container. When the soup is as smooth as you want it, scrape it back into the pot and heat it on medium heat until it's steaming again. Now you can eat it!

FROZEN VEGETABLES IN SOUP

Go ahead and use all frozen vegetables or some frozen and some fresh. As long as you still follow the recipe, the cooking time will be about the same.

★ ★   You've had minestrone, right? Well, that's this—a mixed vegetable soup where you choose exactly what you want from the three groups described on page 131. Then "hard," "soft," and "leafy" vegetables are in the recipe along with some examples so you can pick just one or two or a combination. The steps tell you when to add them to the pot and how long to cook them. When you're done, you will have made dinner for everyone.

ONLY-THE-VEGETABLES-YOU-LIKE SOUP

MAKES: 4 TO 8 SERVINGS (ABOUT 2 QUARTS) ➤➤ *TIME: ABOUT 1 HOUR* ❄

INGREDIENTS

3 tablespoons olive oil, plus more for drizzling

½ onion, chopped

2 or 3 cloves garlic, chopped

Salt and pepper

About 1½ cups chopped hard vegetables like potatoes, winter squash, sweet potatoes, or carrots

1 (15-ounce) can diced tomatoes

4 cups water or vegetable stock, plus more as needed

About 1½ cups chopped soft vegetables like celery, green beans, mushrooms, zucchini, or frozen edamame

About 1 packed cup chopped leafy greens like spinach, kale, arugula, or chard

Grated Parmesan cheese for serving

EAT WITH: lots of bread or Buttery Egg Noodles (page 165).

STEPS

1   Put the oil in a large pot over medium heat. When it's hot and shimmering, add the onion and garlic, sprinkle with salt and pepper, and cook, stirring almost all the time, until the vegetables begin to soften, 2 to 3 minutes.

2   Add the hard vegetables and stir a couple times until they're shiny, then add the tomatoes, juice and all. Raise the heat so the mixture sizzles. Continue stirring until the tomatoes darken and start to become dry, about 3 minutes. Add the water or stock, bring to a boil, and adjust the heat so the soup bubbles gently.

3   Cook, stirring every now and then, until the hard vegetables are fairly soft and the tomatoes have broken up, 15 to 20 minutes.

4   Add the soft vegetables and adjust the heat so the soup bubbles again. Let the soft vegetables have a 5-minute head start in the pot and then add the greens. Adjust the heat so the soup bubbles gently, cover, and cook until the vegetables are quite tender. This will take 10 to 15 minutes, but you'll want to check them and stir every 3 minutes or so. Taste and add more salt and pepper if you like. Eat each bowl drizzled with some olive oil and sprinkled with cheese.

★ ★ See what it's like to make a homemade stock with this shortcut to an amazing chicken noodle soup.

CHICKEN NOODLE SOUP

MAKES: 2 TO 4 SERVINGS ⟫ *TIME: 45 MINUTES*

INGREDIENTS

3 tablespoons butter or olive oil

1 large carrot, chopped

2 celery stalks, chopped

½ small onion, chopped

2 cloves garlic, chopped

2 tablespoons tomato paste

Salt and pepper

5 cups water

1 large or 2 small boneless chicken breasts (about 8 ounces)

4 ounces angel hair pasta or thin egg noodles

¼ cup chopped fresh basil or parsley for garnish

EAT WITH: Raw Snacking Vegetables (page 133) or Steamed Vegetables (page 139) and maybe something crunchy like crackers or croutons (page 243).

STEPS

1 Put the butter or olive oil in a large pot over medium heat. When the butter foams or the oil is warm, add the carrots, celery, onion, and garlic. Cook, stirring every minute or so, until the vegetables are soft, 3 to 5 minutes.

2 Add the tomato paste and sprinkle with salt and pepper. Cook and stir until the paste coats the vegetables. Add the water and stir up any crusty bits from the bottom of the pot. Slip the chicken into the water and adjust the heat so the soup bubbles gently. Cover the pot.

3 Let the soup cook without stirring for 5 minutes, then check to make sure the liquid is still bubbling and stir. Cover the pot and check again in another 5 minutes.

4 Use tongs to carefully lift the chicken out of the soup onto a plate. Cut the thickest part with a small knife. If any pinkness remains in the center, return it to the pot for another 5 minutes (and wash the plate so you don't use it again). When the chicken is ready, put it on a cutting board and use a knife and fork to cut it into chunks.

5 Return the chicken to the pot, add the noodles, and bring the soup to a boil. Cook, stirring every minute, until the noodles are tender but not mushy. Start checking after 3 minutes. Remove the pot from the heat, carefully taste a sip of the broth, and add salt and pepper if you like. Ladle the soup into bowls, sprinkle with the basil and parsley, and eat as soon as it's cool enough.

RECIPE CONTINUES ➡

BEEF OR PORK NOODLE SOUP. Instead of the chicken, use 8 ounces of sirloin steak or boneless pork chops.

MISO CHICKEN NOODLE SOUP. Works with chicken, beef, or pork and has a light, savory flavor from this Japanese soybean paste. Instead of the tomato paste, use 2 tablespoons white miso. Garnish with chopped scallions or cilantro or a sprinkle of sesame seeds instead of the herbs.

CHICKEN-AND-RICE SOUP. Or make it with beef or pork as described in the idea above. Instead of the noodles, add 1 cup leftover cooked rice to the soup in Step 5.

DID YOU KNOW

You can add more vegetables to this soup. Frozen peas, corn, or spinach are all good ideas to stir in with the noodles in Step 5. Use as little or as much as you want.

A creamy soup without cream? Based on your favorite vegetable? How is that even possible? The main recipe is for carrots and a couple more ideas follow to get you rolling. Then you can use the same recipe for cauliflower, broccoli, sweet potatoes, peas, winter squash, or zucchini. Read on!

CREAMY CARROT (OR ANY VEGETABLE) SOUP

MAKES: 2 TO 3 SERVINGS (ABOUT 1 QUART) ➤➤ TIME: ABOUT 1 HOUR ❄ 🍃

INGREDIENTS

2 tablespoons butter or olive oil

½ small onion, sliced

3 cups vegetable or chicken stock, or water, plus more as needed

2 cups chopped carrots (about 12 ounces)

1 small Yukon Gold potato (about 4 ounces), peeled and cut into chunks

Salt

Pepper (if you like)

EAT WITH: something crunchy like croutons or crumbled chips or crackers; be sure to see the ideas on page 112 too.

STEPS

1 Put the butter or olive oil in a 2-quart pot over medium heat. When the butter melts or the oil is hot and shimmers, add the onion and cook, stirring every minute or so, until it softens and starts to turn golden, 3 to 5 minutes.

2 Add the stock or water and the carrots and potato and bring the mixture to a boil. Turn the heat down so that the liquid bubbles gently and cover the pot. Cook, stirring every 5 minutes or so, until the carrots and potatoes break apart easily when you scoop some up with a big spoon and poke them with a fork. To get them super-soft like this will take about 20 minutes.

3 Remove the pot from the heat, uncover, and let it cool for about 10 minutes. Carefully use a ladle to spoon the soup into a blender. It's important NOT to fill the container more than halfway and that you get some help to hold down the lid and start the machine on its lowest setting to start breaking everything up. Stop and scrape down the sides with a soft spatula. Keep going faster and faster as long as the soup isn't splattering high in the container.

4 When the soup is as smooth as you want it, scrape it back into the pot and return it to medium heat. Add more stock or water, 1 tablespoon at a time, until the soup is as thick or thin as you like it. While it's still not too hot, taste and add salt or pepper if you want. Then cook, stirring constantly, until it starts bubbling. Now it's ready.

RECIPE CONTINUES ➡

VARIATIONS

MUSHROOM SOUP. Instead of the carrots, use cremini or button mushrooms and trim and slice them. Everything else stays the same.

SPINACH SOUP. Instead of the carrots, get 10 ounces spinach leaves ready near the stove. In Step 2, wait to add them to the pot until after the potato has been cooking by itself long enough so that you can stick a piece with a fork, 10 to 15 minutes. Then add the spinach to the pot and follow the rest of the recipe.

5 THINGS TO TRY IN CREAMY CARROT (OR ANY VEGETABLE) SOUP

Pick just one of these to add to the pot with the potato:

1. 1 inch piece fresh ginger, peeled and sliced into coins
2. 1 or 2 cloves garlic, chopped
3. 1 teaspoon curry powder
4. ½ teaspoon ground cumin
5. Pinch red chile flakes

DID YOU KNOW

You can add cream, half-and-half, milk, or nondairy milk to any of these soups to make them even creamier. After returning the soup to the pot in Step 4, instead of more stock or water, stir in up to ½ cup of a creamy liquid.

★ ★ ★ (with fresh corn) or ★ ★ (with frozen kernels) A chowder is a chunky, creamy, and thick soup that usually has potatoes in there somewhere. I've written the recipe so that you can use fresh corn (which is a bit of a project; see the illustrations on page 18). Or for a much easier—and still tasty—method, you can use frozen corn. Either way you'll thicken the liquid by cooking flour and butter together to create a white paste known by its French name, *roux* (pronounced roo).

CORN CHOWDER

MAKES: 2 TO 4 SERVINGS (ABOUT 6 CUPS) ➤➤ TIME: 90 MINUTES WITH FRESH CORN; 45 WITH FROZEN

INGREDIENTS

2 cups fresh or frozen corn kernels (if frozen, no need to thaw)

1 small potato (any kind, about 4 ounces)

2 tablespoons butter

2 tablespoons all-purpose flour

1 or 2 scallions, white and green parts separated and chopped

4 cups milk

Salt and pepper, if you like

EAT WITH: Grilled Cheese or Tuna Sandwich (page 91 and 96), Drop Biscuits (page 255), raw or steamed vegetables (page 133 and 139).

STEPS

1 Prepare the fresh corn as shown on page 18. Or measure the frozen corn. Peel the potato if you like and cut it into cubes about ½-inch big. (They don't have to be perfect.)

2 Put the butter in a 2-quart pot over medium-low heat. When it's foaming, stir in the flour. Adjust the heat so the mixture barely sizzles and cook, still stirring all the time, until the mixture (the roux) turns a little golden and smells toasty, not like raw flour. This takes about 5 minutes. Add the chopped white parts of the scallions and stir.

3 Add the milk, using a whisk or a big spoon to dissolve the roux in the liquid. When there are no more lumps, raise the heat to medium and add the potatoes. Cook, stirring every 2 minutes or so, until the soup starts to bubble gently. Cover and cook until the potatoes are tender, 5 to 10 minutes. Check and stir every 3 minutes. To test the potatoes, lift a spoonful out of the pot and see if you can pierce it with a fork.

4 When the potatoes are tender, add the corn and scallion greens. Taste the soup to see if you want to add salt and pepper. Cook, adjusting the heat to keep the soup bubbling gently and stirring every minute, until the corn is hot and tender, about 3 minutes. Ladle into mugs or bowls and eat as soon as it's cool enough.

VARIATIONS

SHRIMP-AND-CORN CHOWDER. When you add the corn in Step 4, stir in 4 ounces shelled raw or cooked shrimp. It's okay if it's still frozen, but if you want it in small pieces, put it in a colander and run it under cold water until it's soft enough to chop. The chowder is ready when the shrimp turns pink (if it was raw) or gets steaming hot (if it was already cooked). This might add a couple minutes to the final cooking time.

CHEESY CORN CHOWDER. When you add the corn in Step 4, stir in ½ cup grated cheddar or Parmesan cheese.

⭐ The all-time American favorite is really just a simple beany soup. Your choice—black or red beans. The main recipe makes a small pot for weeknights. To have a party or have leftovers to freeze, double or triple the quantities and use a big 5-quart pot. And to add different meats, see the ideas that follow.

CHILI

MAKES: 2 TO 3 SERVINGS ➵ ➝ TIME: 45 MINUTES ❄ 🍃

INGREDIENTS

1 (15-ounce) can black or pinto beans (or 1¾ cups cooked beans; see page 210)

2 tablespoons olive oil

½ red bell pepper, cored, seeded, and chopped

½ onion, chopped

1 clove garlic, chopped

2 teaspoons chili powder

1 (15-ounce) can crushed tomatoes

1 cup water

Salt

Pepper (if you like)

Sour cream for serving (if you like)

Grated cheddar or Jack cheese for serving (if you like)

Chopped fresh cilantro for serving (if you like)

Hot sauce for serving (if you like)

STEPS

1 If you're using canned beans, put them into a colander, rinse under running water, and let sit to drain. (For home-cooked beans, just measure the beans. You can use their cooking liquid instead of the water in Step 3 if you have any.)

2 Put the oil in a 2-quart pot over medium heat. When it's hot and shimmering, add the bell pepper, onion, and garlic and cook, stirring almost always, until the vegetables are soft, 3 to 5 minutes.

3 Add the chili powder and stir until you can smell it, about 1 minute. Add the tomatoes, beans, and water and raise the heat to high to bring to a boil. Adjust the heat so the mixture bubbles gently and cover.

4 Cook, stirring every 5 minutes, until the chili thickens and darkens, 10 to 15 minutes. Carefully take a taste and add salt and pepper too if you like.

RECIPE CONTINUES ➡

EAT WITH: Skillet Corn Bread (page 244), Raw Snacking Vegetables (page 133), Guacamole (page 134), warm tortillas (page 107), or chips.

MEATY CHILI. This will make 4 servings. You'll need 8 ounces ground pork or beef. In Step 2, use only 1 tablespoon oil. When it gets hot and shimmers, add the meat and cook, stirring whenever it starts to brown around the edges, until there's no longer any pink anywhere. Then add the bell pepper, onion, and garlic and follow the recipe from there. If the chili looks too thick, you might need to add another ¼ or ½ cup water while it cooks in Step 4.

CHICKEN OR TURKEY CHILI. This will make 4 servings. Instead of black or pinto beans, white beans like navy or cannellini are a fun change to try here. You'll need 8 ounces ground chicken or turkey. In Step 2, keep 2 tablespoons oil. When it gets hot and shimmers, add the meat and cook, stirring whenever it starts to brown around the edges, until there's no longer any pink anywhere. Then add the bell pepper, onion, and garlic and follow the recipe from there. If the chili looks too thick, you might need to add another ¼ or ½ cup water while it cooks in Step 4.

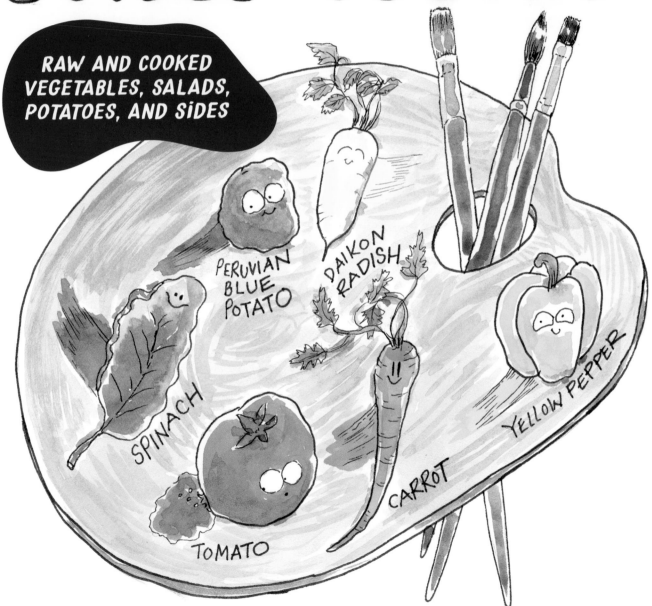

VEGETABLES YOUR WAY

People love to tell kids to eat more vegetables. But does anyone ever explain *how* to eat more vegetables? That's what this chapter is all about. I believe that if you divide vegetables into three groups—Hard, Soft, and Leafy—it's easier to see the big picture and zoom in on the ones you already like. That's the perfect place to start.

The next step is to figure out which vegetables you like to eat cooked and which ones you like raw. Do you like them plain or with salt? What about some butter or olive oil? Or do you think a sauce for drizzling or dipping is best? (There are lots of ideas in the Flavor Bursts chapter beginning on page 67.) Maybe you change things up and eat your vegetables different ways on different days. And as long as I'm asking a bunch of questions, how do you feel about salad?

Talking through these lists with the people you love will help you decide what to try when you're ready for something new. The recipes that follow will teach you many things to do with whatever vegetables you choose. That's *how* to eat more vegetables. Start with your favorites, prepare them exactly how you like them, and then see what happens.

HARD VEGETABLES

BEST RAW
Jicama
Radishes

EAT RAW OR COOKED
Broccoli
Carrots
Cauliflower
Corn on the cob
Garlic
Ginger
Onions
Turnips

NEED TO COOK
Leeks
Potatoes
Sweet potatoes
Winter squash

SOFT VEGETABLES

BEST RAW
Cucumbers

EAT RAW OR COOKED
Bell peppers
Celery
Cherry tomatoes
Chiles
Corn kernels (or baby corn)
Fennel
Mushrooms
Peas
Scallions
Snap peas
Snow peas
Summer squash
Tomatoes
Zucchini

NEED TO COOK
Asparagus
Eggplant
Green beans

LEAFY VEGETABLES

BEST RAW
Lettuce

EAT RAW OR COOKED
Arugula
Brussels sprouts
Cabbage
Escarole
Herbs
Kale
Spinach
Watercress

NEED TO COOK
Bok Choy
Chard
Collard greens

⭐ A rainbow on a plate, or make it shades of green with a little red. Maybe there's a small bowl of sauce for dipping on the side. The best thing about having a bunch of crisp, refreshing veggies all prepped and ready to eat is that you have crisp refreshing veggies all prepped and ready to eat.

RAW SNACKING VEGETABLES

MAKES: 4 TO 6 SERVINGS ⟫→ *TIME: 30 MINUTES* 🍃

INGREDIENTS

1 to 2 pounds of your favorite vegetables to eat raw (see the lists on page 131 for lots of choices)

EAT WITH: Ranch for Real (page 75), Salad Dressing (page 76), Fresh Tomato (or Fruit) Salsa (page 80), any of the sauce ideas from The Condiment Lab (page 78), or simply olive oil and salt.

STEPS

1 Once you pick out the vegetables you want, rinse them and use the drawings on pages 16 to 21 to see how to prepare them. Almost all need trimming, many need peeling, and some are best with the seeds removed.

2 Cut the vegetables into sticks, slices, or coins for easy snacking. Broccoli and cauliflower are nice to break into florets or "little trees." Put the cut vegetables into containers and refrigerate until you want to eat some. How long they'll last depends on how wet they are and how fast you eat them. Pro tip: If you put carrots, celery, and radishes in containers of water in the fridge, they'll keep a few days longer.

VARIATION

CRISP COOKED SNACKING VEGETABLES. Some vegetables you don't like raw will taste better cooked until "crisp-tender" and chilled—like broccoli, cauliflower, and snow or snap peas. Other vegetables need to be cooked until soft before eating—like potatoes, sweet potatoes, and green beans, but they taste awesome cold with dip. So when you want to try cold cooked vegetables, prepare them as shown on pages 16 to 21. Then get a big bowl filled with ice cubes and water, so that after cooking the vegetables you can "shock" them to keep them from getting mushy. Next, steam the vegetables you want on the stove or in the microwave according to the recipe on page 139 and 141. As soon as they're ready, use tongs or a slotted spoon to put them in the bowl of ice water. Swirl the ice water until the vegetables are chilled. Then drain in a colander and eat or refrigerate as described in the recipe.

⭐ Avocados are great sliced and even better mashed into guacamole. You can try adding different flavors every time you make it.

GUACAMOLE

MAKES: ABOUT 1 CUP (2 TO 4 SERVINGS) ⟫ *TIME: 15 TO 30 MINUTES, DEPENDING ON WHAT EXTRAS YOU ADD*

INGREDIENTS

1 large or 2 small avocados (about 12 ounces)

Salt and pepper

EAT WITH: Fresh Tomato (or Fruit) Salsa (page 80) and tortilla chips, on burritos and tacos (pages 102 to 105), in rice bowls, and on toast.

STEPS

1 Before you start, check the list after the recipe to see if you want to add anything to your guacamole. If so, get everything ready. Decide what you want to eat with it and get that ready too.

2 Prepare the avocado as shown on page 16. To quarter it for peeling and removing the pit, cut downward toward the center in 4 places so you can pull wedges of the fruit away from the pit. Scoop the avocado out of the peel in big chunks with a spoon, and put them in a shallow, medium-sized bowl.

3 Use a fork or a potato masher to smush and stir the avocado until it's as chunky or smooth as you like. Add anything you want from the list that follows. (Or keep it simple with all avocado.) Taste and see if you want to season with salt and pepper, then dig in. (Leftovers will turn brown within hours. Pressing a piece of plastic directly on top helps the guacamole stay green a little longer.)

It's best to buy green, hard avocados. You've got to be patient, but once they ripen and become dark and soft on the counter, you can eat them right away or pop them in the fridge, where they'll stay fresh for a few days. If you really love avocados, then a good plan is to have one on the counter and one chilling at all times.

6 THINGS TO ADD TO GUACAMOLE

Start with 1 tablespoon of one or two things and see what you think before adding more.

1. Fresh lime or lemon juice
2. Sour cream
3. Chopped fresh tomato
4. Chopped green onion
5. Chopped cilantro
6. Fresh or frozen corn kernels

SALAD BINGO

CHERRY TOMATOES	RED OR GREEN LEAF LETTUCE	HAM, SALAMI, OR BACON	ROMAINE LETTUCE	CHEESE
RADICCHIO	CARROTS	ENDIVE	CAULIFLOWER	SPINACH
FRISÉE	RED CABBAGE	CUCUMBER	ICEBERG LETTUCE	TOFU CUBES
COOKED SHRIMP, CRAB, OR FISH	FRESH HERBS	BUTTER LETTUCE	RADISHES	ARUGULA
SCALLIONS	CANNED TUNA OR SALMON	NAPA CABBAGE	MESCLUN	COOKED CHICKEN

Is this even a recipe? The size of the salad, what you put in it, and how you dress it are totally up to you. There's also a lot of info here to help you choose and prepare lettuce, spinach, arugula, and other greens. So yeah, let's call it a recipe.

LEAFY SALAD

MAKES: 1 SERVING ⟫ TIME: 15 TO 30 MINUTES, DEPENDING ON HOW MUCH STUFF YOU ADD

INGREDIENTS

Several large leaves or a handful of torn leaves (enough to fill the bowl you want to use)

Additions from the list that follows

Ranch for Real (page 75) or one of the ideas in Salad Dressing (page 76), as needed

EAT WITH: soup, sandwiches, pasta, beans, grains, or mains on the side; or top with cold beans, meat, chicken, eggs, or cheese for a main dish salad.

STEPS

1 Fill a big bowl with cold tap water and get a colander ready in the sink. (Or fill a salad spinner with water.) If you're using a head of lettuce (where the leaves are attached to a hard "core"), pull off and get rid of any brown or wilted outside leaves until you get to fresh inside leaves. If you're using loose unattached leaves, sort through them and throw away any that are brown, wilted, or slimy.

2 With a knife and cutting board or your fingers, trim away any tough edges or stems and cut or tear the leaves into a size that looks best to you. As you work, put them in the bowl of water (or the salad spinner). Swirl to rinse the leaves and lift them into the colander (or lift the spinner basket and pour out the water). If the water looks muddy or sandy, repeat this step.

3 Shake the colander to get most of the water off the leaves and roll them loosely in a clean towel. (Or spin the spinner and pour off the water left in the bowl.)

4 To dress the salad, you have two choices: Put the leaves in the bowl you're going to eat from along with anything you're adding from the list below. Spoon or pour on a little dressing wherever you want it. Or for tossed salad, rinse and dry the bowl you used to rinse the leaves (or the spinner bowl), put your salad in the bowl with a little bit of dressing, and use your hands or a big fork and spoon to toss the leaves until they're lightly coated. Either way, it's better to start with too little dressing than too much. You can add more, but you can't take it away! Eat while the leaves are still crisp.

RECIPE CONTINUES ➡

COLESLAW. Instead of lettuce, use cabbage leaves: Napa cabbage is the mildest; red is the boldest; and green is in between. Stack or fold a few of them and carefully cut across the leaves so they form thin ribbons. If you want them smaller, cut them again in the other direction and keep chopping until they're the size and shape you want. Ranch for Real (page 75) dressing is perfect for slaw. Or you can just toss with some mayonnaise or oil and vinegar until the cabbage is evenly coated.

LEAVES FROM MILD TO BOLD

For those of you new to salads, try starting with the mildest at the top of this list and work your way along the path toward those with the boldest flavor. If you already love salads, you'll probably find some new lettuces here to try.

- Iceberg
- Butter
- Romaine
- Spinach
- Red or green leaf
- Napa cabbage
- Green cabbage
- Red cabbage
- Endive
- Arugula
- Mesclun (which means "mix" in French)
- Frisée
- Radicchio

DID YOU KNOW

You can have salad always ready to make in the fridge. Just fill a salad spinner with torn or baby leaves, rinse them well in cold water, and spin. Dump the water out of the bowl and shake the basket a couple times to fluff the leaves. They'll keep for several days.

17 THINGS TO ADD TO ANY SALAD

Pick as many or as few of the things on this list as you like. You can use a little bit of everything or a lot of just one or two. Then chop everything into bite-sized bits. You can even skip the lettuce!

1. Tomatoes (or cherry tomatoes, whole or cut in half)
2. Celery
3. Carrots
4. Cucumber
5. Radishes
6. Scallions
7. Fresh herb leaves (like basil, mint, or parsley)
8. Any cold cooked vegetables (like broccoli, cauliflower, or green beans)
9. Fruit (like apples, pears, or grapes)
10. Nuts (like peanuts, cashews, or almonds)
11. Cheese (like cheddar, Jack, feta, or grated Parmesan)
12. Cooked chicken
13. Ham, salami, or crumbled cooked bacon
14. Cooked shrimp, crab, or fish
15. Canned tuna or salmon
16. Tofu cubes
17. Croutons (page 243)

✦ When you put food above boiling water, but not actually *in* the water, the heat of the steam cooks it without making it soggy. The trick is to check the vegetables so you can feel how tender they are. The color will also get brighter than raw and then start to turn darker. Leafy vegetables steam the fastest, followed by soft vegetables, then hard. (See the lists on page 131.) It's easiest to choose one vegetable to steam at a time.

STEAMED VEGETABLES

MAKES: 2 SERVINGS ⇉ *TIME: 30 MINUTES* 🌿

INGREDIENTS

8 to 12 ounces any vegetable

1 tablespoon softened butter or olive oil

Salt

Pepper (if you like)

EAT WITH: main dishes made with mostly meat, chicken, fish, or eggs; or sandwiches, burritos, or tacos. You can also try eating steamed vegetables with any of the sauces for Raw Snacking Vegetables on page 133.

STEPS

1 Once you pick out the vegetables you want and rinse them, use the drawings on pages 16 to 21 to see how to get them ready to eat. Almost all need trimming, many need peeling, and some are best with the seeds removed. Cut the vegetables into sticks, slices, chunks, or coins. Broccoli and cauliflower are nice to break into florets or "little trees."

2 Set a steaming basket in a 2-quart pot with a tight-fitting lid. Add enough water to almost touch the bottom of the basket. (If you don't have a basket, see if you have a colander that fits in the pot. Or add about an inch of water in the bottom of the pot so you can steam-boil the vegetables. Or use the microwave method that follows.)

3 Bring the water in the pot to a boil. Put the vegetables in the basket (or directly in the water) and adjust the heat so the water bubbles just enough to make some bursts of steam but not enough to splash all over the food. Cover the pot.

RECIPE CONTINUES ➡

To stop steamed or microwaved vegetables from cooking, in Step 5, set a colander in the sink so you can run the vegetables under cold water. Or to chill them quickly, "shock" them in ice water as explained on page 133. Then you can eat them cold or use them for salads or snacking.

4   After 2 minutes, carefully open the pot so the steam blows away from you. Poke some of the vegetables with a fork or the tip of a small knife to see how tender they are. They will continue to cook and get softer after you remove them from the heat, so stop when they're still a littler firmer than you like to eat them. The tenderest leafy vegetables and smallest chunks will be ready in 2 minutes, hard vegetables will take 15 to 20 minutes, and soft vegetables will be somewhere in between.

5   Use tongs or a slotted spoon to move the finished vegetables to your plate or a serving bowl. Toss with the butter or olive oil, sprinkle with salt and pepper too if you like, and eat.

VARIATION

STEAMED VEGETABLES IN THE MICROWAVE. Honestly, the easiest way to steam vegetables, as long as you know how hot your microwave settings are and you stop frequently to stir and check for tenderness. Put the vegetables on a microwave-safe plate or in a shallow bowl and splash with 2 tablespoons water. Cover with the lid that came with the dish or a clean towel. Cook on high for 1 minute, then check. Repeat until the vegetables are almost ready, then start checking after every 30 seconds. When they're done, pick up with the recipe at Step 5.

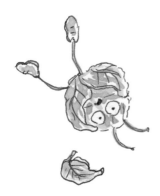

★ ★ For tons of flavor and a little more action, try cooking vegetables in a skillet. The technique is called both "stir-frying" and "sautéing." After coating the pan with a thin layer of butter or oil, there are so many choices. You can brown the outsides. Or not. You can add garlic, ginger, or onions. Or not. Make them saucy when you're feeling saucy. And as with all the vegetable-cooking recipes, you get to choose the vegetables you like. Make sure you have everything ready by the stove. Then if you ever feel things are cooking too fast, adjust the heat or turn it off.

STIR-FRIED VEGETABLES

MAKES: 2 TO 4 SERVINGS ➤➤ TIME: 20 TO 40 MINUTES, DEPENDING ON THE VEGETABLE

INGREDIENTS

1 pound any hard, soft, or leafy vegetable

½ cup water

1 tablespoon butter or olive or vegetable oil, plus more as needed

Salt

Pepper (if you like)

EAT WITH: main dishes made with mostly meat, chicken, fish, or eggs; or toss with plain noodles or add to rice or bowls. For a meatless main dish, add cubes of tofu or cooked or canned chickpeas or other beans.

STEPS

1 Once you pick out the vegetables you want and rinse them, use the drawings on pages 16 to 21 to see how to get them ready to eat. Almost all need trimming, many need peeling, and some are best with the seeds removed. Cut the vegetables into sticks, slices, chunks, or coins. Broccoli and cauliflower are nice to break into florets or "little trees." Get the water ready by the stove.

2 Put the butter or oil in a 10-inch skillet over medium-high heat. When the butter melts or the oil is hot and shimmering, add the vegetables. Adjust the heat so they sizzle without burning.

3 Cook, stirring almost all the time, until the vegetables are as crisp or tender as you like. Start checking after 2 minutes. Poke the vegetables with a fork or the tip of a small knife to see how tender they are. They will continue to cook and get softer after you remove them from the heat, so stop when they're still a littler firmer than you like to eat them. The tenderest leafy vegetables and smallest chunks will be ready in 2 minutes, hard vegetables will take 15 to 20 minutes, and soft vegetables will be somewhere in between. Add more butter or oil to the skillet if the pan starts to look dry. if the bottom of the pan is getting brown, add a small splash of the water, turn the heat down, and stir again.

4 Sprinkle the vegetables with some salt and pepper too if you like and eat hot or let them cool down for a few minutes.

5 THINGS TO ADD TO THE PAN 15 SECONDS BEFORE THE VEGETABLES

You can add one or more of the flavor bombs from this list:

1. 1 or 2 cloves garlic, chopped
2. 1-inch piece fresh ginger, peeled and chopped
3. 1 scallion or small piece of onion, chopped
4. 1 teaspoon spice blend like curry or chili powder
5. ¼ teaspoon single spice like cumin or red chile flakes

5 THINGS TO ADD TO THE PAN WITH THE WATER TO MAKE A SAUCE

1. 2 tablespoons vegetable stock
2. 1 tablespoon lemon or lime juice
3. 1 teaspoon balsamic vinegar
4. 1 teaspoon soy sauce, or more to taste
5. 1 dash hot sauce

★ ★ The thing about roasting vegetables is that they get even more crisp than stir-fried vegetables on the outside, and more tender on the inside. My favorite vegetables to roast this way are cubes of potatoes or sweet potatoes, sliced mushrooms, zucchini coins, broccoli and cauliflower florets, asparagus spears and whole green beans, winter squash, and halved Brussels sprouts. I guess that's a lot to love!

ROASTED VEGETABLES

MAKES: 2 TO 4 SERVINGS >> TIME: 15 TO 60 MINUTES, DEPENDING ON THE VEGETABLE

INGREDIENTS

1 pound any hard, soft, or leafy vegetable

1 tablespoon olive or vegetable oil, plus more as needed

Salt

Pepper (if you like)

EAT WITH: main dishes made with mostly meat, chicken, fish, or eggs; or toss with plain noodles or add to rice or bowls; or use to fill tacos and burritos. You can also try eating roasted vegetables with any of the sauces for Raw Snacking Vegetables on page 133.

STEPS

1 Move the oven rack toward the top setting and heat the oven to 400°F. Once you pick out the vegetables you want and rinse them, use the drawings on pages 16 to 21 to see how to get them ready to eat. Almost all need trimming, many need peeling, and some are best with the seeds removed. Cut the vegetables into sticks, slices, chunks, or coins. Broccoli and cauliflower are nice to break into florets or "little trees."

2 Put the vegetables in a large rimmed baking sheet and drizzle with the oil. Toss a little to decide if you need a little more to coat them all. You want them shiny but not dripping. Spread them out so that they're in a single layer. It's okay if they touch in places. When the oven is ready, carefully slip the baking sheet onto the rack.

3 Start checking after 10 minutes. Use a stiff spatula to look at the bottom of one piece. The vegetables are ready to stir when they're golden and crisp and are easy to scrape off the pan. Don't force them if they're still stuck. You only need to stir them once or twice. Poke a piece with a fork or the tip of a small knife to see how tender they are. That will give you an idea of how much longer they have to go and the next time you need to check and try to stir. The tenderest leafy vegetables and smallest chunks will be ready to eat in 15 to 20 minutes total roasting time, hard vegetables will take 30 to 60 minutes, and soft vegetables will be somewhere in between.

4 When the vegetables are ready, sprinkle them with some salt and pepper too if you like and eat hot or warm.

⭐ Some vegetables have enough natural sugar that cooking transforms them into "candy" without adding anything at all. With this super-slow roasting method, you don't even have to stir or check while they cook. The only thing you need is a few hours to have the oven on a low temperature. The reason this recipe makes a lot is because I bet you're going to love 'em.

CHERRY TOMATO CANDY

MAKES: 4 TO 8 SERVINGS ⟫ *TIME: 2 TO 4 HOURS, WITH HARDLY ANY WORK* ❄

INGREDIENTS

2 pints (4 cups) cherry or grape tomatoes

EAT WITH: other vegetables or salads as a side or flavor bomb; on sandwiches; in tacos or burritos; or dipped in your favorite condiment or sauce (see pages 78 and 79). Or eat with nothing—like candy!

STEPS

1 Heat the oven to 225°F and make sure there's a rack near the middle. Put a sheet of parchment paper in a large rimmed baking sheet.

2 After rinsing the tomatoes, gently move them to a clean towel and pat them dry. There's no need to trim or cut them. Spread them into the prepared pan. They're going to roll around no matter how you try to space them out, so don't worry about that.

3 Put the pan on the rack and walk away for 2 hours before checking. The tomatoes should start to wrinkle and you'll see some liquid oozing. If those by the edges are darker than those in the middle of the pan, carefully stir them around, but no need to mess with them a lot.

4 From now on, peek at the tomatoes every hour. They should be soft, wrinkled, darker, and flatter than when you started but not as dry, brown, or shriveled as raisins. Try one to see if you like it now or want to keep them shrinking and getting dryer.

5 When the tomato candy is ready, let it cool in the pan and eat now, refrigerate in a sealed container for up to 1 week, or freeze for a couple months.

RECIPE CONTINUES ➡

CARROT CANDY. Use 1½ pounds carrots. Everything remains the same except for how you prepare them. After rinsing, trimming, and peeling, cut them crosswise into coins or into sticks about ½ inch thick (see page 17). Now cook and check them the same way as explained for the tomatoes.

SWEET POTATO CANDY. Use 2 pounds sweet potatoes. Everything remains the same except for how you prepare them. After rinsing, trimming, and peeling, cut them into cubes or into sticks about ½ inch thick (see page 156). Now cook and check them the same way as explained for the tomatoes.

TOFU CANDY. Instead of vegetables, use 1 block firm tofu. (It's made from soybeans, so it *is* a sort of vegetable!) Everything remains the same except for how you prepare the tofu. Cut it into cubes about 1 inch thick. Now cook and check them the same way as explained for the tomatoes.

DID YOU KNOW

You can also make "fruit candy" the same way as explained here. The fruits that work best are whole strawberries or blackberries, seedless grapes, thinly sliced oranges, plum or banana slices, and chunks of pineapple or mangoes.

PICK YOUR POTATO

All potatoes can be cooked all ways, so what you choose depends on the texture you like and what you plan to use them for. Try them all and see what you think!

STARCHY POTATOES. Also called baking potatoes or russets. They're big, with thick dark skin, and cook up fluffy. They work best for baking (duh), roasting, stir-frying, and steaming. (And deep-frying, but we aren't doing that in this book.)

ALL-PURPOSE POTATOES. These are smaller than starchy potatoes, bigger than waxy potatoes. They're sort of waxy, sort of starchy, with thin smooth skins. Yukon Gold is a good example found in supermarkets. They work for almost everything, except they don't make fluffy enough baked potatoes in my opinion.

WAXY POTATOES. They're small and either round, oval, or long and skinny, and come in different colors. The skin is thin and usually good to eat. They're called "waxy" because they stay firm after cooking instead of falling apart. They're best roasted or steamed but don't work well as baked potatoes.

STARCHY   ALL-PURPOSE   WAXY

DID YOU KNOW

It takes just as long to bake one potato as it does two, three, or even four. And the leftovers are easy to reheat, or use the insides in soup, burritos, pancakes, or scrambled eggs.

You know 'em. You love 'em. Here's how to cook them the right way. Hint: You won't be using a microwave oven.

BAKED POTATOES

MAKES: 1 BIG POTATO ⟩⟩ *TIME: ABOUT 1 HOUR*

INGREDIENTS

1 large baking potato (also called "russet"; 6 to 8 ounces)

Salt

Pepper (if you like)

Favorite toppings from the list that follows

EAT WITH: meat, chicken, fish, or eggs. Or eat by itself topped with something to make it a meal like grated cheese, fried or scrambled eggs, or chili.

STEPS

1 Heat the oven to 425°F. Scrub the potato with a brush, especially if you like eating the skin. Trim away any dark spots. Use a small sharp knife to carefully poke a couple holes through the skin.

2 When the oven is ready, put in the potato, either right on the middle rack or on a rimmed baking sheet. Wait 30 minutes, then turn the potato. Keep baking until you can easily poke to the center with a long fork or knife, another 20 to 30 minutes more.

3 The potato will be quite hot, so let it rest on your plate for a few minutes. To eat, cut into the top of the potato from top to bottom and use both hands to squeeze the ends toward the middle to open and fluff the insides. Sprinkle with salt and pepper too if you like, then top away.

VARIATION

BAKED SWEET POTATOES OR YAMS. They come in colors ranging from golden to dark orange both inside and out. They have thick skins and taste much different than potatoes, but the sweet ones are very similar to each other. Try them all and see what you think! Bake and top the same way, but you'll probably leave the skin on your plate.

12 TOPPINGS FOR BAKED POTATOES AND SWEET POTATOES

1. Butter
2. Sour cream
3. Olive oil
4. Ranch for Real (page 75)
5. Fresh Tomato (or Fruit) Salsa (page 80)
6. Guacamole (page 134)
7. Hot sauce
8. Grated cheese like cheddar, Jack, or Parmesan
9. Scrambled or fried egg (page 39)
10. Chopped Steamed Vegetables (page 139)
11. Crumbled bacon or sausage (pages 58 and 60)
12. Chili (page 127)

⭐ The funny thing about potatoes is that no matter how you cook and flavor them, they're always awesome. The basic recipe here is perfect for your own creative additions along with the milk. Grated cheese, I'm looking at you.

CREAMY MASHED POTATOES

MAKES: 2 TO 4 SERVINGS ≫ *TIME: 45 MINUTES* ❄

INGREDIENTS

1½ pounds starchy or all-purpose potatoes (see page 149)

Salt

¾ cup milk, plus more as needed

3 tablespoons butter

EAT WITH: dinners like Roasted Chicken (page 225) or Meat Loaf (page 223).

You can make any of these recipes with sweet potatoes. They cook faster, though, so start checking them after 10 minutes of boiling.

STEPS

1 Scrub the potatoes under cold running water with a brush. Trim away any dark spots and peel them if you like.

2 Cut the potatoes into chunks about 1 inch wide. Put them in a 3- or 4-quart pot and add enough cold water to cover them by 3 inches. Add a large pinch of salt. Bring the water to a boil over high heat, stirring once or twice to make sure the potatoes aren't sticking.

3 Adjust the heat so the water bubbles almost at a full boil and cook uncovered until the potatoes are super-tender, 15 to 30 minutes, depending on the type of potato. To test a chunk, scoop it into a big spoon and try breaking it apart with a fork.

4 When the potatoes are done, drain them into a colander. Put the milk and butter into the same pot (no need to wash it) and set it back on the stove over medium-low heat. As soon as the butter melts, remove the pot from the heat and add the cooked potatoes.

5 Use a potato masher to carefully mash and stir the potatoes. (You can also use a fork. It will take a little more work!) Add more milk if they look dry and keep working until they're as smooth and creamy as you like them. Return the pot to medium-low heat and cook and stir until they're steaming hot. Eat right away or cover the pot and keep warm over low heat for up to 30 minutes. Cool and refrigerate leftovers in a sealed container for a few days.

CHUNKY SKIN-ON MASHED POTATOES. Some people call this "rough mash"—a name I sort of like. Use a thin-skinned all-purpose or waxy potato and follow the recipe except for the part where you peel the potatoes. When you get to mashing in Step 5, don't bother to work hard to make them smooth. Keep 'em stiff and lumpy.

BOILED POTATOES. Best with waxy or all-purpose potatoes. Peel them before starting if you like (warning: it's a little bit of a pain) and either keep them whole or cut them into chunks that are at least 2 inches across. Cook them as described in the recipe except you won't need the milk or the masher. Just melt the butter in the pot and stir in the boiled potatoes after draining.

POTATO SALAD. Use any kind of potato you like and decide—peels on or off. You won't need the milk or butter. After following the recipe for cooking and draining the potatoes, fit the colander into a large bowl and let them cool for about 30 minutes. Make a dressing (see pages 76 and 77), or in a small bowl, whisk together ½ cup mayonnaise or sour cream with 2 teaspoons yellow or Dijon mustard. When the potatoes are cool, empty them into the bowl. It's okay if there's some starchy liquid in the bottom. Add ½ cup dressing and toss with a fork. If you add chopped celery, pickles, or scallions, you might want to add more dressing to keep the salad moist. Cover the bowl and refrigerate for at least an hour before eating.

★ ★ I mean big French fries baked in the oven. That's okay, right? As long as they end up crisp on the outside and fluffy on the inside, it doesn't matter how they get cooked. These are way easier than frying in a pot full of oil. And to have them ready for dinner anytime, you can precook the whole potatoes one day and finish them a day or two later. If it's potato cubes like home fries you're after, use the recipe for Roasted Vegetables on page 145.

BIG FRENCH FRIES

MAKES: 2 TO 4 SERVINGS ≫ *TIME: ABOUT 90 MINUTES, INCLUDING RESTING TIME* ❄

INGREDIENTS

2 pounds starchy potatoes
(3 large or 4 medium)

3 tablespoons vegetable oil,
plus more if needed

Salt

EAT WITH: ketchup, mustard, or any of the condiments or sauces on pages 78 and 79. And then hopefully you put something else next to them on your plate like Chicken Mark Nuggets (page 217) or Roasted Chicken (page 225).

STEPS

1 Scrub the potatoes under cold running water with a brush and trim away any dark spots. Use a vegetable peeler to remove the skins if you want them gone. Put the whole potatoes in any 3- to 5-quart pot with enough cold water to cover. Bring the water to a boil over high heat.

2 As soon as the water starts bubbling like crazy, remove the pot from the heat and cover. Let the potatoes sit in the hot water until they're soft enough to squeeze a little with tongs but when you poke them with a small knife it's hard for it to go all the way in. This will take 15 to 25 minutes of sitting depending on the size of the potatoes and whether you peeled them. (You can also do this step in the microwave on high. Put the potatoes on a plate and check them every 2 minutes.)

3 Move the potatoes to a plate and do something else until they're cool enough to hold them. After that, move on to the next step or refrigerate them in a sealed container for up to 2 days before starting Step 4.

RECIPE CONTINUES ➡

4   When you're ready to cut the potatoes, heat the oven to 400°F for light-colored fries or 425°F for well-browned fries. Make sure there's a rack toward the top, and put a large rimmed baking sheet inside to get hot. Carefully cut the potatoes in half from top to bottom and put the flat side down on the cutting board. Now cut downward into slices about ½ inch thick. When you have all the potatoes done, spread them out on the cutting board and cut any that are more than 1 inch wide again top to bottom so that you have sticks that are wider than usual fries but not super-fat. (The photo here will give you the idea.)

5   Put the potatoes in a big bowl with the 3 tablespoons oil. Toss with your hands to coat them totally. They should be pretty slippery and shiny. If not, add another tablespoon of oil and toss again.

BIG SWEET POTATO FRIES. No need to precook sweet potatoes for fries. Just peel 1½ pounds raw sweet potatoes or yams as described in Step 1. Then cut them as explained in Step 4 and follow the rest of the recipe.

6 Carefully remove the hot pan from the oven with oven mitts and use tongs to spread the potatoes into a single layer. They don't have to be in perfect rows or anything, just get them in there without moving them much.

7 Return the pan to the oven to roast the fries, without turning, until they're lightly browned and are easy to scrape from the pan when you try to move them with a stiff spatula. Start checking after 15 minutes, but be patient. A fork should go right in when you poke one. Flip over any fries that aren't browning on both sides. They may take up to 30 minutes depending on how big the sticks were and how hot you set the oven, so keep checking until they're done how you like. (Fries from potatoes you microwaved cook a little faster than if boiled.) When the fries are ready, sprinkle with salt while they're still in the pan, toss gently with the spatula, and put them on a plate to eat.

★ ★ Pancakes meet fritters meet vegetables. You will be shocked at how great these are. The recipe calls for cooked vegetables—perfect for using leftovers. For times you don't have leftovers but want Scattercakes, make a quick batch of Steamed Vegetables in the Microwave from page 141. Or just use frozen peas, carrots, or corn, thawed under running water and drained.

SCATTERCAKES

MAKES: 2 TO 4 SERVINGS ⟫ TIME: 30 MINUTES ❄ 🍃

INGREDIENTS

1 packed cup Steamed Vegetables (page 13), Stir-Fried Vegetables (page 142), or Roasted Vegetables (page 145)

1 recipe Flippy Pancake batter (page 61), made without the sugar

Butter or oil for cooking

Salt and pepper (if you like)

EAT WITH: Ranch for Real (page 75) or any of the condiments and sauces on pages 78 and 79. Extra fantastic with some kind of crisp cooked meat on the side. See page 58 for the possibilities.

STEPS

1 Chop the cooked vegetables into teeny bits not much bigger than peas. If they're wet or saucy, put them on towels. Let the chopped vegetables sit while you make the pancake recipe.

2 Put a 12-inch skillet over medium-low heat (or heat a griddle to the same temperature). Put 1 tablespoon butter or oil into the skillet. When the butter foams and melts or the oil shimmers, use a big spoon to pour a little batter into the pan. Hold the utensil at least an inch above the pan and watch how it spreads. You always want the batter to stop spreading right after pouring and sizzle gently so the pancakes brown without burning and cook on the inside. Raise the heat a little to make that happen and be prepared to adjust the heat as the pancakes cook.

3 Working sort of fast, scatter a little bit of vegetable onto each pancake—not a ton, just a tablespoon or so. Try to use the spoon to spread them around the whole pancake without messing up the batter.

4 Wait until bubbles appear on the pancakes around the vegetables, 3 to 5 minutes. Slip a stiff spatula under an edge to peek and check the color. When the bottom is golden brown, lift the pancake above

RECIPE CONTINUES ➡

CHEESY SCATTERCAKES.
With crisp and melty parts in every bite. After you chop the vegetables, toss them with ⅓ cup grated Parmesan or cheddar cheese. Use that mixture to scatter over the pancakes in Step 3.

the surface with the spatula and turn it, aiming for the empty spot. Do the same with the other pancakes. Keep cooking and checking the bottom until they feel a little firm when pressed and both sides are golden brown, another minute or 2 on the second side.

5 Move the pancakes to a plate and repeat the steps with the rest of the batter, starting with adding more butter or oil to the pan. You should be able to cook all the batter in 2 or 3 batches. Sprinkle with salt and pepper if you like and eat hot or slightly warm.

PASTA AND NOODLES

STARRING

RIGATONI in BAKED ZITI

ALL THE WAYS YOU LIKE TO EAT THEM, PLUS A FEW SURPRISES

RAMEN NooDLES in Squiggly Noodles with Teriyaki

...and a SPECIAL GUEST

?

THE WORLD OF PASTA AND NOODLES

farfalle

lo mein noodles

ramen

soba

WHAT ARE THEY MADE FROM?

Wheat is the grain used for most pastas and noodles. For Italian-style dry pastas, it's a special wheat called "durum" that is ground into a coarse golden flour called "semolina." In recipes "pasta" means these wheat-based shapes and strands. The best come from Italy, but small American companies are making some really good ones too.

Lots of noodles are made from other grains—like white or brown rice, buckwheat, quinoa, or corn—and even beans like chickpeas and mung beans. You can substitute these noodles in any of the recipes, but they will all cook differently. Whenever you want to make a swap, look on the package to see if the directions say to soak or boil them.

During soaking or cooking, make sure you check for doneness early so they don't end up mushier than you want them to be.

Dried egg noodles are slightly golden from the addition of eggs. There are Chinese-, American-, and Italian-style egg noodles. Each have a different thickness and width, but almost all are squiggly and cook to be silky and pleasantly chewy.

Whole wheat pasta and noodles are fun to try too, and they're full of vitamins and fiber, just like whole wheat bread. They tend to get mushy fast, though, and aren't as stretchy as regular wheat or egg noodles. That might be good news for you!

Asian-style noodles are made from all different kinds of grains. The most popular are flat narrow rice sticks and rice vermicelli (super-thin like angel hair), soba (made from buckwheat), udon (fat wheat noodles), and egg noodles (wheat mixed with eggs). There are a few recipes in this chapter that show how to use them. After that I'm guessing you'll want to try more.

Fresh pasta and noodles are made quite differently, and they are a bit of a project, so let's save that recipe for another time. If you want to use store-bought fresh noodles, follow the directions on the package or ask the person behind the counter.

HOW MUCH SHOULD I COOK?

Pastas and noodles almost always come in 1-pound or 12-ounce packages. Some recipes in this chapter call for 4 ounces (1 to 2 servings) or 8 ounces (2 to 4 servings). You might be eating them as a side or as a main dish and the range should give you an idea of what to expect. If you don't have a scale to weigh the pasta, work with an adult to eyeball it—based on the size of the package—until you get the hang of it.

DOES THE PASTA SHAPE MATTER?

Not really. In general, strands—angel hair, spaghetti, fettuccine, soba—are best for thin sauces. Cut shapes—macaroni, orzo, rigatoni, corkscrews—work best with chunky sauces. But you do you. The little windows in pasta and noodle packages are there so you can pick out whatever looks fun to eat.

HOW DO I KNOW WHEN THEY'RE DONE?

As the pasta or noodles are boiling or soaking, you've got to keep checking. The best way is to pluck a strand from the water with tongs or scoop up a couple cut noodles with a slotted spoon. Put them on a clean surface or plate. When the test is cool enough to touch, break into it with a fork or your fingers, and if it's soft, take a taste. It's up to you to know how firm or tender you want it. But it's super important to remember that pasta and noodles will keep cooking after draining, especially if you're going to be tossing them back in the pot with sauce.

HOW DO I COOK ALL THESE?

The specific directions are explained in each recipe. That way you can learn different methods by practicing—and eating!—your way around the world of pasta and noodles.

penne rigate

vermicelli

macaroni

rigatoni

HELP! aiuto!

5 THINGS TO TOSS WITH BUTTERY EGG NOODLES

1. ¼ cup grated Parmesan cheese
2. 1 teaspoon dried herbs like Italian seasoning blend, oregano, or dill
3. 1 or 2 tablespoons chopped fresh herbs like basil, chives, or dill
4. 1 teaspoon (or more) fresh lemon juice or lemon zest
5. ¼ teaspoon (more or less) red chile flakes

⭐ What isn't a good time for buttery egg noodles? They're like silky birthday-present ribbons you can eat. Since they go with everything, the recipe here gives you enough to refrigerate for reheating later—or to share now!

BUTTERY EGG NOODLES

MAKES: 2 TO 4 SERVINGS ➤➤ *TIME: 20 MINUTES* ❄ 🌿

INGREDIENTS

Salt

8 ounces egg noodles (about half a 1-pound package, long or short strands)

1 to 2 tablespoons butter

Pepper (if you like)

EAT WITH: any meat-and-vegetable stir-fry (page 229), Chicken with Orange Sauce (page 219), or Scrambled or Fried Eggs (pages 39 and 43).

VARIATION

BUTTERY WHOLE GRAIN NOODLES. You might not be able to find whole wheat egg noodles, so look for whole wheat fettuccine if you want strands or whole wheat fusilli (corkscrews) or farfalle (butterflies) for cut pastas that are sort of thick and chewy. Cook these the same way as regular egg noodles, checking early and often because they go from firm to mushy pretty fast.

STEPS

1 Fill a 5-quart pot halfway with water and bring it to a boil over high heat. Add 2 big pinches salt.

2 When the water boils, add the noodles. If you have long strands, gently swirl them with tongs until they soften and sink all the way in the water. Adjust the heat so the water boils without bubbling over and cook, stirring every 2 or 3 minutes with the tongs, until the noodles are as tender or mushy as you want. Start checking after 5 minutes. They're going to keep cooking a little after draining.

3 When the noodles are ready, dip a ladle into the pot and save 1 cup of the cooking water near the stove. Drain the noodles into a colander in the sink and return the noodles to the pot with the butter. If you're adding more stuff from the list below, put that in the pot now too.

4 Set the pot over medium-low heat and stir with the tongs until the butter melts. Add a small splash of the cooking water to keep the noodles from sticking and make a little sauce. Eat hot, with a sprinkle of pepper—or not.

You can substitute any kind of oil—like olive or other vegetable or nut oils—for the butter here. Pick one that tastes good to you and stick with it or try a different kind every time you make a pot of noodles.

★ ★ A rainbow of spaghetti sauces all in one place! Perfect for when you want something a little more than plain butter without going full-on tomato sauce. Be sure to check out the variations for all the ideas. All will work with any shape of noodles.

SPAGHETTI WHITE

MAKES: 1 TO 2 SERVINGS ⟫ TIME: 20 TO 30 MINUTES

INGREDIENTS

Salt

4 ounces spaghetti or any pasta (about ¼ of a 1-pound package)

1 tablespoon butter or olive oil, plus more if you like

¼ cup grated Parmesan cheese, plus more for serving if you like

EAT WITH: Leafy Salad (page 137) or Steamed Vegetables (page 139).

STEPS

1 Fill a 3-quart pot a little more than halfway to the top with water, add a big pinch of salt, and set it over high heat. When the water boils, add the pasta. Stir a few times with tongs or a spoon to keep the noodles from sticking.

2 Adjust the heat so it bubbles steadily without overflowing. Cook, stirring every 2 minutes, until the pasta is a teeny bit firmer than you like to eat it. Start checking after 7 minutes. When the pasta is ready, use a ladle to scoop about 1 cup of the cooking water into a measuring cup. Then drain the noodles in a colander in the sink.

3 Return the pot to low heat. (No need to wash it.) Add the butter or oil, the pasta, and the cheese if you're using it. Add a small splash of the pot water you saved and cook, stirring a lot, until the noodles become as soft as you like. Add more butter or oil if you like and just enough of the water to coat the noodles. Eat right away with more salt and cheese if you need any.

VARIATIONS

SPAGHETTI PINK. In Step 3 when you put the pot over low heat, add 1 tablespoon tomato paste with the butter or oil and keep going with the recipe.

SPAGHETTI YELLOW. In Step 3 when you put the pot over low heat, add 1 beaten egg along with the cheese and keep going with the recipe.

SPAGHETTI GREEN. Skip the butter or oil. In Step 3 when you put the pot over low heat, add ¼ cup mashed avocado with the pasta and cheese and keep going with the recipe.

VARIATIONS CONTINUE ↗

SPAGHETTI PURPLE.
In Step 3 when you put the pot over low heat, add 1 cup fresh or frozen blueberries with the butter or oil and keep going with the recipe. Before adding the pasta back to the pot, add a little extra water and stir the berries until a few of them burst. Using a potato masher to squash them will make the sauce less lumpy.

⭐ Looking for noodles with a basic meatless tomato sauce (*marinara* in Italian), or with meatballs or meat sauce? It's all here in one recipe, starting with a super-simple method where you cook the sauce and noodles at the same time in the same pot. The pasta gets perfectly coated without being too gloppy or tomatoey. Try the relatively small portion here or double the batch in a 5-quart pot and feed your friends or family.

ONE-POT PASTA WITH TOMATO SAUCE

MAKES: 2 TO 4 SERVINGS ⟫ **TIME: 30 MINUTES** ❄️ 🌿

INGREDIENTS

2 tablespoons butter or olive oil

½ small onion, chopped

1 (15-ounce) can crushed tomatoes

Salt and pepper

8 ounces any cut pasta

1 cup water, plus more as needed

¼ cup grated Parmesan cheese, plus more for serving

¼ cup chopped fresh basil leaves (if you like)

EAT WITH: Leafy Salad (page 137); Roasted Vegetables like broccoli, green beans, or carrots (page 145); or toast topped with Cheese Butter made with Parmesan (page 242).

STEPS

1 Put 1 tablespoon of the butter or oil in a 2- or 3-quart pot over medium heat. When the butter melts or the oil is hot and shimmering, add the onion and cook, stirring only when it looks like it's getting too dark, until it softens, about 3 minutes.

2 Add the tomatoes, sprinkle with a little salt and pepper, and stir until the mixture looks saucy and starts to bubble. Add the pasta and ½ cup of the water and stir a couple times. Set a timer for 10 minutes.

3 Now you're going to stay close to the stove, stirring every 2 or 3 minutes and adding more water every time the pasta and sauce start sticking to the bottom of the pot. The idea is to keep the sauce bubbling enough to cook the pasta without drowning it or splattering all over the place. Adjust the heat as needed to make that happen, and add the last ½ cup water a little at a time.

4 Begin tasting the pasta when the timer goes off. It should be tender but have some firmness at the center. Check every 2 minutes or so to get to the point where it's almost-but-not-quite as soft as you want it. The pasta might take 10 more minutes to get there.

RECIPE CONTINUES ➡

5 When the pasta is ready, stir in the last tablespoon of butter and the ¼ cup grated cheese. You might need a little more water to coat the noodles in sauce. Taste to see if you need more salt or pepper, stir in the basil if you're using it, and eat hot or warm.

VARIATIONS

ONE-POT PASTA WITH MEATY SAUCE. You'll need 4 ounces ground meat or sausage (any kind). When you add the onion to the pot in Step 1, stir in the meat and break it into bits as it cooks. Adjust the heat so it sizzles and stir whenever the meat starts to stick until it's browned in places, about 5 minutes. Then add the tomatoes and pasta as explained in Step 2 and finish the recipe.

TOMATO OR MEATY SAUCE (WITH OR WITHOUT PASTA). Do you like your sauce on top of your pasta—not mixed together? Then this is the method for you. Get the ingredients ready for the tomato sauce in the main recipe or the meaty sauce idea above. In Step 1, fill a pot a little more than halfway with water, add a big pinch of salt, and bring to a boil over high heat. Make the sauce only—without the pasta— in a separate pot as explained in Steps 1 and 2. While the sauce is bubbling, cook and drain the pasta as described in Spaghetti White on page 166. When the sauce is done, put some pasta on a plate with a spoonful of sauce on top.

HOLDEN'S PASTA WITH DROP MEATBALLS. Start by making the recipe for Meatballs on page 224. Only don't cook them yet, just cover the meat mixture and refrigerate it for up to a day before. Get the ingredients ready for the tomato sauce in the main recipe. In Step 1, fill a pot a little more than halfway with water, add a big pinch of salt, and bring to a boil over high heat. In a separate pot, make the sauce only—without the pasta—as explained in Steps 1 and 2. As soon as the sauce is bubbling, use two spoons to scoop up a rough-shaped meatball from the bowl and drop it in the sauce. Continue until all meatballs are in the sauce. Cover and cook, without stirring, until the meatballs are firm and no longer pink in the center, 10 to 15 minutes. While that's happening, cook and drain the pasta as described in Spaghetti White on page 166. When the meatballs and sauce are done, make your plate the way you like it and eat. (Refrigerate leftover meatballs in a sealed container for up to a few days or freeze for a couple months.)

If you like a chunkier sauce, use 1 large (28-ounce) can diced tomatoes instead of the crushed tomatoes.

★ Moment of truth: Boxed mac-and-cheese this is not. This is better and almost as easy to make. After you try a bite, I'm pretty sure you'll agree. What makes this so special? YOU. From the shape of the noodle—and how chewy or tender you cook it—to the cheese you choose, here's one dinner that will never fit in a box.

SUPER-CREAMY MAC-AND-CHEESE

MAKES: 2 TO 4 SERVINGS ➤➤ TIME: 30 MINUTES ❄

INGREDIENTS

2 cups whole milk, plus more as needed

8 ounces elbow macaroni or other cut pasta

Salt

2 tablespoons cream cheese

1½ cups grated cheddar cheese (about 6 ounces)

EAT WITH: Raw Snacking Vegetables (page 133) or Leafy Salad (page 137) or Coleslaw (page 138).

STEPS

1 Put 1½ cups of the milk and the pasta in a 2- or 3-quart pot over medium-high heat and sprinkle with a little salt. Bring to a boil, stirring slowly almost all the time.

2 Adjust the heat so the mixture bubbles gently. Set a timer for 5 minutes. Keep stirring all the time—you can take little breaks when you need to—and cook until the pasta gets plump and the milk looks thicker. When the timer goes off, check a noodle. It will still be crunchy, but this gives you an idea of how much longer to go.

3 The total cooking time will be 10 to 15 minutes. While you're stirring, notice if the mixture is getting dry and sticking. If so, add some of the milk you measured, 1 tablespoon at a time.

4 When the noodles are just about as firm or tender as you want them, turn the heat down to low. Stir in the cream cheese, grated cheese, and as much milk as you need to make a thick sauce. Keep stirring until everything is melted and looks super-creamy. Taste and add more salt if you like and eat.

RECIPE CONTINUES ➡

SUPER-CRUSTY SUPER-CREAMY MAC-AND-CHEESE.
This makes enough for 4 to 8 servings depending on how big the stomachs sitting at the table are and what else you have on the side. Heat the oven to 375°F. Rub the inside of a 9 x 13-inch baking dish or a 12-inch ovenproof skillet with butter. In a small bowl, combine

1 cup grated Parmesan cheese with 1 cup bread crumbs (to make your own, see page 243) and keep it near the stove. Double the recipe and use a 5-quart pot to cook the mac-and-cheese. In Step 2, when the timer goes off, add all 4 cups of the milk and cheeses and stir until smooth. The mixture should look quite soupy and not very thick. If it

looks dry, add another ¼ cup milk. Spread the wet pasta into the buttered pan, sprinkle with the bread crumb mixture, and bake until the macaroni and cheese is hot, bubbly, and saucy and the topping is golden, 20 to 30 minutes. Let sit for a couple minutes before eating.

You can use almost any cheese in this recipe—anything that melts like grated mozzarella, Jack, Swiss, or Parmesan cheese.

PASTA & NOODLES ♥ VEGETABLES

Here's how to eat them together. You might need some help with the amounts, but basically the idea is to take as many noodles as you want and sauce them with some form of vegetables.

USE LEFTOVERS

Let's say you've got some steamed or roasted vegetables in the fridge from a couple days ago.

Why not invite them to the sauce? Chop them up if you want to, then add them to any of the one-pot pasta sauces on page 169 and 170. It doesn't matter if you've got the pasta mixed in or prefer the sauce on top. Just throw the veggies in the pot when you want and stir until they're hot.

ADD PASTA TO SALAD

Decide if you want Ranch for Real (page 75) or Salad Dressing (page 76). After you make it, boil and drain pasta without making sauce (page 166), and while it's in the colander, run it under cold water to chill. Then make Leafy Salad or the ideas after the recipe (page 137). Or maybe one of the choices with the Tuna Sandwich (page 96)—without the bread. Toss the two things together, adding extra dressing a little at a time to keep things saucy.

STIR NOODLES INTO STIR-FRIES

Sauce your noodles right in the skillet with your vegetables, I always say. Stir-fry your favorite vegetable (page 229). On a back burner, boil some kind of noodle or pasta (page 166) or soak some rice sticks (page 179). When the noodles are ready, add them to the skillet along with some of the cooking or soaking liquid and toss with tongs. Add oil or butter and salt or pepper to make the combo delicious.

DO THE MASH

Cook and drain egg noodles or pasta (page 165 or 166). Remember to save some of the cooking water. Take some steamed, stir-fried, or roasted vegetables and pulse them in the food processor or blender with some of the liquid you saved— enough to make a smooth sauce. Then return the noodles to the pot and toss with some butter or oil and maybe Parmesan cheese. Be sure to taste and add salt or pepper if you like.

★ ★ When it comes to baked ziti, you may as well make a lot. It's perfect for family dinner, to bring to a party, or to pack away in the freezer for a quick meal for yourself later. Pack it up in individual portions and all you need to do is reheat some in a microwave-safe dish on medium until it's hot and bubbly again.

BAKED ZITI

MAKES: 4 TO 8 SERVINGS ➵ *TIME: ABOUT 1 HOUR* ❄ 🍃

INGREDIENTS

3 tablespoons olive oil or butter, plus more for the baking dish

Salt

1 medium onion, chopped

3 or 4 cloves garlic, chopped

Pepper

1 (28-ounce) can crushed or diced tomatoes (for smooth or chunky sauce)

1 pound ziti or other large cut pasta (like rigatoni or bowties)

8 ounces grated mozzarella cheese (or use fresh and cut it into small cubes; about 2 cups)

1 cup grated Parmesan cheese, plus more to pass at the table

EAT WITH: Steamed Vegetables (page 139), Stir-Fried Vegetables (page 142), Leafy Salad (page 137), or toast topped with Cheese Butter made with Parmesan (page 242).

STEPS

1 Heat the oven to 400°F and make sure there's a rack near the middle. Smear some butter or oil inside a 9 x 13-inch baking dish or pan until it's coated all over the bottom and sides.

2 Fill a 5-quart pot almost to the top with water and add 2 big pinches of salt. Put it over high heat to bring to a boil. When it starts boiling, turn the heat down to low until you're ready to cook the pasta.

3 Put the 3 tablespoons oil or butter in a 12-inch skillet over medium heat. When the oil is hot and shimmers or the butter melts, add the onion and garlic, sprinkle with salt and pepper, and stir every minute or so until the vegetables are soft and smell good, 5 to 10 minutes.

4 Add the tomatoes, then adjust the heat so the sauce bubbles without splattering everywhere. Cook, stirring now and then, until the tomatoes darken a little but are still pretty watery, about 5 minutes. Turn off the heat.

5 Cook and stir the pasta in the boiling water until it's a little soft but still too hard to eat, 5 to 7 minutes. Drain the noodles in a colander in the sink, but don't shake the extra water off. It will help make the pasta tender in the oven. Return the noodles to the pot and stir in all of the sauce and half of the mozzarella cheese.

RECIPE CONTINUES ➡

BAKED ZITI WITH SAUSAGE.
Before starting, use the 12-inch skillet to cook 1 pound Italian sausage (4 links or loose) as explained in the recipe on page 60. Move the sausage to a cutting board or plate and make the sauce in the same pan. No need to wash it—in fact, those drippings will add flavor. If using links, slice each across into coins. Stir the sausage into the sauce when it's ready at the end of Step 4. Finish the recipe from there.

6 Spoon the pasta into the prepared pan or dish and spread it evenly. Scatter the rest of the mozzarella cheese and the Parmesan cheese over the top. Move it to the oven and bake until the top is browned and the sauce is bubbling, 20 to 30 minutes. Let the pasta sit for a couple minutes, then eat.

DID YOU KNOW

You can add cooked vegetables to Baked Ziti. See page 175 for some ideas. (Mushrooms or eggplant are soooo good and so are broccoli, cauliflower, or spinach.) Stir the vegetables into the sauce when it's ready in Step 4. Finish the recipe from there.

★ For anyone who likes fresh chiles, here's your chance to use some. Or skip them and it's still an awesome noodle recipe. It's sort of like a warm salad, with bright orange strands of slightly crunchy carrots and silky-chewy rice noodles. You can find at least one kind of rice noodle in most supermarkets. The only thing is the package sizes can vary, so if you don't have a scale, you'll need to do some math to figure out how much you need.

RICE STICKS
WITH CARROT RIBBONS

MAKES: 2 TO 4 SERVINGS >>> TIME: 40 MINUTES

INGREDIENTS

6 cups water

Salt

2 large carrots

6 ounces dried flat rice noodles, about ¼ inch wide (often called "rice sticks," not thin rice vermicelli)

1 red or green hot chile (like jalapeño or serrano; if you like)

4 teaspoons vegetable oil

1 lime, cut in half

Pepper (if you like)

EAT WITH: any of the stir-fries on page 191, Roasted Chicken (page 225), or Dippy Shrimp (page 235).

STEPS

1 Put the water in a 3- or 5-quart pot with a big pinch of salt and bring to a boil over high heat.

2 Trim the tops and bottoms of the carrots, peel off the outside layer, and rinse them under cold water. Put a carrot on a cutting board and, starting at the top, carefully run the vegetable peeler down the carrot to make ribbons. Turn the carrot as you work until you're at the center and can't make any more. Repeat with the other carrot. You should have about 1 packed cup of ribbons.

3 Make sure the water is boiling big time, then add the noodles and carrots, remove the pot from the heat, and cover. You're going to let it sit there until the rice sticks are fully tender and the carrots are a little soft, about 15 minutes.

4 Plenty of time to make the sauce. If you're using the chile, get some rubber gloves on and chop it, with or without the seeds (see the drawings on page 18). Keep it on the cutting board, and carefully get rid of the gloves without touching the fingers. Put the oil in a large bowl and squeeze in the juice from the lime. You can add some pepper if you like. Whisk the sauce with a fork.

RECIPE CONTINUES ➡

5 After 15 minutes, check the noodles and carrots. If they're not tender enough to eat, cover and let them sit another 5 to 10 minutes. When they're ready, ladle out ½ cup of the soaking water and drain the noodles in a colander. If they're too cold for you, run them under super-hot tap water to warm them again.

6 Add the noodles and carrot ribbons to the bowl with the sauce and toss with a big fork and spoon or tongs. Add enough of the soaking water you saved to keep everything moist. If you're adding the chopped chile or anything from the list that follows, now is the time. Taste and add more salt and pepper too if you like and eat.

VARIATION

RICE STICKS WITH PEA POLKA DOTS. Instead of making the carrot ribbons, skip Step 2 and measure ½ cup frozen peas into a colander. Run the peas under cold water for a minute so they thaw. Add the peas to the pot with the noodles in Step 3 and keep going with the recipe.

8 MORE THINGS TO ADD TO RICE STICKS WITH CARROT RIBBONS

Toss any of these with the noodles after draining. If you add a few things, be prepared to make extra sauce from Step 4, but that's no big deal:

1. 2 teaspoons soy sauce
2. 1 teaspoon toasted sesame oil
3. 1 or 2 teaspoons rice vinegar
4. 2 tablespoons chopped fresh herbs (like cilantro, chives, or mint)
5. 1 cup chopped cooked chicken, pork, or beef
6. ½ cup chopped cooked shrimp or crabmeat
7. ½ cup small tofu cubes (heated in the microwave if not already cooked)
8. ¼ cup chopped pistachios or cashews

You can use brown rice noodles here. Cook or soak them as directed on the package and add the carrots to the pot or bowl at the same time.

⭐ Maybe you've had something like this in restaurants. The sauce can be all peanut, all sesame, or a combo. You can try any of those three things—tahini is sesame butter—and cashew, almond, or sunflower butter give you even more choices. Check out the ideas after the recipe for a way to make these without nuts or seeds and another way to turn the noodles into dinner.

COLD NUTTY NOODLES

MAKES: 2 TO 4 SERVINGS ⟫ TIME: 40 MINUTES 🍃

INGREDIENTS

Salt

8 to 12 ounces crunchy raw vegetables (like snow peas, red bell pepper, celery, zucchini, or cucumbers—alone or in combination)

2 tablespoons peanut butter (or see other options in the note above)

1 tablespoon toasted sesame oil

1 tablespoon sugar

1 tablespoon soy sauce, plus more for serving

1½ teaspoons rice vinegar

1 teaspoon chopped fresh ginger (if you like)

Hot tap water as needed

6 ounces thin dried egg noodles or linguini

1 scallion, trimmed and sliced (if you like)

½ cup chopped cilantro leaves (if you like)

Pepper (if you like)

Hot sauce (like sriracha), for serving

STEPS

1 Fill a 3-quart pot a little more than halfway to the top with water, add a big pinch of salt, and set it over high heat to boil. If it's ready before you are, turn the heat down to low.

2 Rinse and trim your vegetables, peel them if necessary, and chop or slice them however you like (see the drawings on pages 16 to 21 for suggestions). You should have 1½ to 2 cups. Put them in a big bowl.

3 Put the peanut or other nut butter in a small bowl with the sesame oil, sugar, soy sauce, vinegar, and ginger if you're using it. Add ¼ cup of hot tap water and whisk with a fork or whisk until the sauce is about the consistency of heavy cream. Let that sit.

RECIPE CONTINUES ➡

EAT WITH: any stir-fried meat and vegetables (page 142), unless you add some to the noodles (see the idea that follows the recipe).

UN-NUTTY NOODLES. For anyone with nut allergies. Instead of the peanut butter, use some Nootchy Butter from the recipe on page 95. Everything else stays the same.

HEARTIER COLD NUTTY NOODLES. Turn the noodles into a full-on meal by topping with any of the following foods: 1 cup chopped cooked chicken, pork, or beef; ½ cup chopped cooked shrimp or crabmeat; or ½ cup small tofu cubes.

4 When the water boils, add the noodles. Stir a few times with tongs or a spoon to keep them from sticking. Adjust the heat so it bubbles steadily without overflowing. Cook, stirring every 2 minutes, until the pasta is as tender as you like to eat it. This is one time you don't undercook it. Start checking after 7 minutes. Drain the noodles in a colander in the sink and rinse under cold running water.

5 Add the noodles to the bowl with the vegetables and pour the dressing over everything. If you're using the scallion and cilantro, add them now too. With a big fork and spoon or tongs, toss the noodles and vegetables until they're coated with the sauce. Taste and add salt and pepper too if you like and eat, passing soy and hot sauces at the table.

★ A sweet-salty Japanese-style sauce that's pretty thin so it soaks into the noodles and shines like crazy. The recipe is for a relatively small amount so you can get it in a bowl fast for lunch, a snack, or as a last-minute side to whatever dinner is going on the stove or in the oven. If you're really in a hurry, you can skip some or all of the vegetables, but they add so much flavor, so in my opinion they're worth it. Double or even triple the recipe if you're expecting a full house. Everyone will love eating these noodles.

SQUIGGLY NOODLES
WITH TERIYAKI

MAKES: 1 TO 2 SERVINGS ➔➔ *TIME: 30 MINUTES* 🍃

INGREDIENTS

Salt

4 ounces dried Chinese-style egg noodles (or use the noodles from 2 packs of single-serving ramen)

1 tablespoon butter

1 or 2 scallions, white and green parts separated and sliced

½-inch piece fresh ginger, peeled and chopped

1 or 2 cloves garlic, chopped

2 tablespoons soy sauce

2 teaspoons sugar

½ teaspoon toasted sesame oil

Pepper (if you like)

Toasted sesame seeds for garnish

STEPS

1 Fill a 3-quart pot a little more than halfway to the top with water, add a big pinch of salt, and set it over high heat. When the water boils, add the noodles. Stir a few times with tongs or a spoon to keep the noodles from sticking.

2 Adjust the heat so it bubbles steadily without overflowing. Cook, stirring every 30 seconds or so, until the noodles are a teeny bit firmer than you like to eat it. Start checking after 3 minutes. When the noodles are ready, use a ladle to scoop about 1 cup of the cooking water into a measuring cup and put it by the stove. Then drain the noodles in a colander in the sink.

3 Return the pot to medium-low heat. (No need to wash it.) Add the butter along with the white parts of the scallion, the ginger, and garlic. Cook, stirring almost all the time, until the vegetables are soft and smell good, 3 to 5 minutes.

RECIPE CONTINUES ➡

EAT WITH: any stir-fried meat and vegetables (page 142), Chicken Mark Nuggets (page 217), and Steamed Vegetables (especially spinach or cabbage, page 139). It's also great with any simply cooked seafood, chicken, pork, or beef.

DID YOU KNOW

You can also make this recipe with un-squiggly noodles like udon, soba (shown in the photo on the next page), or even egg noodles or spaghetti. Cook and check for doneness as described in Step 2.

SQUIGGLY NOODLES WITH MISO BUTTER. A little creamier and so delicious. Eat it with all the same things as the teriyaki noodles. Instead of the soy sauce, use 2 tablespoons white or yellow miso (see page 78). Skip the sugar. Everything else stays the same.

4 Add ½ cup of the noodle cooking water, the soy sauce, sugar, and sesame oil. Raise the heat a little so the teriyaki sauce boils. Then add the noodles and turn off the heat.

5 Use tongs to toss and coat the noodles in the sauce. If they start to look dry, add a small splash of the cooking water. Taste and add a little salt and pepper if you like. To garnish, sprinkle with the scallion greens and sesame seeds before eating.

⭐ I say go for a full-on batch of rice—it's just as easy to make a big pot as a small one. An even bigger plus: Cooked rice keeps in the fridge for several days and a serving reheats perfectly in the microwave in a minute or two. And that means you can have a side dish or base for a whole meal in a flash. Be sure to check out the recipe for Fried Rice on page 193 and the ideas for building bowls on page 213.

WHITE RICE

MAKES: 4 TO 6 SERVINGS ≫ *TIME: 20 TO 30 MINUTES* ❄ 🌿

INGREDIENTS

1½ cups white rice

2¼ cups water, plus more as needed

Salt

Stir-ins from the list on page 191

EAT WITH: Anything. Everything. Or nothing!

STEPS

1 Put the rice in a 2- or 3-quart pot that has a tight-fitting lid. Fill the pot almost to the top with cold tap water and swirl it around with your hand. Carefully pour off as much water as possible, leaving the rice in the bottom of the pot. Repeat a couple more times until the water looks almost clear. Then drain the rice in a strainer over the sink, shake a couple times, and put it back in the pot.

2 Add the 2¼ cups water and a big pinch of salt. Put the pot over high heat. Once the water boils, turn the heat down to medium or medium-low so that it bubbles steadily but gently. Cover the pot and set the timer for 15 minutes.

3 Lift the lid and peek: You want holes to appear in the rice, and when you carefully tip the pot, the rice should be dry but not sticking or burning. If there are no holes and you still see water pool on the side of the pot, cover, keep cooking, and check again in 2 minutes and repeat until it's ready.

4 When the rice does have holes and no water remains in the pot, lift a couple kernels out with a fork and taste. For softer rice, add ¼ cup water and cook for another 2 minutes before checking again. If the rice is just the way you like it, then remove the pot from the heat, add any stir-ins, and fluff them into the rice with a fork. Cover the pot and let the rice rest for at least 5 or up to 15 minutes. Taste and add more salt if you like, fluff with a fork again, then eat.

13 STIR-INS FOR RICE AND GRAINS

1. 1 or 2 tablespoons butter
2. 1 or 2 tablespoons olive or vegetable oil
3. ½ cup (or more) grated Parmesan cheese
4. Up to 1 cup cooked and drained beans
5. Up to ½ cup chopped cooked bacon, ham, or sausage (page 58)
6. Up to 1 can or jar of tuna (5 to 6 ounces) or salmon, or other canned seafood
7. Up to 1 cup chopped cooked chicken, shrimp, or crab
8. About 2 tablespoons chopped fresh herbs like basil, chives, mint, cilantro, or parsley
9. Up to 1 cup frozen peas or corn (no need to thaw first)
10. Up to 1 cup chopped cooked vegetables
11. Up to ½ cup Jammy Onions (page 83)
12. Up to 1 cup Fresh Tomato (or Fruit) Salsa (page 80)
13. Pinch of red chile flakes or black pepper

VARIATIONS

BROWN RICE. More nutritious than white rice and helps you stay full longer than white rice. But the reason you should try it is because it's nutty tasting and a little chewy. All you do in Step 2 after rinsing is increase the water to 2½ cups and set the timer for 25 minutes before checking the first time.

COCONUT RICE. Slightly sweet and nutty. After rinsing, in Step 2, instead of all water, measure 1 (15-ounce) can coconut milk (full- or reduced-fat) and add enough water to make 2¼ cups. Then use that mixture for cooking and follow the recipe.

DID YOU KNOW

Different kinds of rice cook the same way but turn out totally different. Long-grain rice is fluffy and the kernels stay separate. Short-grain rice is pleasantly chewy and sticks together—like sushi rice—or gets creamy when you add more liquid. And medium-grain rice is somewhere in between. To substitute brown rice for white in any recipe that calls for white rice, see page 195.

Nothing is quite like couscous. It looks like teeny seeds the size and shape of sand. But couscous is made from a dough like pastas and noodles. Only instead of cooking in a pot of boiling water, you soak it in boiling water with the heat turned off. What's important to know about couscous is that it's fluffy and mild tasting, soaks up butter or sauces, and is easy and fast to make.

COUSCOUS

MAKES: 2 TO 3 SERVINGS ➤➤ **TIME: ABOUT 10 MINUTES** ❄🍃

INGREDIENTS

½ cup couscous

¾ cup water

Salt

EAT WITH: any of the stir-ins listed on page 191. Couscous is also great with eggs. Or try it instead of rice or noodles.

STEPS

1 If you're making another recipe or stir-ins to eat with this, better get all that ready first, since the couscous cooks fast.

2 Put the couscous and water in a 1- or 2-quart pot with a tight-fitting lid. Add a small pinch of salt, turn the heat to high, and bring the mixture to a boil uncovered.

3 As soon as the water is boiling, remove the pot from the heat and cover it. Let it just sit there for 5 minutes before checking the first time. All the water should be absorbed and the bits will look puffy and light-colored. If it's not ready, cover and check again every 5 minutes until it is. Fluff the couscous with a fork and taste to see if you need more salt before eating.

VARIATIONS

WHOLE WHEAT COUSCOUS. Milder tasting than whole wheat pasta but a little heartier. You make it the exact same way, *except* in Step 3 let it steep at least 10 and up to 20 minutes before fluffing.

PEARL COUSCOUS. These are bigger and chewier like baby balls of pasta or tiny "pearls." (It's also called Israeli couscous.) In Step 2, add an extra 2 tablespoons water to the pot. After it comes to a boil in Step 3, turn the heat down to low so that the water bubbles gently, cover, and let the couscous cook (not just sit) for 5 minutes. Then remove the pot from the heat and let it sit for another 5 minutes before fluffing.

⭐ ⭐ The perfect thing to make with leftover rice. In fact, it's never quite as good with rice you just cooked. You know how cold rice is kind of chalky and stiff? That's exactly how you want it for fried rice. It's the cold starches in the grain that makes it get crunchy in places as you cook. The recipe here includes some basic vegetables and the usual egg. You can skip any of that or add something from the list on page 191 for the last stir.

FRIED RICE

MAKES: 2 TO 3 SERVINGS ≫ *TIME: 30 MINUTES* 🍃

INGREDIENTS

½ bell pepper (any color)

1 scallion

2 tablespoons vegetable oil

Salt

2 cups cooked long-grain white or brown rice (cold if possible)

1 egg

1 tablespoon soy sauce, plus more to taste

1½ teaspoons toasted sesame oil

Red chile flakes or black pepper (if you like)

EAT WITH: Chicken Mark Nuggets (page 217), Roasted Chicken (page 225), or any of the stir-fries on pages 230 and 231.

STEPS

1 Remove the core from the bell pepper if it's still there and chop the rest into small bits. Separate the white and green parts of the scallion and chop them both. Keep the green parts on the side for later, but it's okay to mix the white parts with the bell pepper on the cutting board. Get a plate or shallow bowl ready by the stove.

2 Put 1 tablespoon of the oil in a 10-inch skillet over medium heat. When it's hot and shimmers, add the bell pepper and scallion whites. Sprinkle with salt and raise the heat to medium-high. Cook, stirring only enough to keep the vegetables from burning, until they're soft and browned in places, 3 to 5 minutes.

3 Use a slotted spoon to move the vegetables to the plate. Add the last 1 tablespoon oil to the skillet and tip the pan so it coats the bottom. Right away, scatter the rice into the hot oil, using a stiff spatula to spread it into a thin layer.

4 Cook without stirring until the rice sizzles and browns, about 2 minutes, then stir with the spatula, breaking up any lumps and scraping the bottom of the pan until the rice is hot and crisp here and there, 3 to 5 minutes. *RECIPE CONTINUES* ➡

5 Crack the egg on a small plate and open it into a small bowl. (See page 39.) Beat it with a fork until it's light yellow with hardly any streaks. Use the spatula to clear a small empty spot in the pan, then pour in the beaten egg and start stirring it into the rice with the spatula. Turn the heat down to keep things from burning and stir and scrape until the egg is cooked, just a minute or so. Turn off the heat and return the bell pepper and scallion whites to the skillet along with the scallion greens, soy sauce, and sesame oil. Stir to combine. Taste and add salt and some red or black pepper if you like and eat hot or let it cool for up to 15 minutes.

WANT TO TRY MORE BROWN RICE?

You can use brown rice in any of the recipes in this chapter. All it needs is a little head start. Measure the same amount of brown rice, long or short grain as directed. For the very first thing, fill the pot halfway with water, add a pinch of salt, and bring it to a boil over high heat. Add the brown rice and adjust the heat so the water bubbles neither too crazily nor too gently. Don't stir. Set the timer for 12 minutes. Then drain it in a strainer, shake a couple times, and use that "par-cooked" (short for partially cooked) rice for whatever recipe you're making.

★ ★ Do you know what risotto is? It's an Italian dish that you stir almost the whole time you're cooking to make rice that's creamy enough to eat like oatmeal. There's almost always a lot of Parmesan and butter involved, and usually other things—like vegetables, seafood, or herbs—stirred in too. This is sort of like that, only with a lot less stirring and using any kind of cheese. If you want to add something from the list on page 191, use half of the amount or double this recipe and use a bigger pot.

CREAMY RICE
WITH BUTTER AND CHEESE

MAKES: 2 TO 3 SERVINGS ⟫ *TIME: 30 MINUTES* 🌿

INGREDIENTS

¾ cup white rice (a short-grain kind like Arborio will be creamiest)

Salt

2 cups water, plus more as needed

2 tablespoons butter or olive oil

½ cup grated Parmesan or other melting cheese, plus extra for eating

EAT WITH: any tomato sauce (page 170), simply cooked chicken or sausage, or cooked vegetables (especially spinach or peas and carrots, which you can also stir right into the rice with the cheese).

STEPS

1 Put the rice in a 1- or 2-quart pot with a pinch of salt and the 2 cups water. Bring to a boil, then turn the heat down so the liquid bubbles gently. Cover and cook without stirring for 10 minutes.

2 Check the rice. Add enough water to cover it by about ½ inch and stir, scraping up any dried bits that might be stuck to the bottom of the pot. Cover and cook again for 3 minutes.

3 This time when you check, carefully dip a fork into the pot and lift out a couple kernels to taste. You want them soft enough to eat and a little bit soupy. If they're not there yet, add enough water to keep the rice wet, cover, and cook for another 2 minutes.

4 By now the rice is ready. Stir in the butter or olive oil, cheese, and enough water, 1 tablespoon at a time, so the rice is creamy. Taste and add salt if it needs more. Eat with another sprinkling of cheese on top.

★ ★   What if you could eat sundaes for dinner? You can! All you have to do is believe that a scoop of something delicious with sauce on top counts as a sundae. Farro is a mellow-tasting whole grain that's popular in Italy and the United States. Cooked this magical way and drizzled with warm olive oil on top, it's perfect for putting the sundae theory to the test. And the method here works for steel-cut oats too. Check out the list that follows in case you want to try adding something to the topping.

FAR OUT FARRO SUNDAE

MAKES: 2 TO 3 SERVINGS ≫→ TIME: 45 MINUTES ❄ 🌿

INGREDIENTS

¾ cup farro

1½ cups water, plus more as needed

Salt

3 tablespoons olive oil or butter

EAT WITH: White Beans with Parmesan (page 209), sausage or other cooked meat (page 60), Leafy Salad (page 137).

STEPS

1 Put the farro in a 2-quart pot that has a tight-fitting lid. Fill the pot almost to the top with cold tap water and swirl it around with your hand. Carefully pour off as much water as possible, leaving the farro in the bottom of the pot. Repeat a couple more times until the water looks almost clear. Then drain the farro in a strainer over the sink, shake a couple times, and put it back in the pot.

2 Add the 1½ cups water and a small pinch of salt. Put the pot over high heat. Once the water boils, turn the heat down to medium or medium-low so that it bubbles steadily but gently. Cover the pot and set the timer for 20 minutes.

3 Lift the lid and peek: You want holes to appear in the farro, and when you carefully tip the pot, the farro should be puffy and starting to burst a little but not sticking or burning. If it doesn't look like that and the pot is dry, add another 2 tablespoons water, cover, keep cooking, and check again in 2 minutes and repeat until the farro is ready.

4 When the farro is ready and no water remains in the pot, lift a couple kernels out with a fork and taste to make sure it's soft and has enough salt. Stir once or twice with a big spoon or stiff spatula to scrape up any starchy bits stuck on the bottom. Cover the pot and let the farro rest for at least 5 and up to 15 minutes while you make the sauce.

RECIPE CONTINUES ➡

5 Put the olive oil or butter in a 1-quart pot over medium-low heat. (If you're adding anything to the sauce, put it in at the same time.) Cook, watching the whole time and stirring once or twice, until the butter foams or the oil smells good and shimmers, 1 to 2 minutes. (Or a little longer if you added toppings.) Cover and remove the pot from the heat.

6 Use an ice cream scoop or serving spoon to dip into the farro and grab a sticky mound and put it in a bowl or on a plate. It's okay if it's not a perfect ball. Spoon some of the sauce on top and eat.

8 YUMMY EXTRAS FOR FAR OUT SUNDAE SAUCE

As little or as much as you like. Warm them in the sauce in Step 5 until they're soft or scatter them on top after drizzling.

1. Seedless grapes (cut in half—or not)
2. Blueberries
3. Chopped fresh tomatoes or halved cherry tomatoes
4. Chopped pistachios, peanuts, cashews, or other nuts
5. Sunflower, sesame, or green pumpkin seeds
6. Chopped garlic or scallions
7. Chopped sweet or dill pickles
8. Chopped black or green olives

★ One good thing about making your own refried beans is that you get to pick the kind of bean and how you season it. Another good thing is that you can use beans from a can or those you cooked yourself from dried. (There's a recipe on page 210.) And the last good thing is that it's sort of wild to mash and stir the beans in the skillet and watch them change.

REFRIED BEANS

MAKES: 2 TO 3 SERVINGS ⟫ *TIME: 20 MINUTES*

INGREDIENTS

1 (15-ounce) can pinto or black beans (or 1¾ cups cooked)

¼ cup butter or vegetable oil

1 scallion or ½ small onion, chopped (if you like)

Water as needed

1½ teaspoons chili powder

Salt

Hot sauce, dried red chiles, or black pepper (if you like)

EAT WITH: any tacos or burritos (pages 105 and 102); Quinoa Cooked with Salsa (page 202); or as a dip for tortilla chips with Guacamole (page 134), sour cream, and any salsa.

STEPS

1 Put the beans in a colander and run cold tap water over them, shaking until they're rinsed. Let them drain. If you're using the chopped scallion or onion, make sure it's ready to go. Put about 1 cup of water next to the stove too.

2 Put the butter or oil in a 10-inch skillet over medium heat. When the butter foams or the oil is hot and shimmers, add the beans, the scallion or onion if you're using it, and the chili powder. Cook, stirring almost the whole time, until the mixture starts sizzling, about 1 minute.

3 Use a potato masher to start mashing the beans, carefully pressing straight down into the skillet. Add a small splash of water and adjust the heat so that the beans bubble a little without sticking. As you refry the beans, you can use the masher or fork to stir if you need to or switch back to the spoon.

4 Keep mashing, stirring, and adding water until the refried beans are as chunky or smooth as you want them. This will take between 5 and 10 minutes. They'll get a little stiffer as they cool on your plate. Taste and add salt and some hot sauce, dried red chiles, or black pepper if you like the beans spicy. Then eat hot or warm.

⭐ ⭐ Rather than using just water to cook these teeny grains—which are somehow both fluffy and a little crunchy at the same time—you build in flavor right from the start by toasting them in butter or olive oil, then cooking them in a liquid that's a mixture of salsa and water. You can use whatever homemade cooked or jarred salsa you like and stir in whatever you want from the list on page 191. Now that's a party in a pot.

QUINOA COOKED WITH SALSA

MAKES: 2 TO 4 SERVINGS ⟩⟩ *TIME: 45 MINUTES* ❄ 🍃

INGREDIENTS

¾ cup quinoa

1 tablespoon butter or olive oil, plus more for eating

1 cup any jarred or cooked salsa (see page 80)

½ cup water

Salt and pepper (if you like)

Chopped fresh cilantro (if you like)

EAT WITH: any tacos or burritos (pages 105 and 102), Refried Beans (page 201), or Meat Loaf (page 223).

STEPS

1 Put the quinoa in a mesh strainer (also called a sieve) and run cold tap water over it. As you rinse the kernels, stir with your hands or a big spoon until everything is wet. Shake off the extra water and let the quinoa sit over a bowl until you need it.

2 Put the butter or oil in a 2-quart pot that has a tight-fitting lid and turn the heat to medium. When the butter melts or the oil gets hot and shimmers, add the quinoa and stir so it all looks shiny. Adjust the heat so you can hear and see the kernels sizzle. Keep stirring until they smell like toast, about 1 minute.

3 Add the salsa and water and stir until combined. Raise the heat a little so the mixture bubbles gently without splattering all over. Cover the pot and let it cook without stirring. Set the timer for 15 minutes.

4 Carefully open the lid and tip the pot to see if there is still liquid in it. Taste a little quinoa to see if it's soft. When it's ready, the grains will look puffier than when you started and there will be little rings around each kernel. To keep cooking, add a tablespoon or 2 of water if the pot is dry and check again in 5 minutes.

5 When the quinoa is ready, add salt and pepper too if you like and some more butter or oil. Add some chopped cilantro too if you like. Fluff with a fork and eat hot or warm. The leftovers are good cold or reheated in the microwave and will keep in the fridge for 1 week.

VARIATION

CORNY BLACK BEAN QUINOA COOKED WITH SALSA. This makes a whole vegetarian meal. When you add the salsa and water in Step 3, stir in ½ cup frozen or fresh corn kernels and ½ cup drained canned or cooked black beans.

DID YOU KNOW

You can cook long- or short-grain white rice, bulgur, or farro this exact same way. And if you want to try this recipe with brown rice, check out the shortcut on page 195.

★ ★ ★ Humans have been eating hummus for thousands of years. And maybe you've been eating it a while too. The reason the recipe is tagged "Advanced" is because you need a food processor or blender to get the beans smoother than you can by mashing—in other words, to purée them. History, machinery, and vocabulary all in one delicious dip!

HUMMUS

MAKES: 4 TO 6 SERVINGS ➤➤ TIME: 30 MINUTES

INGREDIENTS

1 (15-ounce) can chickpeas (or 1¾ cups cooked; see page 210)

1 clove garlic, peeled

⅓ cup tahini

3 tablespoons olive oil, plus more as needed

¼ cup water, plus more as needed

1 tablespoon fresh lemon juice

1 teaspoon ground cumin

Salt and pepper

EAT WITH: Raw Snacking Vegetables (page 133), pita bread or crackers, or as a filling for sandwiches.

Chickpeas are also called garbanzo beans. (Or use whatever beans you like.) Tahini is like peanut butter, only made by grinding toasted sesame seeds.

STEPS

1 Put the chickpeas in a colander and run cold tap water over them, shaking until they're rinsed. Let them drain.

2 Put the garlic in a food processor or blender and pulse the machine until the clove bounces around into bits. Add the chickpeas, tahini, oil, water, lemon juice, cumin, and a sprinkle of salt and pepper.

3 Turn on the machine and let it run for 30 seconds. Stop and scrape down the sides with a soft spatula. To make the hummus saucier, add 1 tablespoon water and 1 teaspoon olive oil and turn the machine on again.

4 Stop, scrape, taste, and add more salt and pepper if you think it needs it. And if you want the hummus even saucier, repeat Step 3. Carefully remove the blade if you used a food processor and scrape the hummus into a bowl. Eat right away or cover tightly and refrigerate for up to 1 week.

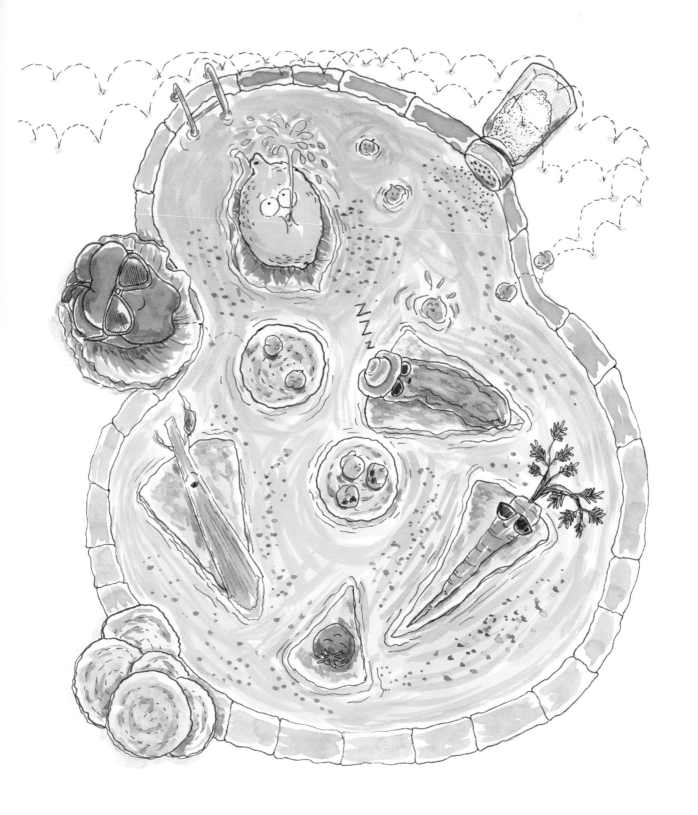

★ These sort of crunchy beans look like green peanuts and taste a little nutty. They're actually young soybeans. You'll find edamame with frozen vegetables either out of their pods or still in them. The variation gives the steps for cooking them in the shell—and eating them with your fingers.

SHINY EDAMAME

MAKES: 2 TO 3 SERVINGS >> *TIME: 15 MINUTES*

INGREDIENTS

½ cup water

1 teaspoon toasted sesame oil

2 teaspoons soy sauce

1 teaspoon sugar

1 tablespoon vegetable oil

1½ cups frozen edamame (out of the pods)

Salt (if you like)

Additions from the list that follows (if you like)

EAT WITH: White Rice (page 190), Fried Rice (page 193), Cold Nutty Noodles (page 182), or Squiggly Noodles with Teriyaki Sauce (page 185).

STEPS

1 Put the water in a small bowl with the sesame oil, soy sauce, and sugar. Stir with a fork to make a little sauce.

2 Put the vegetable oil in a 10-inch skillet over medium heat. When it's hot and shimmering, add the edamame and stir until the beans are shiny all over, about 1 minute.

3 Add the sauce to the skillet and adjust the heat so it bubbles a little and gives off some steam. Cook, stirring every minute or so, until the sauce becomes thick and shiny and the beans soften and get hot, about 5 minutes. If the pan gets dry before the beans are ready, add more water 1 teaspoon at a time.

4 Turn off the heat, taste, add a little salt if you like, and stir. (If you're adding any extras from the list that follows, stir them in now too.) Eat the beans hot or warm or refrigerate them for later to eat cold. (They'll keep in an airtight container for several days.)

RECIPE CONTINUES ➡

Any bean works great stir-fried. As long as they're not too mushy and you don't stir them too much, they'll turn out fine. Chickpeas and frozen lima beans are the firmest. Black beans are a close second.

SHINY EDAMAME IN THE POD.
Fun for snacking. The recipe
stays the same *except* use
3 cups frozen edamame in their
pods and make the sauce with
¾ cup water. The beans will take
between 5 and 10 minutes to
get tender. To eat, let them cool,
then grab a pod between your
teeth and squeeze the beans
into your mouth like toothpaste
or sideways like you're gnawing
on corn on the cob. (They're also
good cold.)

4 EXTRAS TO ADD TO SHINY EDAMAME

In or out of the shell, add any or
all of these just before your last
couple stirs:

1. 1 tablespoon toasted
   sesame seeds
2. 1 chopped scallion
3. Red chile flakes or chopped
   fresh red chile to taste
4. A squeeze of lemon juice

★ ★ ★ You will learn a lot from cooking a pot of dried beans and then baking them. Patience, for one thing, since it can take an hour or more for them to get soft. You don't have to babysit them. You can either cook something else to eat with them at the same time or do homework or whatever. Think of it like watching a video in slow motion, where you can see all the ways a food changes when it's heated, stirred, and seasoned.

WHITE BEANS WITH PARMESAN

MAKES: 3 TO 4 SERVINGS (3 TO 4 CUPS) ⟫→ TIME: 1½ TO 2 HOURS ❄ 🌿

INGREDIENTS

8 ounces dried cannellini or large navy beans (about 1¼ cups)

Salt

3 tablespoons olive oil

½ cup grated Parmesan cheese, plus more for serving

½ cup chopped fresh basil leaves for garnish

Pepper (if you like)

EAT WITH: White Rice (page 190), any roasted or stir-fried vegetable, Leafy Salad (page 137), Drop Biscuits or toast topped with Garlic Butter (page 255 or page 243), or your favorite bread or cracker.

STEPS

1 Put the beans in a colander and rinse them under cold tap water. As you spray the water around, use your hands to toss them and remove any that look super-strange.

2 Pour the beans into a 3-quart pot and add enough water so they're covered by about 2 inches. Bring the water to a boil over high heat, then turn the heat down so the liquid bubbles gently. Cover the pot and set a timer for 20 minutes.

3 Every time you check the beans, stir them and ask yourself how they're doing. As the beans cook, they'll get plumper and softer and the water in the pot will go down and get thicker. This is because the beans are soaking up the water like a sponge. If the beans are no longer covered in water, add enough so they are, adjust the heat so the liquid bubbles gently again, then cover and set the timer for another 20 minutes.

4 Repeat Step 3. Only this time the beans are probably starting to look closer to being ready. If that's true, set the timer for 10 minutes. If they still look pretty raw, set it for 15.

5 The next time you check, taste a bean. They're probably tender but not quite soft enough to eat. Add 1½ teaspoons salt, stir, adjust the heat so the liquid bubbles gently, cover, and set the timer for 5 minutes. Next time you stir, test again. Don't add more

RECIPE CONTINUES ➡

I JUST WANT A POT OF BEANS FROM SCRATCH

Your wish is my command! If you stop making White Beans with Parmesan after Step 5, you'll have plain beans—like what comes from a can—only way better. This recipe makes about 3 cups cooked beans, so you might even consider starting with a full pound. It takes just as long. After cooking, let them cool, transfer them to an airtight container, then refrigerate for up to 1 week or freeze for several months. See the list on page 191 for flavoring grains. Everything also works great with plain-cooked beans.

HOW TO MAKE WHITE BEANS WITH PARMESAN WITH CANNED BEANS

Whenever you don't have time for homemade beans, skip to Step 6 and use two 15-ounce cans of beans for every 8 ounces of dried beans. Drain and rinse them. Instead of the cooking liquid, use tap water or chicken or vegetable stock to moisten them before topping and baking.

salt, but add more water if the beans look dry and keep cooking until the beans are as firm or tender as you like. (You can cool and refrigerate the beans and liquid in an airtight container for up to 5 days.)

6   When you're ready to finish the beans, heat the oven to 400°F. Smear an 8-inch skillet or square or round baking dish with 1 tablespoon of the oil. Make sure the cheese and basil are ready to go. Use a slotted spoon to move the beans into the prepared skillet or baking dish. Use a regular spoon to add enough liquid from the pot to make the beans look moist but not drowning. (You can refrigerate or freeze the rest of the cooking liquid in an airtight container to use for soup.) Drizzle the remaining 2 tablespoons oil over the beans. Sprinkle the top with the cheese and put the pan in the oven.

7   Bake until the beans are bubbly and the cheese is melted, about 15 minutes (longer if the beans came out of the fridge). Garnish the top with the basil and pepper if you like, put some extra Parmesan on the table for sprinkling, and eat. (Refrigerate leftovers in an airtight container for up to several days or freeze for a few months.)

VARIATIONS

CHICKPEAS WITH FETA CHEESE. Use dried chickpeas instead of the cannellini or navy. They'll probably take longer, but honestly the time can vary a lot, so just keep checking. In Steps 6 and 7, use crumbled feta cheese and garnish with chopped fresh dill or parsley.

BLACK BEANS WITH JACK CHEESE. Use dried black beans instead of the cannellini or navy. They'll cook a little more quickly. In Steps 6 and 7, use grated Jack cheese and garnish with chopped fresh cilantro.

DID YOU KNOW

You don't have to soak beans before cooking. You can, of course, but you don't really save much time and you have to plan ahead. For this recipe, let's stick to the basics.

BUILD-a-BOWL

GRAB A BOWL. OPEN THE FRIDGE. OPEN THE PANTRY. Go through the steps and pick as many foods as you want, heating some or all in the microwave as you go. After making a few of your own special formulas, you'll be making recipes specially for building bowls later.

1

Rice or grains
(pages 190 to 203)

Beans (canned or home-cooked; page 209)

Noodles or pasta
(pages 161 to 187)

Potatoes (page 145 or pages 150 to 153)

Steamed greens (page 139)

Lettuce

Sprouts

2

Vegetables—raw snacking (page 133), steamed (page 139), or roasted (page 145)

Jammy Onions (page 83)

Tomatoes

Avocado

Pickles

Fresh or dried chiles

3

Eggs (pages 39 to 43)

Scrambled Tofu (page 41)

Bacon, sausage, ham, and stuff like that (page 58)

Chicken (pages 225 to 227)

Shrimp (page 237) or fish (page 238)

Meatballs (page 224)

Canned tuna

Peanut butter

Grated or crumbled cheese

4

Crunchy Bread (page 242)

Chopped nuts

Seeds—sunflower, sesame, or pumpkin

Crackers or chips

5

Ranch for Real (page 75)

Soy Sauce Glaze (page 71)

Salad Dressing (page 76)

Honey Mustard Sauce (page 74)

A fresh or cooked salsa (page 80)

Your secret sauce from The Condiment Lab (page 78)

Chopped fresh herbs
(page 72)

Olive or vegetable oil

Yogurt

Soy sauce

Hot sauce

Squeeze of lemon or lime

★ ★ ★   You won't believe how easy it is to make crispy tidbits of chicken in the oven. And they're waaayyyy better than what you get at a drive-up window. If you double this recipe, you'll have enough for a lot of hungry people, or make enough to freeze the leftovers in an airtight container to heat later in the microwave. There are a couple ways....instead. And check out the next page for more nugget and some sauce ideas.

CHICKEN MARK NUGGETS

MAKES: 4 SERVINGS ≫→ *TIME: 30 MINUTES* ❄

INGREDIENTS

1 pound boneless chicken (tenders, breasts, cutlets, or thighs)

Salt and pepper

1 cup whole milk

4 cups corn flakes

3 tablespoons good-quality vegetable oil, plus more as needed

EAT WITH: Raw Snacking Vegetables (page 133) or Big French Fries (page 155).

STEPS

1   Heat the oven to 400°F. Cut the chicken into chunks about 2 inches long. Put them in a medium bowl, sprinkle with a little salt and pepper, and pour in the milk. Toss with a fork until the pieces are all coated with the milk. Let the chicken sit while you get everything ready to cook.

2   Put the corn flakes in a shallow bowl and crumble them with your hands or a potato masher. Crush the flakes into crumbs about the size of coarse bread crumbs. (For a more even coating, make finer crumbs by pulsing the cornflakes in a blender or food processor.)

3   To set up for breading and baking: Put a large rimmed baking sheet on a counter or table and smear the bottom with the oil. On one side (depending on whether you like to work from the left or the right), put the bowl with the crumbs. Next to that, put the bowl with the chicken.

4   Toss the chicken again with the fork to make sure all the pieces are wet. With tongs (or your hands), one at a time lift a piece of chicken from the bowl and roll it in crumbs until coated all over. As you work, put the pieces on the oiled pan, spreading them out so they're evenly placed without touching. (Be sure to wash your hands once you're done with this step.)   *RECIPE CONTINUES* ➡

5 Set a timer for 10 minutes and let the chicken bake without touching. You're looking for a crunchy-looking golden brown crust to form on the bottom as the oil sizzles. You'll see it around the edges when the pieces are ready, and you'll be able to turn them easily without tugging. Tongs are the best tool to avoid splatters, but sometimes a stiff spatula can help loosen every bit from the pan. If they're not ready to turn when the timer goes off, set it for another 5 minutes and check again to see if they're ready to turn.

6 If you used breasts or tenders, bake the second side for another 5 minutes (or 8 minutes for thighs). You want the second side to be about the same color as the first. To test for doneness, carefully remove the pan and cut into a piece with a fork and small knife so you can peek. The meat should feel firm against the fork and cut easily and you'll see no pink. The juices should be clear. You don't have to check every piece once you get the hang of what they look like.

7 Sprinkle the nuggets with a little salt and pepper if you like. Serve them plain, or with a condiment or homemade sauce for dipping on the side.

VARIATIONS

FISH MARK NUGGETS. Instead of the chicken, use firm thick fish fillets like salmon, cod, catfish, or halibut. Everything else in the recipe stays the same. Follow the cooking times for chicken breasts in Step 6.

PORK OR BEEF MARK NUGGETS. Instead of the chicken, use boneless beef or pork sirloin or loin chops or steak. Everything else in the recipe stays the same. Follow the cooking times for chicken thighs in Step 6.

3 DIP IDEAS FOR CHICKEN MARK NUGGETS

Besides ketchup or mustard, nuggets made with chicken, fish, pork, or beef all go with your favorite sauces in the Flavor Bursts chapter that starts on page 67. My top three picks:

1. Honey Mustard Sauce (page 74)
2. Hot Soy Sauce Syrup (page 71)
3. Ranch for Real (page 75)

★ ★　Feel like a total chef when you whip up perfectly golden chicken and a bright, buttery sauce. It's easy, especially if you have some help. To wow friends or family, double the recipe and cook the chicken in two batches before moving on to the sauce in Step 6.

CHICKEN WITH ORANGE SAUCE

MAKES: 2 TO 3 SERVINGS →→ TIME: 45 MINUTES

INGREDIENTS

½ cup all-purpose flour

½ teaspoon salt, plus more if you like

12 ounces boneless, skinless chicken tenders or thighs

1 tablespoon olive oil

2 tablespoons butter

1 cup orange juice

Pepper (if you like)

2 tablespoons chopped fresh mint, parsley, or chives for garnish

EAT WITH: Creamy Mashed Potatoes or Buttery Egg Noodles (pages 152 or 165), steamed or roasted vegetables (pages 139 or 145), or Leafy Salad (page 137).

STEPS

1　Spread the flour out in a large shallow bowl next to the stove. Add the salt and stir with a fork to combine. Add the chicken to the bowl and toss the pieces in the mixture until every nook and cranny is covered.

2　Put the oil and 1 tablespoon of the butter in a 12-inch skillet over medium-high heat. When the butter foams and the oil is hot and shimmering, quickly but carefully use tongs to lift a piece of chicken above the bowl, shake off the excess flour, and put it in the pan. Smooth side down first is best, but if you can't, no big deal. Try with some of the other pieces. It's more important that the chicken is spread out as much as possible.

3　When all the pieces are in, adjust the heat so the edges sizzle without burning. If the flour is getting dark fast, turn the heat down under the pan. Cook without touching until the chicken smells like toast and you can see the edges curling up from the bottom of the pan, 3 to 5 minutes for breasts and 5 to 7 minutes for thighs. While the chicken cooks, dump the flour out of the bowl, wash and dry it, and put it next to the stove again.

4　Tug on the thinnest piece of chicken with the tongs to see if it will lift easily and peek at the bottom. It should be golden brown. If it is, turn the pieces over, using a stiff spatula. If the chicken isn't ready, set the timer for another minute and check again.

RECIPE CONTINUES ➡

PORK CHOPS WITH APPLE PAN SAUCE. Perfect for fall when the weather gets chilly. Instead of the chicken, use pork chops that are about ½ inch thick. For the cooking times, treat the boneless chops like chicken breasts or bone-in chops like thighs. Use apple cider instead of the orange juice. Everything else stays the same.

5 Repeat Step 4 to cook and brown the other side. As the pieces finish browning, move them to the clean shallow bowl and turn the heat under the skillet to medium-low. Even though the outsides are brown, the chicken will probably still be pink inside. That's okay. It will finish cooking in the sauce, but you're going to need to use a clean platter or dinner plates for serving. (Unless you want to just serve from the skillet—your choice.)

6 Add the orange juice to the skillet and adjust the heat so it steams and bubbles. Use a stiff spatula to scrape up all the browned bits from the bottom of the pan. Then add the last 1 tablespoon butter and stir until it melts and the sauce bubbles again.

7 Return the chicken to the skillet and cook, using the spatula to move it around and coat it in the sauce until the thickest piece is no longer pink inside, about 5 minutes. To check, use a small knife to cut a slit and peek inside. Taste the sauce and see if it needs more salt, then move the chicken to the platter or plates and spoon the sauce over the top. Garnish with chopped herbs and eat.

The old-school name for thin boneless chicken is "cutlets." You don't have to cut them, though, if you use boneless chicken tenders or thighs, or find precut cutlets where you buy meat. You can use big boneless breasts too, but you'll need to bash them between two sheets of plastic wrap with a pounding tool so they're an even thickness.

★ ★ One easy mixture gets you three favorite foods. Shape it into a log for meat loaf, make patties for burgers, or roll it into balls. And if you want to make the recipe with ground pork, lamb, chicken, or turkey, go right ahead. It's all better than good.

MEAT LOAF, BURGERS, AND BALLS

MAKES: 4 TO 6 SERVINGS ⇒→ TIME: 30 TO 60 MINUTES, DEPENDING ON THE SHAPE ❄

INGREDIENTS

1 tablespoon olive oil

1 cup grated Parmesan cheese

1 egg

¼ cup bread crumbs

2 teaspoons dried Italian seasoning blend

2 tablespoons chopped fresh parsley leaves (if you like)

½ teaspoon salt, plus more if you like

¼ teaspoon pepper (if you like)

1 pound ground beef

EAT WITH: For meat loaf: Creamy Mashed Potatoes (page 152), Baked Potatoes (page 151), or steamed or roasted vegetables (pages 139 and 145). For sauce: see The Condiment Lab (page 78) or make a batch of Tomato Sauce (page 170). See the variations for burger and meatball "eat with" ideas.

STEPS

1   Heat the oven to 350°F. Smear the olive oil on the bottom of a small rimmed baking sheet.

2   Put the grated cheese in a large mixing bowl and set a small plate next to it on the counter. Smack the side of an egg on the plate hard enough to hear it crack but gently enough that the shell doesn't break into pieces. Use both hands to carefully hold the egg over the mixing bowl and open it so the insides slide out.

3   Add the bread crumbs to the bowl. Then add the Italian seasoning, parsley leaves if you're using them, and the ½ teaspoon salt. (If you really like salt, add a teeny pinch more, but remember the cheese is a little salty.) Add the pepper if you're using it. With a whisk or fork, beat until the mixture is all the same color.

4   With your hands or a soft spatula, fold in the ground meat. It's okay if the egg mixture isn't perfectly mixed in. You don't want to overstir the meat or it will get dry and tough. Scrape the meat mixture onto the baking sheet and shape it into a log that's the same thickness from one end to the other so the meat loaf will cook evenly.

5   Bake the meat loaf until it's browned on the top and sides and firm when you press on it. Set a timer for 30 minutes to check the first time. There shouldn't be any pinkness inside at all. Make a slit with a small sharp knife and take a peek or stick a quick-read thermometer into the thickest part. It should say 160°F or a little more. When the meat loaf is ready, take the pan out of the oven and let it sit for 5 minutes before cutting and eating. *RECIPE CONTINUES* ➡

BURGERS. Don't bother to heat the oven. You have two choices: Make the meat loaf recipe and divide the mixture into 4 big or 6 medium-sized pieces. Or just use the 1 pound of ground meat (without mixing it with any other ingredients) and divide that into 4. Smash each hunk of meat between your hands or on a plate into patties no more than 1 inch thick. Try not to press and squeeze them too much, just enough so they hold together. Then sprinkle them with some salt. Put a dry 12-inch skillet over medium heat. When it's hot, put in the burgers, giving them as much room as possible. Adjust the heat so the meat sizzles without burning and cook (no touching!) until the edges brown and you can easily slip a stiff spatula underneath to turn them, about 5 minutes. Cook the other side the same way. Eat as a sandwich on your favorite bun or bread with the toppings you like best. Fries (page 155) or slaw (page 138) are good sides, as are pickles.

MEATBALLS. Again, you have choices: Skip Step 1, and follow Steps 2, 3, and 4 (stop after folding in the ground meat). Then use the meat mixture to make Holden's Pasta with Drop Meatballs (page 170). Or for just the balls to eat with something else, follow the recipe through Step 4 (stop after folding in the ground meat). Instead of shaping the mixture into a loaf, scoop a heaping teaspoon out of the bowl, then use another teaspoon to scrape the meat onto the prepared baking sheet. Repeat until the bowl is empty. Bake the meatballs for 20 minutes before checking the first time. If they're not ready, check again every 5 minutes until they are.

★ ★　The awesome thing about simply roasted chicken is all the ways you can eat it. Hot out of the oven, chilled for picnics or snacks, or pulled from the bones and chopped for salads, sandwiches, and soups. One recipe and a couple variations cover all the possible choices for how you like your chicken best, starting with your favorite bone-in parts like drumsticks. The steps also tell you how to turn the pan juices into a little sauce. Or make your favorite sauce recipes from the Flavor Bursts chapter beginning on page 67.

ROASTED CHICKEN,
WITH OR WITHOUT BONES

MAKES: 6 TO 8 SERVINGS ≫→ *TIME: 30 TO 90 MINUTES, DEPENDING ON THE CUT* ❄

INGREDIENTS

2 tablespoons olive oil

3 to 4 pounds bone-in chicken parts (any mix of wings, legs, thighs, breasts)

Salt

EAT WITH: baked or mashed potatoes (pages 151 and 152), White Rice (page 190), Buttery Egg Noodles (page 165), Steamed Vegetables (page 139), or Leafy Salad (page 137).

STEPS

1　Make sure the top oven rack is in the middle or one notch higher. Turn the heat to 450°F. (That's super-hot, so be careful from now on.) Put the oil in a 9 x 13-inch roasting pan that's at least 2 inches deep.

2　Add the chicken parts to the pan skin side up. If you see any big chunks of skin or fat, cut them off with kitchen scissors. Sprinkle the pieces all over the top with salt. Spoon the oil on top and use your hands or tongs to toss and coat the chicken all over with the oil and salt. (Hands are the best for this job.) Spread the chicken into a single layer, skin side up. Let it sit until the oven is ready.

3　Put the chicken in the oven and set the timer for 20 minutes. Stand back from the oven when you open the door to peek inside. (The steam coming out will be hot!) If any chicken parts are getting too dark, carefully remove the pan and use tongs to move the chicken around. But if everything looks fine, shut the oven and keep roasting for another 10 minutes before checking again. After that, check the chicken every 5 minutes. Total roasting time will be 30 to 40 minutes.

RECIPE CONTINUES ➡

4 The chicken is ready when the skin is crisp and golden and the meat and the juices in the pan are no longer pink. Use the tongs and a small sharp knife to cut a piece right down to the bone and peek inside. (Or use a quick-read thermometer to poke the thickest piece without touching any bones. It should say about 160°F.) You can also take the breast meat and wings out first and put the rest back in the oven to make sure it's cooked all the way through.

5 When the chicken is ready, use tongs to move the pieces to a platter or rimmed baking sheet to sit while you make the sauce. Add 1 cup water to the pan and scrape up any stuck bits from the bottom with a stiff spatula. Carefully pour all the juices and browned bits into a 1-quart pot and bring to a boil over high heat.

6 Turn the heat down so the sauce bubbles gently and add anything you like from the list after the recipe. Taste the sauce and add more salt if you want, then serve the chicken and pass the sauce at the table. (Put any leftovers in airtight containers. They'll keep in the fridge for up to 5 days or the freezer for months.)

Chicken and turkey drumsticks, wings, and thighs are called "dark meat" and take longer to cook than the "white meat" found on breasts. You can totally see the difference in color and texture, especially after cooking.

VARIATIONS

ROASTED WHOLE CHICKEN.
Super juicy and pretty coming out of the oven. You will probably need some help cutting it up after roasting. Instead of the parts and a roasting pan, use a 3- to 4-pound whole chicken and a 10-inch ovenproof skillet. If you want, cut off the pointy wing tips and extra fat from the chicken with kitchen scissors. After coating with salt and the oil in Step 2, put the chicken breast side up in the skillet and transfer the skillet to the heated oven. Roast for 40 minutes before checking the first time. Total cooking time will be 45 minutes to 1 hour. Resting and making the sauce stays the same, only you can make it right in the skillet while an adult carves the chicken into pieces and slices.

ROASTED BONELESS CHICKEN. No skin and bones to mess with and much faster. Thighs will be a little juicier and chewier than breasts. Instead of the parts and a roasting pan, use 1½ to 2 pounds boneless, skinless chicken breasts or thighs and a large rimmed baking sheet. After coating with salt and the oil in Step 2, put the chicken smooth side up in the pan and put the pan in the heated oven. Roast for 15 minutes before checking the first time. Total cooking time will be 20 to 30 minutes. Resting and making the sauce stays the same as in the main recipe.

5 WAYS TO SEASON ROASTED CHICKEN PAN SAUCE

1. Up to 2 tablespoons chopped fresh herbs like basil, mint, dill, parsley, or chives (or 1 tablespoon rosemary)
2. Up to 2 teaspoons dried herbs like dried Italian seasoning blend or oregano
3. Up to 2 teaspoons ground spice or spice blend like curry or chili powder
4. Up to 1 tablespoon mustard
5. A pinch red chile flakes or black pepper

Museum of Roasted Chicken

drumstick

thigh

breast

★ ★ If you learn one recipe in the book, this is it—a recipe that lets you pick any meat, vegetable, or tofu (see the variations below) combo you want. Everything you need to know about how to choose and swap hard, soft, and leafy vegetables starts on page 131. For drawings that will help you prep all sorts of foods, see pages 16 to 21. Since stir-frying is a super-quick cooking method, it's best to have everything chopped, measured, and next to the stove. And get your sides rolling or done before you start too, so you'll be all set to eat as soon as your stir-fry is ready.

BEEF-AND-VEGETABLE STIR-FRY

MAKES: 2 TO 3 SERVINGS ⟩⟩ TIME: 45 MINUTES ❄

INGREDIENTS

8 ounces beef sirloin, flank, skirt, or strip steak

8 ounces favorite vegetable (like red bell pepper, broccoli, carrots, or green beans)

1 scallion, white and green parts separated and chopped

1 teaspoon chopped garlic

1 teaspoon chopped fresh ginger

1/2 cup water

2 teaspoons soy sauce, plus more as needed

2 tablespoons vegetable oil

Salt and pepper

EAT WITH: plain white, brown, or coconut rice (pages 190 and 191); Rice Sticks with Carrot Ribbons (page 179); or Cold Nutty Noodles (page 182). Lemon or lime wedges are always good too, for squeezing.

STEPS

1 To make the meat easier to slice thinly, put it in the freezer for 15 to 20 minutes. That gives you time to get everything ready. Start by trimming the vegetable you're using. Peel it and remove the seeds if you need to. Then decide if you want to slice it thinly or chop it into chunks and do that too. Put the vegetables close to the stove.

2 Get the scallion, garlic, and ginger chopped and by the stove too. The scallion white parts, garlic, and ginger can all be together, but keep the green scallion tops separate. Measure the water and soy sauce into a small bowl next to the stove too. Put 1 tablespoon of the oil in a 10-inch skillet, but don't turn on the heat yet. Get a clean plate ready for when you start cooking. You may as well get a spoon or stiff spatula out now too.

3 Take the meat out of the freezer and slice it thinly or cut it into bite-sized chunks. If you're slicing, look for the way the meat has very faint stripes, usually the long way. That's called the "grain" of the meat. Cutting across the grain (so your knife breaks those stripes) will get you more tender pieces. All will still be fine if you cut the wrong way. RECIPE CONTINUES ➡

4 Turn the heat on under the skillet to medium-high. When the oil shimmers, add the meat so it's in a single layer. Sprinkle with a little salt and maybe some pepper. Wait until the meat sizzles and you see and smell it browning before stirring for the first time, 2 or 3 minutes. It should scrape up easily from the pan and not be very watery. Keep stirring until little or no pink remains, then move the meat to the empty plate.

5 Add the last 1 tablespoon oil to the skillet and turn the heat down to medium. Add the mixture of scallion whites, garlic, and ginger and stir a couple times. Add the vegetables and keep stirring until everything in the pan is sizzling and shiny. Keep cooking, stirring every 30 seconds or so, until the vegetables are as soft as you like, 3 to 5 minutes.

6 Add the water–soy sauce mixture, stir a couple times, then scrape the steak and all the juices from the plate into the skillet. If the sauce isn't bubbling, turn the heat up a little. Cook and stir until the sauce coats the meat and vegetables, then turn off the heat and stir in the scallion greens. Taste and add soy sauce, salt, and pepper if you need more seasonings and eat right away.

Some stores carry beef, pork, or chicken already sliced for stir-frying. It's not that hard to cut it up yourself, but you might want to try this shortcut sometime if the choices don't look too fatty.

CHICKEN-AND-VEGETABLE STIR-FRY. Any of the vegetables from the main recipe work well with chicken. So does celery, asparagus, or mushrooms. Instead of the beef, use boneless, skinless chicken breast or thighs. Everything stays the same, except you don't need to freeze the chicken in Step 1. And in Step 4, cook the chicken slices or chunks until no pink remains, about 5 minutes total for breast meat and 8 to 10 minutes for thighs.

PORK-AND-VEGETABLE STIR-FRY. Any of the vegetables from the main recipe work well with pork, but I really like chopped greens like cabbage or bok choy. Instead of the beef, use boneless pork loin chops or pork sirloin steaks. Everything stays the same, except in Step 4, cook the pork slices or chunks until no pink remains, about 5 minutes total.

SHRIMP-AND-VEGETABLE STIR-FRY. Any of the vegetables from the main recipe work well with shrimp, but snow or snap peas are amazing. Instead of the beef, use peeled medium-sized raw shrimp. (There's no need to freeze it. But you can use frozen shrimp—just put it in a colander and run it under cold tap water to thaw it a little.) Leave them whole or cut them if you like that better. Everything stays the same, except in Step 4, cook the shrimp until it just turns pink, 3 to 5 minutes depending on how cold and big the pieces are.

TOFU-AND-VEGETABLE STIR-FRY. One of my all-time favorite stir-fries. Any of the vegetables from the main recipe work well with tofu, but I especially like frozen peas or chopped Brussels sprouts or cabbage. Instead of the beef, use 8 ounces firm tofu (about ½ block). Everything stays the same, except you don't need to freeze the tofu in Step 1. And in Step 4, add another 1 tablespoon of oil, use medium (instead of medium-high) heat, and be sure you wait to stir the tofu the first time until it's browned and no longer sticks, 5 to 10 minutes.

★ This creamy, crunchy tuna bake is a little different from most old-fashioned casserole recipes and a lot like pot pie, only with a potato chip crust. Instead of starting with a can of soup for the sauce, you're going to make a thick white sauce called *béchamel* (said bay-shaw-mel; see the Did You Know note below for more info).

TUNA-POTATO-CHIP POT PIE

MAKES: 2 TO 4 SERVINGS »→ *TIME: ABOUT 1 HOUR*

INGREDIENTS

2 tablespoons butter or olive oil, plus more for the baking pan

2 tablespoons all-purpose flour

1¼ cups milk (preferably whole), plus more if needed

1 cup grated mild or sharp cheddar cheese

1 can or jar of tuna (5 to 6 ounces)

1 cup frozen peas or frozen peas and carrots (no need to thaw them)

Salt

Pepper (if you like)

2 snack bags potato chips (about 3 ounces total)

EAT WITH: Leafy Salad (page 137) or Steamed Vegetables (page 139), but you don't really need anything on the side.

STEPS

1 Heat the oven to 350°F. Use a little butter or oil to smear in an 8- or 9-inch square baking pan or dish. (It should be able to hold 6 to 8 cups.)

2 Put the butter or oil in a 2- or 3-quart pot over medium-low heat. When the butter melts or the oil is hot, add the flour to the pot and stir it in with a whisk. Turn the heat down to low and cook, whisking without stopping, until the mixture gets a little darker and smells like toast, about 3 minutes.

3 To be sure the sauce is smooth, not lumpy, pour in the milk slowly, whisking the whole time. Keep cooking and whisking until the sauce thickens enough to look like gravy, another 2 or 3 minutes. When you dip in a spoon and pull it out, the sauce should cover the spoon completely and slowly drip off. Remove the sauce from the heat.

4 Add ¾ cup of the cheese, the tuna, and frozen vegetables. Stir and try plopping a spoonful back into the bowl. If it seems too stiff, add 2 tablespoons milk and try again. Taste and add salt and pepper if you like. Scrape the mixture into the baking pan or dish, using a soft spatula to make sure you got it all and to smooth the top.

5 Put the potato chips in a medium bowl and crumble them with your hands or a potato masher. You want most of the pieces to be the size of quarters, so don't get too into it. Stir in the last ¼ cup cheese and sprinkle everything over the top of the tuna mixture.

RECIPE CONTINUES ➡

FISH IN CANS, JARS, AND POUCHES

Tuna fish you probably know, and maybe canned salmon too. These are two of the most popular cooked fish that are sold in cans, jars, or pouches so that you can eat them right out of the container. Sardines, mackerel, clams, and anchovies also come this way. I love fish, so of course I'm going to say, "Try 'em and see what you like!"

A lot of people call all of this "tinned fish." But you have other choices besides cans. I like fish packed in jars, but it's sometimes hard to find and will be more expensive than cans, which are my second pick. For both cans and jars, the fish is packed tight inside with either water or oil (which is richer, with a taste that might be described as "fishy"). Tuna and salmon also come in pouches. In the packages the fish tends to be milder and smoother, less chunky. You might like that. But skip the kits and flavored stuff. Whatever you choose will be best if you buy it plain and add your own seasonings and dressing.

6 Bake until the topping is golden, the cheese is melted, and the sauce is bubbling, 25 to 35 minutes. Remove from the oven and let the tuna bake sit for 5 minutes before eating.

VARIATIONS

CHICKEN–POTATO–CHIP POT PIE. Use about 1½ cups packed chopped or shredded cooked chicken instead of the tuna. Light or dark meat or cooked ground chicken—all good. Everything else stays the same.

SALMON–PUFFED–RICE POT PIE. Make some easy swaps: Use canned or jarred (or home-cooked) salmon for the tuna, Jack instead of cheddar cheese, and unsweetened puffed rice cereal instead of the potato chips. Everything else stays the same.

TOMATOEY BEANS WITH TORTILLA CHIPS. Skip making the béchamel in Steps 2 and 3. Drain 1 (15-ounce) can black, kidney, or pinto beans (or 1¾ cups cooked beans) into a colander and rinse them under cold tap water. Put them in a medium mixing bowl with 1½ cups jarred or cooked tomato salsa (page 80), ¾ cup grated mozzarella cheese, and 1 cup frozen corn. Use tortilla chips instead of potato chips, and after you crumble them in Step 4, add ½ cup more mozzarella. Everything else stays the same.

Watching béchamel go from watery to gravy-like seems like magic. The sauce is good plain or with crumbled cooked sausage or bacon on Drop Biscuits (page 255) or like it is here with cheese melted into it and spooned over toast (page 242). The minute you taste béchamel, you'll think of all sorts of ways to eat it.

⭐ The easiest way to cook shrimp ever. The trick is to keep the boiling time quick. I've made a list of possible ways to flavor the water, in the hope that you try some or all of them. Though it might seem like a lot of seasonings to add, they season the whole pot of water, so only a little soaks into the shrimp. This is one of those recipes that's perfect for feeding your family or a crowd. As you double, triple, or quadruple the ingredients, increase the pot size too. More water will take longer to bring to a boil, but the cooking time stays the same.

DIPPY SHRIMP

MAKES: 2 TO 4 SERVINGS ⟫ *TIME: 20 MINUTES*

INGREDIENTS

2 cups water

Salt

Anything from the list after the recipe

1 pound large peeled raw shrimp (frozen is fine)

1 tablespoon butter

EAT WITH: Coleslaw (page 138), Skillet Corn Bread (page 244), White Rice (page 190), or your favorite bread with butter. And for dipping: bottled hot sauce or ketchup or any of the sauces or dressings from the Flavor Bursts chapter beginning on page 67.

STEPS

1 Put the water in a 3-quart pot with a tight-fitting lid over high heat. Add a big pinch of salt and anything you want from the list of seasonings. Bring the water to a boil. If you added seasonings, let them cook for 5 minutes before going to the next step. (Adjust the heat so the liquid isn't splattering everywhere.)

2 Return the liquid in the pot to a full boil and add the shrimp. Right away, carefully remove the pot from the heat, cover, and let sit until the shrimp is bright pink on the outside and white on the inside. Start checking after 1 minute. (Super-big frozen shrimp might take up to 3 minutes.)

3 Use tongs or a slotted spoon to move the shrimp from the pot to a big bowl. Scoop 1 cup of the cooking water into a small pitcher or measuring cup and add the butter so it melts. Eat the shrimp with the buttered cooking water for dipping, plus whatever other sauces and sides you made.

RECIPE CONTINUES ➡

VARIATIONS

DIPPY SHRIMP WITH POTATOES AND CORN ON THE COB. After salting (and maybe seasoning) the water in Step 1, add 1 pound scrubbed small red or white potatoes. If they're bigger than 2 inches across, cut them into big chunks first. Bring the water to a boil and cook, stirring once or twice, until you can poke the potatoes easily with a fork, 10 to 15 minutes. Use this time to husk 2 ears fresh corn if you need to (see page 18) and carefully cut or break each cob into two or three chunks. When the potatoes are tender, pick up the recipe at Step 2 and add the corn to the pot with the shrimp.

YOU–PEEL DIPPY SHRIMP WITH OR WITHOUT POTATOES AND CORN ON THE COB. Cooking shrimp with the shells still on always makes the cooking water taste a little more like the ocean than with pre-peeled. It's fun to make a little mess at the table to get to the good stuff inside. Follow the main recipe or the variation with potatoes and corn, only instead of the peeled large shrimp, use 1¼ to 1½ pounds peel-on frozen raw shrimp. Everything else stays the same.

7 SEASONINGS FOR THE BOILING WATER

Add as many of these as you like to the water before adding the shrimp.

1. 2 or 3 lemon or lime wedges
2. 1 small onion, peeled and cut in half
3. 3 or 4 cloves garlic, peeled
4. 1 or 2 teaspoons spice blend (like chili powder, curry powder, or a seafood-specific mix like Old Bay Seasoning)
5. 1 bay leaf
6. 1 dried hot chile
7. 1 teaspoon black peppercorns or ground pepper

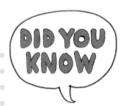

DID YOU KNOW

Many people around the United States make versions of this dish and call it a "boil." It's big-time party food. Some kind of shell-on seafood goes in the pot—shrimp, yes, but it could also be crab, lobster, mussels, clams, or crawfish—and sometimes smoked sausage, along with corn on the cob, onions, and potatoes.

★ ★ ★ When she was little, my youngest daughter, Emma, loved this meal. (And she still does!) Mild white fish like cod is easy to cook and a nice change from chicken. The potatoes should be sliced as thinly as possible, so you might need help from an adult. A food processor fitted with the slicing blade is a great solution.

EMMA'S FISH

MAKES: 2 TO 4 SERVINGS ≫→ TIME: 1 HOUR

INGREDIENTS

1½ pounds Yukon Gold potatoes

3 tablespoons butter

Salt

About 1 pound cod fillets

1 lemon, cut into wedges

EAT WITH: Coleslaw (page 138) and any sauce you like best from the Flavor Bursts chapter beginning on page 67.

You can also use catfish or rockfish in this recipe.

STEPS

1 Heat the oven to 425°F. Peel the potatoes and slice them as thinly as possible, ideally no more than ¼ inch thick. Pile them up in a 9 x 13-inch baking pan or rimmed baking sheet.

2 Melt 2 tablespoons of the butter in a small pot or in the microwave. Drizzle the melted butter over the potatoes and toss to coat them all over. Spread the potato slices flat into the bottom of the baking dish. (It's okay if they overlap as long as the layer is pretty even.) Sprinkle the top with some salt.

3 When the oven is hot, put the pan in the oven and set a timer for 10 minutes. Every 10 minutes, turn the potatoes with a stiff spatula. In 30 to 40 minutes, they should be lightly browned all over. Spread them out again and put the cod on top. Pinch the last tablespoon of butter into little bits and "dot" the top of the fish with them. Sprinkle on a little more salt if you like.

4 Roast the cod with the potatoes until it turns solid white and easily breaks into flakes at the thickest part, 8 to 12 minutes depending upon the thickness of the fillets. The best way to check is to peek with a small knife. Try to avoid overcooking so it doesn't get dry. Cod begins to "gape"—its sections separate—when it is done. Remove from the oven and use the spatula to cut the fish and scoop potatoes onto plates. Eat right away.

CRUNCHY BREAD

You got toast, right? Put bread in a toaster or toaster oven, and it pops up the toast or dings when it's done. Maybe you let it cook some more if it's not brown enough or the slices—or bagel—are thick. Then what do you put on it? Butter probably. Maybe some jam or honey. But have you ever tried . . .

YUMMY BUTTER

Start with 4 tablespoons (½ stick) butter (or coconut oil). It's got to be soft enough to mash, so put it in a small mixing bowl and let it sit out on the counter for about an hour. Then mash and stir to get these spreads to eat on toast. Or after smearing the butter on the toast, try melting the Yummy Butter by putting it back in the toaster oven or under the broiler. Just be sure to watch the whole time so it doesn't burn.

CINNAMON SUGAR BUTTER
Add 2 teaspoons sugar and ¼ teaspoon cinnamon.

CARAMEL BUTTER
Add 1 tablespoon dark brown sugar.

HONEY BUTTER
Add 2 tablespoons honey.

CHOCO–BUTTER
Add 2 teaspoons each sugar and cocoa powder.

CHEESE BUTTER
Add 2 tablespoons grated cheddar, Parmesan, or Jack cheese.

GARLIC BUTTER
Add 2 tablespoons grated Parmesan cheese, ½ teaspoon dried Italian seasoning blend, and ¼ teaspoon granulated garlic (or 1 minced clove garlic).

BIRTHDAY CAKE BUTTER
Add 2 tablespoons confetti sprinkles, jimmies, or other sprinkles.

CROUTONS

The best way to use up bread that's getting dry is also a terrific way to add lots of crunch to soups and salads, or to simply make a fantastic snack. Make cubes of toasted bread called croutons. First heat the oven to 400°F. Then pick whatever bread you want to use—sandwich slices, leftover Italian or French bread, whole grain rolls or English muffins, even corn bread. Cut away the crust if you like, and cut the bread into cubes. It doesn't matter what size as long as they're pretty close to the same. Measure them and pile them up on a rimmed baking sheet. For every cup of cubes, drizzle with 1 tablespoon olive oil, toss with your hands or a stiff spatula to get a little on most of the bread, then spread the croutons into an even layer. Bake until browned and crunchy, 5 to 15 minutes depending on how big they are. Store in an airtight container and eat within a couple days.

CRUMBS

Store-bought bread crumbs are fine—buy coarse ones like panko-style and make sure they're unseasoned—but homemade are even better. For fresh bread crumbs, tear leftover bread that's starting to get dry into bite-sized pieces and put them in the bowl of a food processor fitted with a metal blade. Pulse a few times, then let the machine run for 30 seconds, or until they break into crumbs the size of wet sand. Now you can fry them in a little olive oil over medium heat, or spread them out in a rimmed baking sheet and dry-toast them in a 300°F oven until crisp, about 30 minutes.

CRAZY CRUMBS

Instead of throwing out all those crumbs at the bottom of bags, save 'em to decorate and flavor ice cream, yogurt, mashed potatoes, plain rice, or noodles—everything! Anytime you finish a box or bag of chips, cereal, or crackers, shake the crumbs into an airtight container like a small jar. Keep adding crazy crumbs for up to a month, then use what's left at the bottom and start a clean jar.

★ ★ Making your own corn bread for dinner (or snacks) is a simple recipe for learning to bake and a fun way to contribute to family meals. Be sure to check out the list of things you can add to the batter on the opposite page.

SKILLET CORN BREAD

MAKES: 6 TO 8 SERVINGS ⇒ TIME: 1 HOUR

INGREDIENTS

2 tablespoons butter or olive oil, plus more for greasing the pan

1½ cups cornmeal

½ cup all-purpose flour

1 teaspoon baking soda

1 teaspoon salt

1 tablespoon sugar (or 2 if you like it sweet)

1 egg

1¼ cups buttermilk or whole-milk yogurt, plus more if needed

EAT WITH: Guacamole (page 134); Creamy Tomato Soup (page 110); Chili (page 127); Corn Chowder (page 124); any meat loaf, burgers, or balls (page 223); or warm with butter and honey.

STEPS

1 Heat the oven to 375°F. Use some butter or oil to smear all around a 10-inch ovenproof skillet. (Cast iron is great, or you can use a 9-inch square baking dish.)

2 Put the cornmeal into a large bowl with the flour, baking soda, salt, and sugar. In a medium bowl, whisk together the egg and buttermilk or yogurt. (For egg-cracking directions, see page 39.)

3 Pour the liquid mixture into the dry mixture and use a slow stirring and folding motion with a big spoon or soft spatula just enough to make the dry ingredients wet and form a batter. It's okay if there are lumps, but if the mixture looks too dry, add more buttermilk or yogurt 1 tablespoon at a time.

4 Melt the 2 tablespoons butter in the microwave or a small pot over medium-low heat. (Or skip this if you're using oil.) Add the melted butter or oil to the batter and stir a couple more times.

5 Pour or ladle the batter into the prepared skillet or pan, then use the soft spatula to scrape in what's stuck inside the bowl. Spread the top with the spatula to make an even layer. Bake until the top is lightly browned and the sides have pulled away from the pan, 25 to 30 minutes. You'll know it's ready when you poke a toothpick into the center and it comes out clean. Cool for at least 10 minutes, then slice into wedges or squares with a pretty big knife and eat warm if possible.

5 THINGS TO STIR INTO CORN BREAD BATTER

If you want to add more than one thing, adjust the quantities so you add no more than 1½ cups total.

1. 1 cup corn kernels (fresh or frozen)
2. 1 cup grated cheddar or Jack cheese
3. ½ cup cooked and crumbled bacon, ham, or sausage
4. ½ cup chopped roasted red peppers
5. 1 chopped fresh or pickled jalepeño chile

★ These are perfectly sweet with less sugar than cake and a lot of fruit. Plus, they're fun to make. Paper or foil liners to put in the pan—called a "tin" from the old days—are a little easier than smearing butter into each cup, and they help keep the muffins fresh.

BLUEBERRY MUFFINS

MAKES: 12 MEDIUM-SIZED OR 24 MINI MUFFINS ⟫ TIME: 1 HOUR

INGREDIENTS

4 tablespoons (½ stick) butter, plus more if needed for the cups

2 cups all-purpose flour

½ cup sugar

2 teaspoons baking powder

½ teaspoon salt

1 egg

1 cup milk (preferably whole), plus more if needed

1 cup blueberries (fresh or frozen)

EAT WITH: butter and jam, honey, or maple syrup; Scrambled Eggs (page 39).

STEPS

1 Heat the oven to 375°F. Put 1 paper or foil liner into each of 12 medium or 24 mini cups in a muffin tin or tins. (If you're not using liners, smear some softened butter into the bottom and sides of each cup—enough so you can see it.)

2 Melt the 4 tablespoons butter in a microwave or in a small pot over medium-low heat. Put the flour in a large bowl along with the sugar, baking powder, and salt and stir until evenly mixed. Put the melted butter, egg, and milk in a small bowl and whisk until there are no streaks and the color is light yellow. It's fine if the butter clumps up into bits. (For egg-cracking directions, see page 39.)

3 Pour the liquid mixture into the dry mixture and use a slow stirring and folding motion with a big spoon or soft spatula just enough to make the dry ingredients wet and form a batter. It's okay if there are lumps, but if the mixture looks too dry, add more milk 1 tablespoon at a time.

4 Carefully stir the blueberries into the batter without overmixing. Spoon the batter into the prepared cups in the muffin tin. The cups won't be filled to the top. The batter will puff and grow the rest of the way during baking.

RECIPE CONTINUES ➡

CHOCOLATE CHUNK MUFFINS.
Use any kind of chocolate you
like, but for me, something on
the dark side is always best.
Instead of the blueberries, chop
2 to 3 ounces chocolate into bits
(or use about ⅓ cup chocolate
chips) and add them to the batter
in Step 4.

5 Bake until the top is lightly browned and firm when you carefully
press on one, 15 to 20 minutes for mini muffins and 20 to
30 minutes for the normal-sized kind. (Frozen berries will slow
down baking time a little.) You'll know they're ready when you poke
a toothpick into the center and it comes out clean. Cool the pans
on a wire rack for 10 minutes before removing the muffins from
the cups. Eat warm or within a day or 2. (Freeze leftover muffins
in an airtight container for up to several months. Thaw and warm
them in the microwave, or wrapped in foil in a 300°F oven for about
30 minutes.)

★ ★   I've been making this exact banana bread since I first learned to cook, and it's one of my most popular baking recipes. You can either use an electric mixer (see page 266) or mix the batter with a spoon. If you're not crazy about bananas, the variations will point you in three other directions.

BANANA BREAD

MAKES: 8 TO 12 SERVINGS ➢→ *TIME: 90 MINUTES* ❄ 🌿

INGREDIENTS

8 tablespoons (1 stick) butter, softened, plus more for greasing the pan

2 cups all-purpose flour

½ teaspoon salt

1½ teaspoons baking powder

1 cup sugar

3 very ripe medium bananas

2 eggs

1 teaspoon vanilla extract

½ cup chopped walnuts (if you like)

½ cup unsweetened shredded coconut (if you like)

EAT WITH: a smear of butter or cream cheese, a scoop of vanilla or caramel ice cream, or nothing!

STEPS

1   Heat the oven to 350°F. Grease a 9 x 5-inch loaf pan with butter by smearing about 1 tablespoon around the sides and bottom of the pan.

2   Whisk together the flour, salt, baking powder, and sugar in a large bowl.

3   Mash the bananas with a fork or potato masher in a medium bowl until very smooth. You should have about 1½ cups. Mash in the butter. Add the eggs and vanilla and stir or beat with an electric mixer until well combined. (For egg-cracking directions, see page 39.)

4   Add the banana mixture to the dry ingredients and use a slow stirring and folding motion with your spoon or soft spatula just enough to make the dry ingredients wet and form a batter. It's okay if there are lumps. Gently fold in the nuts and coconut if you're using them.

5   Pour or spoon the batter into the prepared pan. Bake until the bread is golden brown and firm when you carefully press on the loaf, 50 to 60 minutes. You'll know it's ready when you poke a toothpick into the center and it comes out almost entirely clean.

6   Cool the pan on a wire rack for 15 minutes, then carefully turn the pan upside down to release the loaf. Serve warm or at room temperature. (Or wrap airtight and store at room temperature for up to 2 days or freeze for up to several months.)   *RECIPE CONTINUES* ➡

PUMPKIN BREAD. Instead of the bananas, use one 15-ounce can plain pumpkin purée (not pumpkin pie filling). Add 1 teaspoon cinnamon and ½ teaspoon ground ginger and skip the vanilla. Everything else stays the same.

APPLESAUCE BREAD. Instead of the bananas, use 1½ cups chunky applesauce (like the one on page 261). Add 1 teaspoon cinnamon if you like and skip the vanilla. Everything else stays the same.

SWEET POTATO BREAD. Instead of the bananas, use 1½ cups mashed baked sweet potatoes (see page 152, or use one 15-ounce can plain sweet potato purée). Add 1 teaspoon cinnamon if you like and skip the vanilla. Everything else stays the same.

DID YOU KNOW

When you smear pans with butter or oil for baking, that's called "greasing" the pan. The butter or oil keeps the batter from sticking to the pan as it bakes. It's important to get a thick layer on the sides and bottoms and into the corners. And sometimes after greasing, you'll be directed to also flour the pan. There are directions for that in Step 1 on page 295.

★ ★ You want pizza? There are a couple ways to get there without pulling a box out of the freezer or calling for delivery. This way gets you a deep-dish pie with the toppings you love.

PIZZA

MAKES: 4 TO 8 SERVINGS ⟫ *TIME: ABOUT 1 HOUR*

INGREDIENTS

⅓ cup olive oil, plus more for the pan

3 cups all-purpose flour, plus more if needed

1 tablespoon baking powder

¾ teaspoon salt, plus more to taste

About 1 cup warm water

½ cup tomato paste

½ teaspoon dried Italian seasoning blend (if you like)

3 cups grated mozzarella cheese (about 12 ounces)

1 or 2 extra toppings from the list below (if you like)

EAT WITH: Raw Snacking Vegetables (page 133), Leafy Salad (page 137), or Steamed Vegetables (page 139).

STEPS

1 Heat the oven to 400°F and make sure there's a rack in the bottom half. Coat the sides and bottom of a 9 x 13-inch baking pan or dish (glass or ceramic is okay too) with some olive oil.

2 Put the ⅓ cup olive oil in a large bowl. Add the flour, baking powder, and ¾ teaspoon salt. Use a soft spatula to stir in ¾ cup of the warm water with a tossing and pressing motion. The dough should be wet but crumbly. If there are dry bits of flour, add more water, 1 tablespoon at a time, being careful not to overmix. Grab clumps of the dough and press them into the prepared pan or dish so that you make an even layer in the bottom, all the way to the edges.

3 Scrape the tomato paste into a small bowl. Add 2 tablespoons warm water, the Italian seasoning, and a pinch of salt if you like. Stir with a fork until smooth. Spread or dab the tomato sauce on top of the crust, careful not to tear the dough. It's okay if it's not smeared perfectly evenly.

4 Put the pan in the lower half of the oven and set the timer for 15 minutes. Then when the timer goes off, take the pan out of the oven.

RECIPE CONTINUES ➡

DID YOU KNOW You can turn bread into pizza. Heat the oven to 400°F and put 1 or more split sub rolls or English muffins on a rimmed baking sheet. For each roll or muffin, you'll need 1 tablespoon tomato paste mixed with 1 teaspoon water, plus ½ cup grated cheese. Sauce and top the halves as described in the recipe and bake until toasted and bubbly, about 10 minutes. (Or try the Pizzillas on page 88.)

5 Carefully scatter the cheese on top of the sauce and put 1 or 2 toppings over the top if you're using them. Return the pizza to the oven and set the timer for another 15 minutes.

6 The pizza is ready when the crust is golden around the edges, puffed in the middle, and the cheese is hot and bubbly. If it's not ready when the timer goes off, check again in 5 minutes. Let the finished pizza cool for 5 minutes before cutting. You can cut it into any size squares you like. For triangles, cut each square in half across from one corner to another. (Freeze leftovers in an airtight container for up to a couple months and reheat in the microwave for 1 to 3 minutes.)

VARIATION

WHITE PIZZA. Skip the tomato paste and don't make the tomato sauce in Step 3. When you top the pizza with the mozzarella cheese in Step 5, sprinkle ½ cup grated Parmesan cheese on top along with the Italian seasoning if you like. Bake with or without extra toppings as described in Step 5.

10 EXTRA TOPPINGS FOR PIZZA

1. 3 to 4 ounces sliced pepperoni
2. 2 cooked Italian sausage links (about 8 ounces total), crumbled or sliced
3. ½ cup grated Parmesan cheese
4. 6 sliced button or cremini mushrooms, tossed in 1 tablespoon olive oil
5. 1 cup chopped cooked spinach or broccoli
6. ½ red or green bell pepper, chopped
7. ½ small white or red onion, thinly sliced or chopped
8. ½ cup sliced black or green olives
9. Sliced pickles (don't laugh until you try it!)
10. Pinch red chile flakes

★ ★ As with cookies, biscuit dough can be shaped by rolling and cutting with a shaped tool or simply by dropping blobs by the spoonful. See the last two variations for patting and cutting circle-shaped biscuits and doughnuts. And if you don't have a food processor—or just want to make the dough by hand—there are directions here for how to do that too.

DROP BISCUITS

MAKES: 12 MINI, 6 MEDIUM, OR 4 LARGE BISCUITS ⇒⇒ TIME: 45 MINUTES

INGREDIENTS

4 tablespoons (½ stick) cold butter, plus a little more softened butter for greasing the pan

2 cups all-purpose flour, plus more if needed

1 teaspoon salt

1 tablespoon baking powder

1 teaspoon baking soda

1 cup buttermilk or plain whole milk yogurt, plus more if needed

EAT WITH: eggs cooked any way (pages 39 to 41), any crisp cooked meat (pages 58 to 60) or filling you like to make a sandwich, Jammy Onions (page 83), or one of the Yummy Butters on page 242.

STEPS

1 Heat the oven to 450°F. Grease a large rimmed baking sheet with some softened butter. Cut the 4 tablespoons cold butter into small cubes.

2 Put the flour in a food processor with the metal blade. Add the salt, baking powder, and baking soda. Pulse 3 or 4 times to mix. Add the cold butter to the food processor and pulse at least 5 times, until the bits of butter are the size of peas.

3 Add the buttermilk or yogurt and pulse just until the mixture forms a loose ball. (If the dough seems very sticky and wet, pulse in more flour, 1 tablespoon at a time, until the ball comes together. If it's too dry, do the same with buttermilk or yogurt.)

4 With help from your finger or an extra spoon, drop heaping tablespoons of the dough onto the baking sheet. You want them to be about the same size. Press down slightly with the back of a spoon. (To make bigger biscuits, use a large spoon or ice cream scoop.)

5 Bake the biscuits until golden brown, 7 to 9 minutes for minis (or 10 to 15 minutes for medium and large). To test, poke a toothpick into the center of a biscuit. It should come out clean.

RECIPE CONTINUES ➡

DID YOU KNOW

You can make these biscuits by hand. In Step 2, put all the dry ingredients in a large bowl and add the butter cubes. Grab handfuls of the mixture and rub your fingers together so you smush the butter and break it into bits as you mix it into the flour. After the dough has clumps the size of peas, pick up with the recipe at Step 3.

6 Cool the pan on a wire rack for 5 to 10 minutes. When the biscuits are cool enough to handle, cut them in half so you have a top and bottom like a hamburger bun. (They're best within a few hours, but you can store leftovers in an airtight container for a couple days. Split and toast them right before eating.)

VARIATIONS

CINNAMON-RAISIN BISCUITS. In Step 2, add ½ teaspoon cinnamon to the dry ingredients. After the dough forms a ball in Step 3, move it to a bowl and fold in ½ cup raisins. Then bake as directed.

CHEESE BISCUITS. After the dough forms a ball in Step 3, move it to a bowl and fold in ½ cup grated cheddar or mozzarella cheese. Then bake as directed.

PATTED-AND-CUT BISCUITS. Works for the main recipe and both variations. Sprinkle a clean, flat work surface with 2 tablespoons flour and have more flour ready. Use your hand to spread the flour out in an even layer. After the dough forms a ball in Step 3, move it to the floured surface and sprinkle a little more flour on top. Press and fold the dough a couple times to "knead" it. Gently press the dough until it's about ¾ inch thick. The shape doesn't matter, but try not to stretch it. Use a round biscuit cutter or a sturdy drinking glass to make circles 1 to 2 inches across. Move them to the baking sheet. Press together the scraps, pat them out, and cut the same way. Shape a little biscuit out of whatever you have left. Bake as directed.

BAKED-AND-GLAZED DOUGHNUTS. Amazing! Start by making a recipe for your favorite glaze, on page 283. (Or put 1½ cups powdered sugar on a plate.) Follow the variation for Patted-and-Cut Biscuits, only instead of cutting one circle, use a doughnut cutter (or 1 big and 1 small circle) to cut rings and holes. Start checking the doughnuts and holes after 7 minutes. They'll cook faster than large biscuits. In Step 6, cool the doughnuts and holes on the wire rack, set over a baking sheet or cutting board. When the doughnuts are cool enough to touch, dip one of the flat sides in the glaze (or powdered sugar) then put it back on the rack glaze side up to let it drip. Then roll the holes around in the glaze (or powdered sugar) and put them back on the rack too.

SWEETS

CAKES, PUDDINGS, FRUIT TREATS, WHIPPED CREAM, AND EVERYTHING CHOCOLATE

⭐ The big deal about making applesauce yourself is peeling the apples. So, in this recipe you can peel them, or not—your choice. Chopping up the fruit with the peels makes things so much easier and gives the sauce a ton of fruity flavor—and a slight pink or green color. Another solution is to keep the peels on and then turn everything into a smooth sauce. After cooking, let the sauce cool for 30 to 60 minutes. Put half in a blender or food processor to purée, then pour it into an airtight container that will hold at least 1 quart. Repeat with the rest.

APPLESAUCE

MAKES: ABOUT 1 QUART ≫→ *TIME: 1 HOUR* ❄️ 🍃

INGREDIENTS

Water as needed

2 to 3 pounds apples (any kind or a mix)

Salt

½ teaspoon cinnamon, or more to taste (if you like)

EAT WITH: plain yogurt or vanilla ice cream; on top of French Toast, Flippy Pancakes, or Waffles (pages 45, 61, and 63).

STEPS

1 Put about ½ inch water in a 2- or 3-quart pot with a tight-fitting lid. Core and peel the apples if you like. Chop them into bite-sized pieces. (The illustrations on page 16 show you how.) As you work, put the apples in the pot and add a pinch of salt. Cover and turn the heat to medium.

2 When the water starts to boil and you see steam coming out of the pot, remove the lid. Cook, stirring every 5 minutes, until the apples break apart and become mushy, 30 to 40 minutes. When you stir, adjust the heat so the applesauce bubbles constantly, but if the bottom starts to stick, turn the heat down a little and add water, 1 tablespoon at a time.

3 Taste the applesauce and add the cinnamon and more salt if you like. Eat warm or cool and refrigerate in an airtight container for up to 1 week (or freeze for a few months).

RECIPE CONTINUES ➡

DID YOU KNOW You don't need to sweeten fruit sauce. Cooking naturally makes it sweeter than raw fruit. And a little bit of salt brings out the fruity flavors.

PEACHSAUCE. So great in summer. Use peaches instead of the apples. To prepare them, see the drawings on page 20. You have the same choice to use peels or not, but if you do, consider making a smooth peachsauce as explained in the recipe note. Instead of cinnamon, ½ teaspoon vanilla extract is the way to go.

PEARSAUCE. Use pears instead of the apples. Peeling them is usually a good idea. To prepare them, see the drawings on page 16. If you like cinnamon, it's good with the pears too.

BERRYSAUCE. Instead of the apples, use 4 pints berries. (Frozen are fine. You'll need about 3 to 4 pounds or 6 to 8 cups.) Don't add any water to the pot in Step 1 and get them started on medium-low until they release some juice. Then you can raise the heat and bring to a boil. Skip the cinnamon.

PLUMSAUCE. Use any kind of plum instead of the apples. They're a pain to peel, so I suggest puréeing the sauce after cooking as explained in the recipe note. To prepare them, see the drawings on page 20. If you like cinnamon, it's good with plums too.

CHERRYSAUCE. Supereasy because frozen fruit is almost always pitted. (Check the label.) Use 1½ pounds frozen sweet or tart—also called "pie"—cherries instead of the apples. With tart cherries, add ½ cup sugar in Step 1. Don't add any water to the pot in Step 1 and get them started on medium-low until they release some juice.

⭐ The easiest, fudgiest brownies ever. Go ahead and chunk them up with up to ½ cup chopped nuts or chocolate bits when you mix the batter together in Step 4. Just know that they're pretty perfect just the way they are.

BROWNIES

MAKES: 9 LARGE OR 12 MEDIUM BROWNIES »» *TIME: 45 MINUTES* ❄

INGREDIENTS

12 tablespoons butter (1½ sticks), plus more for the pan

1 cup cocoa powder

½ cup all-purpose flour

¼ teaspoon salt

1¼ cups sugar

2 eggs

1 teaspoon vanilla extract

EAT WITH: a scoop of vanilla or chocolate ice cream, a dollop of Whipped Cream (page 267), or any of the fruit sauces on page 262.

STEPS

1 Heat the oven to 325°F and make sure there's a rack in the middle. Smear butter around the sides and bottom of an 8- or 9-inch square baking pan. You should be able to see it, even in the corners. Put the cocoa, flour, and salt in a medium bowl and whisk until all the streaks become a light brown color. You'll use this dry mixture in a minute.

2 Melt the butter in the microwave or a 1-quart pot over medium-low heat. Scrape it into a large mixing bowl with a soft spatula, then whisk in the sugar until the mixture cools a little. (Just use the same whisk. No need to wash it.)

3 Crack the eggs and open them into the same bowl (see page 39) and measure in the vanilla. Use the whisk to beat everything together until the color is the same. It's okay if the butter makes little clumps or looks weird.

4 Switch back to the soft spatula and stir the dry mixture into the wet mixture. You want everything to come together into a batter, but it's okay if there are still some lumps. Pour or spoon the batter into the prepared pan and use the spatula to scrape as much as you can out of the bowl.

5 Move the pan to the oven and set the timer for 15 minutes if using a 9-inch pan and 20 minutes for an 8-inch pan. You want the center of the brownies to still be a little jiggly when you gently shake the pan. If they're not ready, keep baking for 5 minutes, then check again.

RECIPE CONTINUES ➡

6 Cool the brownies in the pan on a wire rack until they're almost completely cool. For 9 squares, cut the brownies into three rows across in both directions. For 12 rectangles, go 4 rows one way and 3 the other. Keep leftovers in an airtight container for a day or freeze leftovers for up to a couple months. (They're great gently warmed in the microwave!)

CREAM IT! BEAT IT! WHIP IT! FOLD IT!

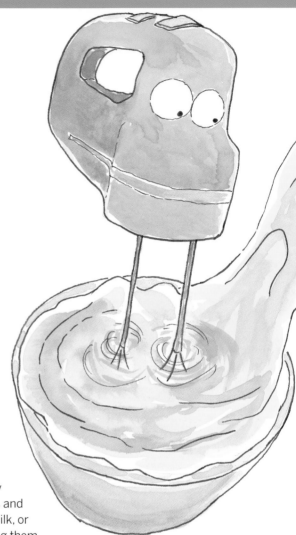

With words like "chop," "slice," "cook," "stir," "whisk," and "roast," you're learning action words or "techniques" as you make recipes. Baking has some special words too.

CREAMING

Mixing softened butter and sugar together (sometimes with eggs) gives many cookies, cakes, and frostings their rich fluffiness. You can cream butter and sugar by hand with a balloon whisk, but it takes some work and time. An electric mixer—either the kind that you hold in your hand or one that sits on a stand—is easier and faster. Swirl the beaters or whisk in the center of the bowl back and forth and in circles, then scrape the sides down with a soft spatula 1 or 2 times until the mixture has no streaks and you see ripples or ribbons in the top. You'll probably need help creaming the first couple times, but then you'll be a pro.

BEATING

Making scrambled eggs (page 39) is a perfect example of beating—the word to describe taking two separate, usually very different things (like yolks and whites, whole eggs and milk, or oil and vinegar) and mixing them until they turn into one thing. The tools for beating are a balloon whisk, electric mixer, or just a fork. The recipes help point to the best choices.

WHIPPING

Almost like magic, whipping turns a liquid into a soft cloudlike pillow (like cream into whipped cream). The more you bake, the more you'll see other recipes that do the same thing with other foods. You'll need a balloon whisk or an electric mixer. Food processors don't work as well for cream because they whip unevenly and too intensely. Run the beaters or whisk around the outside of the bowl toward the center, stopping to scrape the sides down with a soft spatula 1 or 2 times as you whip.

FOLDING

The gentlest way to mix two or more things into one. Like stirring, you can use a big spoon, but a soft spatula is even better, since you can scrape the sides of the bowl. When you stir, you're making a sort of circle motion around the bowl, pot, or pan. To fold you slowly scoop and lift from the bottom and sides toward the top. Whenever a recipe says to mix gently or to "stir the batter until just mixed," folding is a good technique to practice.

So easy and fun and much tastier than anything out of a can. Look for "heavy" or "whipping" on the label—or just "cream." Half-and-half won't work. And for the best results make sure your tools and bowl are clean and dry.

WHIPPED CREAM

MAKES: ABOUT 2 CUPS » TIME: 5 MINUTES

INGREDIENTS

1 cup cold cream

FLAVORING WHIPPED CREAM

Pick a sweetener and one flavor from this list. After the cream is whipped, keep the mixer going and add them slowly.

- 1 or 2 tablespoons granulated or golden brown sugar
- 2 or 3 tablespoons powdered sugar
- 1 tablespoon fruit jam
- ½ teaspoon vanilla extract
- 1 teaspoon grated lemon, lime, or orange zest
- ¼ teaspoon cinnamon

STEPS

1 Pour the cream into a cold clean medium mixing bowl or the bowl in a stand mixer.

2 Use a whisk in a fast circular motion or an electric mixer on a medium to medium-high setting to beat the cream until you get the fluffiness you want. The stages are: frothy, foamy, fluffy with soft peaks, and fluffy with stiff peaks.

3 The cream will go from liquid to whipped with stiff peaks in 2 to 5 minutes depending on how fast you or the machine are working. You will be able to see the different stages in Step 2 if you pay attention. It's even okay to stop and scrape the sides with a soft spatula to get a feel for the changes.

4 As soon as you see stiff peaks, stop so you don't overbeat to the point the cream forms clumps. (If that happens, add 1 tablespoon cream or milk and stir with a spoon to try to smooth things out.)

5 Add a flavor from the list here and eat a spoonful right away on hot chocolate, with cakes or brownies, or on top of pies and crisps. (Refrigerate the rest in an airtight container for up to 2 hours.)

★ ★ Most kids love chocolate chips just the way they are so I won't try to talk you into chopping your own chunks for cookies. But since that's how I like 'em, there's a variation after the recipe in case you want to try. Just be sure to get chips that aren't too sweet or milky. Darker chocolate keeps its shape a little better, and the cookie dough is perfectly sweet. "Bittersweet," "semi-sweet," or dark chocolate with somewhere around 70% "cacao" (or "cocoa") written on the label are a good place to start.

CHOCOLATE CHIP COOKIES

MAKES: 24 TO 36 ⟶ **TIME: 45 MINUTES** ❄ 🍃

INGREDIENTS

2 sticks butter, softened to room temperature

2 cups all-purpose flour

1 teaspoon salt

¾ teaspoon baking soda

¾ cup granulated sugar

¾ cup packed brown sugar

2 eggs

1 teaspoon vanilla extract

8 ounces chocolate chips (about 1⅓ cups)

EAT WITH: your favorite ice cream between two cookies for a sandwich, or a simple glass of ice-cold milk.

STEPS

1 Heat the oven to 375°F. Get 2 large baking sheets out. You'll be using them dry (without greasing them). Make sure you take the butter sticks out of the fridge 30 to 60 minutes before making the cookies. It really needs to be soft. Mix the flour, salt, and baking soda in a small bowl. You'll use that dry mixture in a minute.

2 To cream together the butter and sugars, put the butter in a large mixing bowl and measure in the sugars. Use a whisk, or a hand-held or upright mixer on a medium to medium-high setting, to beat until the mixture is light and fluffy, about 3 minutes by machine, a couple minutes longer by hand. (See page 266.)

3 One at a time, crack and open the eggs into a small bowl (see page 39) and add them to the butter-sugar mixture. Beat the first egg into the mixture before adding the second. Scrape the sides of the bowl down in between each egg.

4 Measure in the vanilla and add the dry ingredients to the bowl. Switch to a soft spatula and stir until a stiff dough forms. You want it to be all the same color without overmixing. Stir in the chocolate chips.

RECIPE CONTINUES ➡

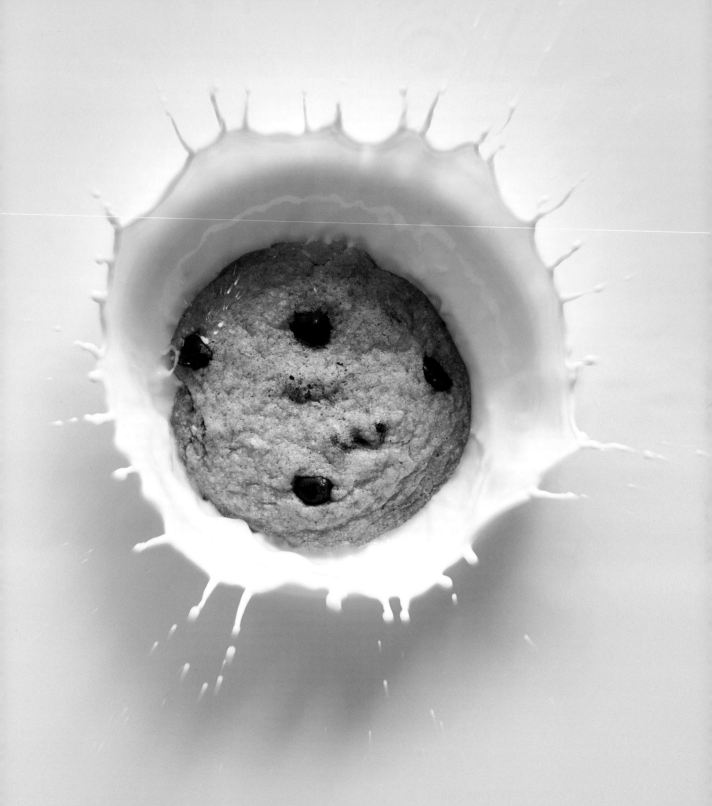

5 Use two spoons—teaspoons for small cookies or tablespoons for large—or 1 spoon and your finger to scoop up mounds of dough and drop them onto the baking sheets. Keep the dough about 2 inches apart. Bake until lightly browned around the edges and on the bottom, 8 to 12 minutes, depending on the size of the cookie. To check, take them out of the oven, carefully slip a stiff spatula under one, and peek. If they're not ready, put them back in the oven and check again in 2 minutes.

6 Cool the cookies for about 5 minutes on the sheets before moving them to a wire rack with a stiff spatula. These will keep in an airtight container for a couple days or freeze for a few months.

VARIATIONS

CHOCOLATE CHUNK COOKIES. Instead of the chips, use 3 large chocolate bars. (Most are about 3 ounces each.) Open them flat onto a cutting board and use a meat pounder or the back of a heavy metal spoon to bash the bars into chunks no bigger than ½ inch across. (Or if you're comfortable, use a knife and a rocking motion to chop them.) It's okay if they're all different sizes. Use the chunks instead of the chips in Step 4.

NUTTY CHOCOLATE CHIP OR CHUNK COOKIES. Add up to ½ cup chopped peanuts, walnuts, almonds, or pecans to the batter along with the chocolate chips or chunks.

COCONUTTY CHOCOLATE CHIP OR CHUNK COOKIES. Add up to ½ cup unsweetened shredded coconut to the batter along with the chocolate chips or chunks.

DID YOU KNOW You don't need an electric mixer to "cream" together butter and sugar for cookies. It's a lot more work to stir them together by hand until fluffy, but it can be done. To use a mixer, see page 266.

★ ★   Everyone's favorite way to eat oatmeal is buttery, chewy, and crisp all at the same time. I'll leave the choice of extra stuff—raisins, chocolate chips, nuts, or coconut to you. See the list that follows the recipe for ideas.

OATMEAL COOKIES

MAKES: 24 TO 36 ⟫ *TIME: 45 MINUTES* ❄

INGREDIENTS

12 tablespoons butter (1½ sticks), softened to room temperature

1½ cups all-purpose flour

2 cups rolled oats

1 teaspoon baking soda

2 teaspoons cinnamon

1 teaspoon salt

½ cup granulated sugar

1 cup packed brown sugar

2 eggs

1 teaspoon vanilla extract

¼ cup milk

EAT WITH: ice cream or a glass of milk, or make sandwich cookies by pressing together the flat sides of two cookies with a dab of Vanilla Frosting (page 298).

STEPS

1 Heat the oven to 375°F. Get 2 large baking sheets out. You'll be using them dry (without greasing them). Make sure you take the butter out of the fridge 30 to 60 minutes before making the cookies. It really needs to be soft. Mix the flour, oats, baking soda, cinnamon, and salt in a medium bowl until there are no more streaks. You'll use that dry mixture in a minute.

2 To cream together the butter and sugars, put the butter in a large mixing bowl and measure in the sugars. Use a whisk, or a hand-held or upright mixer on a medium to medium-high setting, to beat the butter until the mixture is light and fluffy, about 3 minutes by machine, a couple minutes longer by hand. (See page 266.)

3 One at a time, crack and open the eggs into a small bowl (see page 39) and add them to the creamed sugars. Beat the first egg into the mixture before adding the second. Scrape down the sides of the bowl in between each egg.

4 Measure in the vanilla and add the dry ingredients and the milk to the bowl. Switch to a soft spatula and stir until a stiff dough forms. You want it to be all the same color without overmixing. (If you're adding any extras, stir or fold them in now.)

RECIPE CONTINUES ➡

EXTRA STUFF FOR OATMEAL COOKIES

When you stir in the dry ingredients in Step 4, add as many things from this list as you like, as long as the total is no more than ¾ cup.

- Raisins
- Chocolate chips or chunks
- Chopped nuts (really any kind!)
- Chopped dried fruit
- Unsweetened coconut flakes
- Crumbled shredded wheat flakes or bran flakes
- Crumbled unsalted potato chips

5 Use 2 spoons—teaspoons for small cookies or tablespoons for large—or 1 spoon and your finger to scoop up mounds of dough and drop them onto the baking sheets. Keep the dough about 2 inches apart. Bake until lightly browned around the edges and on the bottom, 8 to 12 minutes, depending on the size of the cookie. To check, take them out of the oven, carefully slip a stiff spatula under one, and peek. If they're not ready, put them back in the oven and check again in 2 minutes.

6 Cool the cookies for about 5 minutes on the sheets before moving them to a wire rack with the spatula to cool completely. These will keep in an airtight container for a couple days or freeze for a few months.

★ ★ Smooth or chunky? That's the big question with this recipe. Only you can decide if you want to add chopped peanuts or not. Be sure to check out the variation and the Did You Know note here before you stick around. (Hah! Get the joke? Peanut butter? Sticky?)

PEANUT BUTTER COOKIES

MAKES: 24 TO 36 ⟫ *TIME: 45 MINUTES* ❄

INGREDIENTS

8 tablespoons (1 stick) butter, softened to room temperature

1 cup all-purpose flour

½ teaspoon baking soda

¼ teaspoon salt

½ cup granulated sugar

1 cup packed light brown sugar

1 cup peanut butter (any kind, but stirred well if there's a layer of oil floating on top)

2 eggs

1 teaspoon vanilla extract

1 cup roasted peanuts, chopped (if you like)

EAT WITH: chocolate or vanilla ice cream (on the side or sandwiched), a glass of cold milk or mug of hot chocolate, or for a next-level treat, drizzle with Cocoa Glaze (page 283).

STEPS

1 Heat the oven to 375°F. Get 2 large baking sheets out. You'll be using them dry (without greasing them). Make sure you take the butter out of the fridge 30 to 60 minutes before making the cookies. It really needs to be soft. Mix the flour, baking soda, and salt in a small bowl. You'll use that dry mixture in a minute.

2 To cream together the butter and sugars, put the butter in a large mixing bowl and measure in the sugars. Use a whisk, or a hand-held or upright mixer on a medium to medium-high setting, to beat the butter until the mixture is light and fluffy, about 3 minutes by machine, a couple minutes longer by hand. (See page 266.) Add the peanut butter and beat for another minute.

3 One at a time, crack and open the eggs into a small bowl (see page 39) and add them to the creamed sugars. Beat the first egg into the mixture before adding the second. Scrape down the bowl in between each egg.

RECIPE CONTINUES ➡

DID YOU KNOW

You can make these cookies (or the PB&J Cookies) with almond, cashew, or sunflower seed butter. Just follow the recipe with the same quantities, exactly the same way.

VARIATION

PB&J COOKIES. After you drop the dough onto the baking sheets in Step 5, turn to page 279 and follow the directions for making Thumbprint Cookies with your favorite jam or preserves.

4 Measure in the vanilla and add the dry ingredients to the bowl. Switch to a soft spatula and stir until a stiff dough forms. You want it to be all the same color without overmixing. Stir in the peanuts if you're using them.

5 Use 2 spoons—teaspoons for small cookies or tablespoons for large—or 1 spoon and your finger to scoop up mounds of dough and drop them onto the baking sheets. Keep the dough about 2 inches apart. Bake until lightly browned around the edges and on the bottom, 8 to 12 minutes, depending on the size of the cookie. To check, take them out of the oven, carefully slip a stiff spatula under one, and peek. If they're not ready, put them back in the oven and check again in 2 minutes.

6 Cool the cookies for about 5 minutes on the sheets before moving them to a wire rack with the spatula to cool. These will keep in an airtight container for a couple days or freeze for a few months.

★ ★ You know why I'm giving you a recipe that makes a ton of cookies? Because this is the best cookie for freezing and slicing like those logs you can buy at the store, only wayyyy better. You can also make cut-out cookies with this dough—in all different shapes, decorated with frosting, glaze, sprinkles, whatever. (See page 283.) And wait, there's more! You can also use the same recipe for "thumbprint" cookies that you fill like teeny pies.

SUGAR COOKIES

MAKES: 36 TO 48 ➤➤ TiME: 45 MiNUTES, PLUS A COUPLE HOURS TO CHiLL

INGREDiENTS

2 sticks butter, plus
2 tablespoons, softened to
room temperature

3 cups all-purpose flour

1 teaspoon baking powder

¼ teaspoon salt

½ cup powdered sugar

½ cup granulated sugar

1 egg

1 teaspoon vanilla extract

EAT WiTH: Decorations
(see page 283)!

STEPS

1 Make sure you take the 2 sticks of butter out of the fridge 30 to 60 minutes before making the cookies. It really needs to be soft. Mix the flour, baking powder, and salt in a small bowl. You'll use that dry mixture in a minute.

2 To cream together the butter and sugars, put the butter in a large mixing bowl and measure in the powdered and granulated sugars. Use a whisk, or a hand-held or upright mixer on a medium to medium-high setting, to beat the butter until the mixture is light and fluffy, about 3 minutes by machine, a couple minutes longer by hand. (See page 266.)

3 Crack and open the egg into a small bowl (see page 39) and add it to the creamed sugars. Measure in the vanilla and add the dry ingredients to the bowl. Switch to a soft spatula and stir until a sandy dough forms. You want it to be a crumbly dough that's all the same color.

4 With your hands, gather the dough into one big blob in the bowl. To shape it into a ball you'll need to press pretty hard, fold, and squeeze. Put the dough on a clean work surface or large plate. Cut the dough in half with a sharp knife and roll each piece into a log about 2 inches across and 6 inches long. It's okay if they're not perfect. Wrap tightly in parchment paper, put in an airtight container, and chill until firm, about 2 hours or overnight. (This is

RECiPE CONTiNUES ➡

VARIATIONS

THUMBPRINTS. Go from dough to cookies without chilling logs! Get the filling ready: 3 cups jam, preserves, or any frosting (page 298). Use your hands to grab and roll tablespoon-sized pieces of dough into balls. Put however many cookie balls will fit on the baking sheet, 2 inches apart. (Save the rest for a second batch or roll, wrap, and freeze the dough as described in Step 4.) Press down lightly with your thumb a couple times on each ball to make a pocket. It's okay if the edges crack. Bake the cookies as per Step 6. Once they're totally cool, drop teaspoons of the filling into each pocket.

CUTOUT SUGAR COOKIES. Pick out some cookie cutter shapes you like. Then follow the directions for shaping and chilling the dough, and rolling and cutting Gingerbread People on page 280, starting with Step 4. You can make sugar people or cut out different shapes. Use the ideas on page 283 to help you decorate.

when you'd freeze one or both of the logs. They will keep for a couple months. Thaw overnight in the refrigerator before making cookies.)

5 When you're ready to bake, heat the oven to 400°F and take the last 2 tablespoons of butter out of the fridge if you haven't already. Get 2 large baking sheets out. Smear each with some of the extra 2 tablespoons butter. (You want to barely see it.) Unwrap one of the doughs and put it on a cutting board. Use the tip of a small sharp knife to mark notches on top of the log for where you want to cut. The notches should be ¼ inch apart. Use the notches to help you slice downward with the knife to make the cookies. The tricky part is working carefully and slowly so the knife stays steady and the cookies are as evenly thick as you can cut them. It's okay if they're not perfect. Move the cookies to the baking sheets about 1 inch apart. (You'll probably have to work in two batches, but there's no need to grease the pans again.) Bake until the edges start to dry and turn golden and the centers are puffed and soft. Check after 6 minutes and if they're not ready, check again every 2 minutes until they are.

6 The cookies will still be very soft and almost seem raw when you take them out of the oven. That's perfect. Let them sit for 1 minute on the sheets, then use a stiff spatula to transfer the cookies to a wire rack to finish cooling. Repeat the baking steps with the cookies left on the cutting board. (Store these in an airtight container for a day or two or freeze for a couple months.)

7 When the cookies are totally cool, see page 283 for decorating ideas. Or eat them just as they are.

★ ★ ★ These spiced cookie folks are a fun group project for any time of year, especially over the holidays. Plus, there are a couple different ways to cut this dough. You can shape two logs, refrigerate or freeze, and slice like Sugar Cookies (page 277). Or you can roll the dough as you do for gingerbread people, only use different cookie-cutter shapes. Whatever you choose, decorating is a must. See the directions on page 283 for some ideas.

GINGERBREAD PEOPLE

MAKES: 36 TO 40 ⟩⟩ **TIME: ABOUT 1 HOUR, PLUS TIME TO CHILL THE DOUGH AND DECORATE** ❄ 🍃

INGREDIENTS

2 sticks butter, softened to room temperature

3¼ cups all-purpose flour, plus more for rolling the dough

1 heaping tablespoon ground ginger

1 tablespoon cinnamon

1 teaspoon baking soda

1 teaspoon salt

1 cup molasses

½ cup granulated sugar

½ cup packed brown sugar

EAT WITH: hot chocolate, warm apple juice, or a glass of milk.

STEPS

1 Make sure you take the butter out of the fridge 30 to 60 minutes before making the cookies. It really needs to be soft. Mix the flour, ginger, cinnamon, baking soda, and salt in a small bowl. You'll use that dry mixture in a minute.

2 To cream together the butter and sugars, put the butter in a large mixing bowl and measure in the molasses and sugars. Use a whisk, or a hand-held or upright mixer on a medium to medium-high setting, to beat the butter until the mixture is light and fluffy, about 3 minutes by machine, a couple minutes longer by hand. (See page 266.)

3 Switch to a soft spatula or big spoon and slowly sprinkle in the dry ingredients, stirring the whole time. Stop if you need to scrape down the sides of the bowl and take a break. You want the dough to be all the same color and to be able to pinch the soft dough in your fingers. It's okay to mix this cookie a little more than the other doughs in this chapter.

4 Divide the dough in half and use your hands to shape each piece into a disk about 1 inch thick. It's okay if it's not perfect. Wrap tightly in parchment paper, put in an airtight container, and chill until firm, about 2 hours or overnight. (This is when you'd freeze one or both of the disks. They will keep for a couple months. Thaw overnight in the refrigerator before making cookies.)

DID YOU KNOW

Molasses is a liquid sweetener made by cooking raw sugarcane. The taste is richer than maple syrup and it's thicker too. It might taste strong out of the bottle, but in cookies it's mild like caramel. Use regular—not blackstrap—molasses for this recipe.

5 When you're ready to bake, heat the oven to 350°F. Get 2 large baking sheets out. You'll be using them dry (without greasing them). You'll need a sturdy rolling pin and a flat, clean, dry workspace like a counter or large cutting board. Take one disk out of the fridge, open the wrapping, and press. Your fingers should make a dent, but if they sink in, rewrap the dough and refrigerate for another 15 minutes before trying again. If the dough is too hard to press, let it sit out for a few minutes.

RECIPE CONTINUES ➡

6 To keep the dough from sticking, you will sprinkle flour on the workspace and the top of the dough, and rub it all over the rolling pin both before you start and once or twice as you roll. This is called "dusting with flour," since the plan is to use as little flour as you can. Too much will make the cookies crumble! The easiest way is to put some flour in a tea strainer and shake it where you want it and then rub your hand to smear it evenly. Once you get the hang of it, you'll use less and less.

7 Start rolling from the middle of the disk outward, crossing to the left and right in a V shape. Rotate the rolling pin and the dough to make sure it's rolled evenly between ¼ and ½ inch thick. As you roll, press on the pin evenly and firmly (but not hard!). If anything starts to stick, dust with more flour. To get under the dough, lift it with a stiff spatula. Fix any holes or tears with tiny scraps of dough from the edges. Add a dab of water to help seal your patches in place. Don't try to pinch holes closed.

8 Dip your cookie cutter in some flour from the workspace and start cutting out the people (or other shapes). Make the cutouts as close to each other as you can, dipping in flour whenever the dough starts to stick. Carefully remove the dough between the shapes and make a pile of scraps on the side. Move the cookies to the baking sheets about 2 inches apart.

9 Gather up the scraps into a disk and refrigerate the dough if it's too soft. You'll roll and cut them the same way. Then repeat Steps 5 through 8 with the second disk of dough. (You'll have to work in at least two batches.) Bake until the edges are firm but the centers are still soft, 6 to 10 minutes, depending on how thick they are.

10 The cookies will still be very soft and almost seem raw when you take them out of the oven. That's perfect. Let them sit for a minute on the sheets, then use a stiff spatula to transfer the cookies to a wire rack to finish cooling. Repeat the baking steps with the cookies left on the cutting board. (Store these in an airtight container for a day or two or freeze for a couple months.) When the cookies are totally cool, see page 283 for decorating ideas. Or eat them just as they are.

DECORATING COOKIES

★ Here's an easy sauce called "glaze" for cookies that you can make in different flavors. Drizzle it from a spoon, smear it with a knife, or make drops with a toothpick. It's the perfect "glue" to help candies, jimmies, sprinkles, and colored sugar stick to cookies. To decorate and write with frosting or glaze, see page 299.

VANILLA GLAZE

MAKES: ABOUT 2 CUPS ⟫ TIME: 15 MINUTES 🌿

INGREDIENTS

3 cups powdered sugar, plus more as needed

½ cup whole milk

1 teaspoon vanilla extract

STEPS

Put the 3 cups powdered sugar, milk, and vanilla in a medium bowl and use a whisk or electric hand mixer to beat into a smooth and shiny glaze. It will harden a little as it sits, but you want it stiff enough to slowly drizzle from a spoon. Add more sugar ¼ cup at a time to get it there. Use right away or refrigerate in an airtight container for up to 1 week.

VARIATIONS

COCOA GLAZE. Use 2½ cups powdered sugar and ½ cup cocoa powder. If you need to make the glaze thicker, stir in 2 tablespoons more powdered sugar and 2 tablespoons more cocoa at a time.

LEMON GLAZE. Skip the milk and vanilla. Squeeze ¼ cup juice from 1 or 2 lemons and mix with ¼ cup water. Everything else stays the same.

ORANGE GLAZE. Skip the milk and vanilla. Squeeze ¼ cup juice from 1 orange and mix with ¼ cup water. Everything else stays the same.

★ There's so much to love about crisps. Juicy, soft fruit underneath a cookie-like crust that you can and should eat warm. And whatever fruit you like, go for it. I put apples in the main recipe since they're good all year round. The variations tell you how to use special summer fruits like the nectarines in the photo.

FRUITY CRISP

MAKES: 4 TO 8 SERVINGS ⟩→ *TIME: 1 HOUR*

INGREDIENTS

5 tablespoons butter, plus more for smearing the pan

About 2½ pounds apples

Juice of ½ lemon

⅔ cup packed brown sugar, plus 1 additional tablespoon

½ cup rolled oats (not instant)

½ cup all-purpose flour

Pinch of salt

¼ cup chopped nuts (if you like)

EAT WITH: ice cream, Whipped Cream (page 267), or a spoonful of cream drizzled on top.

STEPS

1 Heat the oven to 400°F. Smear about 1 tablespoon butter on the sides and bottom of an 8- or 9-inch square baking pan. Cut the 5 tablespoons butter into pea-sized bits, spread them out on a plate, and put it in the freezer while you get everything else ready.

2 Follow the directions for peeling, coring, and slicing apples as described on page 16. You want about 6 cups for this recipe. Same deal there as here: peels or no peels, your choice. Put the apples in a large bowl, and toss them with the lemon juice and extra 1 tablespoon brown sugar. Let them sit.

3 Take the butter out of the freezer and scrape it all into a medium bowl. Add the last ⅔ cup brown sugar, the oats, flour, salt, and nuts if you're using them. Use your hands to mix until a crumbly topping comes together. Rubbing and squeezing as you go will get you there fast.

4 Spoon the apples into the baking pan and spread them into an even layer. Scrape all the juices out of the bowl over the apples. Scatter the topping over the fruit.

5 Bake until the topping is browned and crisp and the apples are soft and bubbling, 40 to 50 minutes. You can poke them with a fork to make sure. Let the pan rest on a wire rack for just a few minutes and eat warm or at room temperature. Cover the pan if anything is left, refrigerate, and eat within a day or 2. *RECIPE CONTINUES* ➡

CHERRY CRISP. Easier since there's nothing to slice. Instead of the apples, use 1½ pounds frozen tart—also called pie—cherries. Keep the brown sugar in the topping, but in Step 2, toss the cherries with 2 tablespoons cornstarch and ½ cup granulated sugar and skip the lemon. Top and bake the crisp the same way as in the main recipe.

BERRY CRISP. Choose blueberries, blackberries, or raspberries—or a mix. Fresh or frozen. Instead of the apples, use 1½ pounds (3 pints). Keep the brown sugar in the topping, but in Step 2, toss the berries with 2 tablespoons cornstarch and 2 tablespoons granulated sugar and skip the lemon. Top and bake the crisp the same way as in the main recipe.

PEAR CRISP. Same recipe with pears instead of apples.

PEACH OR NECTARINE CRISP. You can make the same recipe with peaches or nectarines instead of apples. The only change is that you'll need 3 to 4 pounds of fruit.

★ ★ Turning milk, sugar, and eggs into pudding is a cooking magic trick. After heating and whisking, the refrigerator is where the warm thick goo turns to rich and creamy pudding. So, find something to do for a few hours to keep your mind off dessert.

VANILLA PUDDING

MAKES: 4 TO 8 SERVINGS ⟫ *TIME: ABOUT 30 MINUTES, PLUS TIME TO CHILL* 🌿

INGREDIENTS

2 tablespoons butter, softened to room temperature

6 eggs

⅔ cup sugar

2½ cups half-and-half or whole milk

¼ teaspoon salt

1 teaspoon vanilla extract

EAT WITH: any of the fruit sauces on page 261 or a Sugar Cookie (page 277).

STEPS

1 Take the butter out of the fridge and let it warm up by the stove while you make the pudding. Get ready to separate the yolks from the whites of 4 eggs. (It's fun and easy.) Put a large bowl next to a small bowl on the counter with a little plate close to you in between the bowls. Crack an egg on the plate and, super-slowly, open it over the small bowl so that you're pouring the whole egg from one half of the shell into the other. The idea is to catch the yolk in the shell and let the whites pour off into the bowl.

2 Next, pour the yolk into the empty shell in your other hand, again so the whites slide off into the bowl. One or two more times and you should have only the yolk left. (It's okay for this recipe if it breaks, but try not to get any yolk in the white part.) Put the yolk in the large bowl. Repeat with 3 more eggs. Then crack the last 2 eggs on the plate and open the whole thing into the large bowl. (See page 297 for some ideas about what to do with the leftover egg whites.) Add the sugar to the bowl and whisk it with the eggs and yolks until it's smooth and evenly colored, about 1 minute.

3 Put the half-and-half in a 2- or 3-quart saucepan over medium-low heat. Stir every minute just until it begins to steam, 2 to 3 minutes. Remove the pot from the burner and turn off the heat.

4 Use a soup ladle to scoop up some of the hot half-and-half and slowly pour it into the bowl with the egg and sugar mixture, whisking constantly. (You might ask someone to help hold on to the bowl while you juggle everything.) Repeat with another ladle.

RECIPE CONTINUES ➡

5 Whisk the egg mixture into the half-and-half that's still in the pot and set the heat to medium-low again. Cook, whisking the whole time, until the pudding thickens enough to coat the back of a spoon without just pouring off. This will take about 10 minutes, so if you need to take a break, move the pot to a cold burner. (Or ask someone to help!)

6 When it's ready, remove the pot from the heat and whisk in the butter, salt, and vanilla until the butter melts completely. Pour or ladle the mixture into 1 large heatproof bowl or 4 to 8 small bowls. Press a piece of plastic wrap directly on top of the pudding to prevent the top from drying out. Refrigerate until chilled, at least 2 hours, and eat within a day or 2.

VARIATIONS

CHOCOLATE PUDDING. Presto! Chop 4 ounces dark chocolate. In Step 6, when you add the butter and vanilla, whisk it into the pot and keep stirring until it melts. Then finish the recipe.

BUTTERSCOTCH PUDDING. Tastes like a cross between honey and caramel with one easy switch. Use ⅔ cup packed dark brown sugar instead of the granulated white sugar.

★ ★ Does anyone you know call a refrigerator an "icebox"? That's what people used to say back before the electric kind we have now. They were just a box with a big block of ice to keep things cool. The point is, you don't need an oven to make this cake. All you need is a refrigerator.

ICEBOX CAKE

MAKES: 4 TO 6 SERVINGS ⟫ TIME: 30 MINUTES, PLUS 8 HOURS TO CHILL 🌿

INGREDIENTS

2 cups cream

½ cup sugar

1 box or bag cocoa snaps or other chocolate wafers (about 12 ounces)

Extras from the list that follows

EAT WITH: fresh sliced strawberries or bananas, or whole raspberries or blueberries.

You can make an Icebox Cake—and the variations on the next page—with gluten-free cookies or crackers.

STEPS

1 Line a standard 8 x 5-inch glass or metal loaf pan with 2 sheets of plastic so that one covers lengthwise and the other covers across the long sides. Have your cookies and extras ready to go.

2 Follow the recipe on page 267 for whipping the cream and adding the sugar. You want your whipped cream to end up with stiff peaks.

3 Use the back of a big spoon to spread a little whipped cream in the bottom of the pan. Put a tightly packed single layer of cookies on top. Start by pressing in whole cookies so they're touching, then use broken pieces to fill in any gaps and open corners.

4 Cover the cookies with a thick layer of whipped cream (about ½ inch deep) and sprinkle some extras on top of the cream. Put another layer of cookies on top of that, just like you did before, then top with cream and extras. (You get the idea!) Keep going so that the last of the whipped cream is on top. Decorate with the last extras. (You may have cookies left over, but that's okay, right?)

5 Refrigerate the cake for at least 8 hours. (It's great to make it in the morning to eat after dinner, or before you go to bed to have for lunch or a snack.) To serve, cover the pan with a large plate or platter and carefully flip it upside down so the cake flops out of the pan. Remove the plastic. Then use a serrated knife (the kind with sharp ridges like a saw) to cut slices across the cake and eat cold. Leftovers keep in the refrigerator for a few days.

VARIATIONS

VANILLA ICEBOX CAKE. Skip the chocolate cookies and use vanilla wafers. When you make the whipped cream, add 1 teaspoon vanilla extract with the sugar. Everything else stays the same.

GRAMMY ICEBOX CAKE. Plain graham crackers are less sweet than cookies, so you can add sweeter extras. The square corners also make them perfect for square pans but not so great for round pans. Flavor the whipped cream with 1 teaspoon vanilla (or not) when you add the sugar. Everything else stays the same.

5 EXTRAS TO SCATTER IN AND ON ICEBOX CAKE

You'll need about 1 cup of any of these:

1. Chopped chocolate or chocolate chips (any kind)
2. Unsweetened shredded coconut
3. Your favorite nuts
4. Chopped candy
5. Sprinkles or jimmies

★ ★ There's nothing babyish about these small chocolate cakes. There is a surprise inside, however—warm gooey fudge that pours onto your plate the minute you stick in your fork. (Or spoon!)

HOT LAVA FUDGE CAKES

MAKES: 4 INDIVIDUAL CAKES ⟫ *TIME: 45 MINUTES*

INGREDIENTS

8 tablespoons (1 stick) butter, plus more softened butter for smearing

4 ounces dark chocolate, finely chopped

4 eggs

¼ cup sugar

2 teaspoons all-purpose flour

¼ teaspoon salt

EAT WITH: ice cream, Whipped Cream (page 267), Berrysauce or Cherrysauce (page 262), or fresh raspberries.

STEPS

1 Smear four 4-ounce (½-cup) ceramic, glass, or metal baking dishes with lots of softened butter. You want to see it covering the sides and bottom, and in that crack where they meet.

2 Melt the 1 stick butter in the microwave or in a 1-quart pot over medium-low heat. Take the butter off the heat and add the chocolate. Stir until it's melted into the butter. Use a soft spatula to scrape the mixture into a large bowl and let it sit while you move on.

3 Crack 2 of the eggs into a medium bowl and add 2 more yolks (see the directions on page 287 and save the extra whites for another time). Add the sugar and beat with a whisk or an electric mixer until light and thick, about 1 minute (1 or 2 minutes longer by hand).

4 Add the egg mixture, flour, and salt to the melted chocolate and whisk or stir until combined. Spoon the batter into the prepared dishes. (At this point you can refrigerate them for up to 3 hours; just bring them back to room temperature before baking.)

5 When you're ready to bake, heat the oven to 450°F. Put the baking dishes on a rimmed baking sheet and bake until the cakes have puffed up a bit, the tops are no longer shiny and liquid, and the center of the cakes still jiggles slightly when shaken, 7 to 9 minutes. It's way better to bake them too little than too much. Take the pan out of the oven and let the cakes rest for 1 minute.

6 Put a plate on top of each dish and use and potholder and get some help to carefully turn the cake upside down onto the plate. Count to 10-one-thousand, then lift up the dish and eat right away.

★ ★   Party cake for sure. Or just an everyday cake. Golden, rich, and tender in that classic vanilla way that everyone loves. The main recipe is for a rectangle with plenty of room to write on and decorate. The variations turn the same batter into a layer cake, ring-shaped cake, or cupcakes.

CONFETTI CAKE

MAKES: 8 TO 12 PIECES ➢➢ **TIME: ABOUT 90 MINUTES, BEFORE DECORATING**

INGREDIENTS

10 tablespoons (1¼ sticks) butter, softened, plus more for greasing

2 cups all-purpose flour, plus more for dusting

2½ teaspoons baking powder

¼ teaspoon salt

1¼ cups sugar

8 egg yolks (see page 287 for how to separate egg yolks from the whites)

1 teaspoon vanilla extract

¾ cup whole milk

One of the frosting or glaze recipes from page 298 or 283

Candy confetti or other sprinkles as needed

EAT WITH: vanilla, chocolate, or strawberry ice cream—or really any flavor you love.

STEPS

1   Heat the oven to 350°F and make sure there's a rack in the middle. Smear a layer of butter on the bottom and sides of an 8 x 13-inch cake pan or dish to grease it. To flour the pan, sprinkle in about 2 tablespoons of the extra flour and tip and shake the pan so that the flour sticks to the butter all over. Turn the pan upside down over the sink and tap it so the extra flour falls out.

2   Whisk together the 2 cups flour, the baking powder, and salt in a medium bowl and set aside. Put the butter in a large bowl and use a whisk or an electric mixer to beat—or cream—it until smooth and fluffy. Slowly add the sugar, whisking or beating the whole time until the butter gets a little lighter in color and even more fluffy, 3 to 4 minutes. (See page 266.)

3   Keep whisking or beating while you spoon in the yolks, one at a time. (It's okay if some break.) Stop to scrape down the sides with a soft spatula once or twice. When all the eggs are mixed into the butter-sugar mixture, mix in the vanilla.

4   Use the soft spatula to stir in about ¾ cup of the flour mixture, then add a splash of the milk. Repeat until all the milk and flour are gone. Stir only enough to form a pretty smooth batter (it's okay if there are still some small lumps).

RECIPE CONTINUES ➡

5 Spoon the batter into the prepared pan and then scrape out the rest of the batter from the bowl too. Set the timer for 35 minutes and put the cake in the oven to bake. The cake is ready when a toothpick poked into the center of the cake comes out clean or with a few moist crumbs. If it's not ready, check again in 5 minutes.

6 You can let the cake cool all the way in the pan (set on a wire rack) and decorate and cut it from there. Or you can turn it onto a platter or cutting board so you can frost the sides too. If so, let the cake cool in the pan for 5 minutes. Then carefully run a knife around the edge of the cake to loosen it and turn it upside down onto a clean towel. Use the towel to turn it right side up again onto the wire rack to finish cooling. Scootch the cake onto the platter or board to frost or glaze and decorate. (Leftover cake keeps covered at room temperature for a day and then move it to the fridge for up to a couple more days.)

CONFETTI LAYER CAKE. Use two 8- or 9-inch round cake pans and prepare them as described in the main recipe. (The larger pans will make slightly thinner layers.) Start checking for doneness after 20 minutes. Cool and remove from the pans as described in the main recipe before decorating. To frost, put one cake upside down on a big plate or cake stand and frost the top. Put the other layer on top right side up and frost that. Then frost the sides. Decorate with sprinkles however you like.

CONFETTI RING CAKE. For party fun, fill the center with scoops of ice cream. Use a standard size tube or Bundt pan and grease and flour it as described in Step 1. Start checking for doneness after 30 minutes. Cool and remove from the pan as described in the main recipe before decorating. Choose any glaze to drizzle over the top and let drip down the sides of the cake.

CONFETTI CUPCAKES. Makes about 24 cupcakes. Skip Step 1, and put a paper cup into each well of 1 or 2 standard-sized muffin tins. Fill each cup two-thirds full with batter. Start checking the cupcakes for doneness at 15 minutes. (You test them the same way as a big cake.) Let them rest in the pan for 10 minutes, then move them to a rack to finish cooling before you frost or glaze and decorate them.

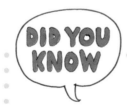

DID YOU KNOW

You can refrigerate the leftover egg whites in an airtight container for up to three days or freeze them for several months. They're great for egg-white omelets and vegetable scrambles (see pages 52 and 39).

FROSTING ON THE CAKE

Is the frosting or the cake your favorite part? I love them both. The frosting here gives you a few flavor choices. The best tool for spreading it is called an "offset spatula," with a long and narrow piece of metal that bends down from the handle so it lies flat on the counter when you hold it. But a non-sharp knife (like a butter knife) or soft spatula work fine too.

VANILLA FROSTING

MAKES: ENOUGH FROSTING AND FILLING FOR 1 LAYER OR RECTANGLE CAKE, 2 DOZEN CUPCAKES, OR 3 TO 4 DOZEN COOKIES ⟫ TIME: 20 MINUTES

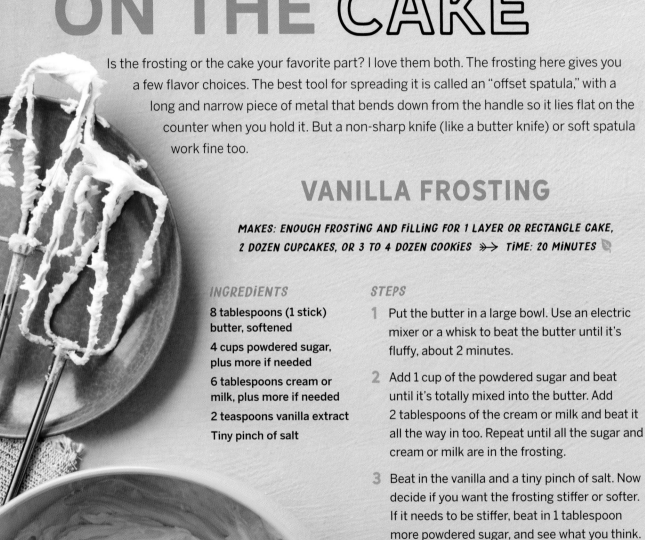

INGREDIENTS

8 tablespoons (1 stick) butter, softened

4 cups powdered sugar, plus more if needed

6 tablespoons cream or milk, plus more if needed

2 teaspoons vanilla extract

Tiny pinch of salt

STEPS

1 Put the butter in a large bowl. Use an electric mixer or a whisk to beat the butter until it's fluffy, about 2 minutes.

2 Add 1 cup of the powdered sugar and beat until it's totally mixed into the butter. Add 2 tablespoons of the cream or milk and beat it all the way in too. Repeat until all the sugar and cream or milk are in the frosting.

3 Beat in the vanilla and a tiny pinch of salt. Now decide if you want the frosting stiffer or softer. If it needs to be stiffer, beat in 1 tablespoon more powdered sugar, and see what you think. For softer frosting, beat in 1 tablespoon more milk or cream. Refrigerating the frosting in an airtight container will keep it fresh for several days and makes it stiffer too.

MILK CHOCOLATE FROSTING.
Use only 1 teaspoon vanilla. Chop 2 ounces dark chocolate. Melt it in the microwave or in a 1-quart pot over low heat. Let it cool for 10 minutes. After you add the first cup of powdered sugar in Step 2, whisk or beat in the chocolate. Then keep going until all the sugar is added.

CREAM CHEESE FROSTING.
Works with any of the flavors here. Instead of the butter, use 8 tablespoons (½ cup) cream cheese.

CINNAMON FROSTING.
Great on Gingerbread People (page 280) or Banana or Pumpkin Bread (page 249). Use just 1 teaspoon vanilla and add 2 teaspoons cinnamon at the same time.

LEMON, LIME, OR ORANGE FROSTING.
Use only 4 tablespoons of cream or milk to start and add 2 tablespoons fresh lemon, lime, or orange juice. Adjust the stiffness of the frosting by adding more cream or milk as described in Step 3.

The time to scatter confetti, jimmies, sprinkles, crushed candy, or colored sugar onto cake is after you frost and before you write. (Just be sure to leave some space for the words if you're going to add them.) To get extras to stick to the sides, put some in your hand and press them gently into the frosting. Scoop up what falls on the plate with a small spoon and use them too. Then the very last thing are the candles.

WRITING ON CAKES (OR COOKIES)

Ask if you've got a pastry bag in your house you can use. It needs to be pretty small for kids. If you don't, then all you need is a square piece of parchment 12 to 13 inches across. Fold it in half corner-to-corner to make a triangle. Then fold the triangle in half again, then in half again. Look into the layers and find a pocket that will hold a little frosting or glaze. Fill the pocket almost to the top and fold the edges over to close the cone if you like. Snip off a teeny bit of the tip of the cone so that you have the right size hole for your writing. Then squeeze the frosting through the hole like toothpaste!

⭐ ⭐ Proof that yes, you can make candy! The only reason this recipe is marked "Intermediate" is for the food processor. Other than that, you won't believe how easy these are.

CHOCOLATE-CHERRY BONBONS

MAKES: ABOUT 2 DOZEN SMALL BALLS ➵ *TiME: 45 MiNUTES, PLUS TiME TO CHiLL* ❄ 🍃

INGREDiENTS

2 tablespoons butter

3 ounces milk, dark, or white chocolate, chopped, or chips (about 1/2 cup)

1 1/4 cups unsweetened dried bing (dark) cherries (about 8 ounces)

2 cups powdered sugar, plus more as needed

1/4 cup all-purpose flour

1/2 teaspoon vanilla extract

1/8 teaspoon salt

Water as needed

EAT WiTH: a glass of milk or mug of mint tea.

STEPS

1 Put the butter and chocolate in a small microwave-safe bowl and melt the mixture on high heat for 30 seconds. Check and stir and repeat once or twice until the butter and chocolate melt without bubbling or burning. (You can also do this step in a 1-quart pot over medium-low heat.) Stir with a soft spatula until the mixture is cool enough to touch.

2 Put the cherries and the chocolate mixture into a food processor fitted with a metal blade. Add 1 1/2 cups of the powdered sugar along with the flour, vanilla, and salt. Let the machine run until the paste-like mixture is smooth and forms a ball. If a ball doesn't form after a minute, add 1 tablespoon water through the feed tube. After that, add water 1 teaspoon at a time until you get a ball shape, careful not to add too much. You want the paste to be stiff enough to pinch with your fingers into a damp glob. Carefully take the blade out, scrape the paste into a large bowl, cover, and refrigerate for at least 1 hour or up to a day.

3 When you're ready to roll the bonbons, put a sheet of parchment paper in a large rimmed baking sheet. Sprinkle the last 1/2 cup powdered sugar onto a plate and smash any clumps with a fork. Use your hands to grab and roll big pinches of the cold paste into 1-inch balls. Then roll them in the sugar so they're coated all over and put them on the prepared pan. Use more as needed until all the paste is turned into bonbons. Enjoy your candy! Keep the leftovers in an airtight container in the refrigerator for up to a few days or in the freezer for several weeks.

RECiPE CONTiNUES ➡

VARIATIONS

CHOCOLATE–COCONUT BONBONS. For a snowball look, try white chocolate. Instead of the dried cherries, use unsweetened shredded coconut. Everything else stays the same.

PEANUT BUTTER BONBONS. Skip the dried cherries and water and use 1 cup unsweetened peanut butter—chunky or smooth, your choice. No need to use the food processor. After melting the chocolate and butter in Step 1, mix everything (except the extra powdered sugar for rolling) together in a large bowl with a soft spatula until smooth. Continue with the recipe at Step 3.

ABOUT THE KIDS

The children who appear in these pages are friends and family of the team who worked together on the book. The kids offered to share their experiences cooking—and sometimes eating!—the recipes in this book and are photographed by the people who love them. I'm so grateful for the enthusiasm and joy. Here's a little bit about them:

Dedication and page 296: Max Robin Freeman is Mark's daughter Emma's son. Max loves to eat and is excited to learn how to cook. He and his cousin, Holden Traverse (7), are just getting acquainted when the photo on the Dedication page was taken by Holden's mom, Kate Bittman. And later in the book Max is eating cake at his 1st birthday party. That photo was taken by his dad, Jeff Freeman.

Dedication and pages 2, 29, 30, and 226: In addition to appearing with Max on the dedication page (see above) Holden makes smoothies and applesauce with his Gumps, Mark. (Ghazalle Badiozamani took those photographs.) Holden's dad, Nick Traverse, and his mom, Kate, took the photos of him trying out the electric mixer and enjoying a piece of chicken on the fly. The more often Holden is in the kitchen, the more he wants to do!

Pages 7, 8, and 11: Makenna (5) and her sister Raven (7) learn about something new every time they hang out in the kitchen. Their "Mimi," Gina, took these photos at her home in Bremerton, Washington.

Pages 9 and 13: Brothers Marcel (8) and Naeem (2) have a blast whenever they're together in their kitchen. The photos were taken by their dad, Mike Diago.

Pages 14, 23, and 63: Mika Milova (5) happily eats lunch at school and demonstrates cooking and mixing pancakes at home in New Jersey. The photos were taken by Taylor Milova, Mika's parent.

Page 39: Ava (2) and Rowan (6) crack and scramble eggs together in their home in New York City. The photo was taken by their mom.

Page 74: Making your own Honey Mustard Sauce is easy. Just ask Alexandra from Brooklyn. The photo was taken by her mom, Janelle.

Page 87: Popping popcorn helped Joshua Slavin (10) from Lusaka, Zambia, learn to control heat when cooking. His father is J. P. Slavin and his sister is Cheswa. The photo was taken by Joshua's mother, Kalumba Chisambisha-Slavin.

Page 130: Sisters Maya (10) and Juliet (7) use teamwork to prepare and cook all kinds of vegetables. Their dad took these photos.

Pages 156 and 157: Isaiah (9) and his little sister Phoebe (4) show how easy it is to make French fries. The photos were taken by their mom, Sandy Chen.

Page 187: Jack (14) is smart to get all his ingredients ready for fast-cooking recipes. We met him through the Rachel Lynn Henley Foundation—a nonprofit organization in Tacoma, Washington, that supports families with childhood cancers. When he made the Squiggly Noodles, Jack had just finished two and a half years of treatment for leukemia, and his family is thrilled to report that he is in remission. The photos were taken by his mom, Demorie.

Page 204: Levi (9) and Zara (11) from San Diego focus on peeling garlic for their first batch of Hummus, which they made with black beans. Their father, LaRon Lindsay, took this photo.

Page 208: Bellamie (9) demonstrates how to squeeze beans from the pod for the Shiny Edamame recipe variation. The photo was taken by her mom (and the book's designer), Melissa Lotfy.

Page 224: Using your hands to mix meatballs works great and is lots of fun. Nora Mead (7) from New York City shows how. Her dad, Robert Mead, took these photos.

Page 243: Nuriel (Nuri) Badiozamani Beylin (8) delighting his grandparents in San Diego. The photo was taken by his mom, Ghazal Badiozamani.

Page 254: Monte Greene (16) demonstrates pressing a super-simple pizza dough into the pan at home in New York City. His mom, Karen, took the photo.

Page 265: Rafa Spack (4) and his grandmother, Joan Eisenberg, measure cocoa for Brownies. The photo was taken over summer vacation in Cape Cod by Rafa's mom, Nicole.

Pages 274 and 275: Lalitha (7) and Meenakshi (4) had a blast making—and eating—Peanut Butter Cookies with their mom, Maya, who took these photos.

Page 279: Belle Harris (9) from Irvington, New York, loves to cook, especially when cookies are involved. Here she is getting the dough shaped before chilling and making the thumbprint variation. Her mom, Keach Hagey Harris, took the photo.

Page 291: Anna (9) and Caroline ("Cara," 4) Ford took their fabulous Icebox Cake outside to enjoy at their home in Vienna, Virginia. The photo was taken by their mom, Katie.

Page 302: Vera Fox-Glassman (8) melts chocolate and safely uses a food processor to make Chocolate-Cherry Bonbons, a fruity homemade candy. Her mom, Katherine, took these photos, and her brother Milo helped eat the delicious results..

The Collages on the Inside Covers
The kids who appear in the photographs on these opening and closing collages include vintage images from the Bittman family, along with a few of our young recipe testers and new friends. From left to right by row, they are:

Front
Row 1: Kate and Mark Bittman, Josie, Holden, Willa and Hadley Sutherland, Zoe, Myles Kim
Row 2: Nick Traverse, Kate Bittman, Josie, Willa Sutherland, Holden, Charlie, Sadie Gant
Row 3: Holden, Binah and Emmanuel Boudy, Emma Baar-Bittman, Virginia Catherine, Nora Gant, Anouk Benayoun, Vivanta Vijaychandran

Back
Row 1: Eloise and Bea, Hadley Sutherland, Oz, Josie, Holden, Charlie
Row 2: Emmanuel Boudy, Taj Harley, Rishi Kumar, Kate Bittman, Isabella Fernando, Ari, Charlie
Row 3: Holden, Eva Cassidy, Kate Bittman, Josie, Zoe Clark, Penny Jones and Ellie Coleman, Mika

INDEX

Note: Page references in *italics* indicate photographs or illustrations.